D0205579

# CELEBRATING WOMEN COACHES

# CELEBRATING WOMEN COACHES
## COACHES

*A Biographical Dictionary*

## Nena Rey Hawkes
## and John F. Seggar

*Foreword by*
Russell L. Sturzebecker and Linda J. Carpenter

**Greenwood Press**
Westport, Connecticut • London

**Library of Congress Cataloging-in-Publication Data**

Hawkes, Nena.
    Celebrating women coaches : a biographical dictionary / Nena Rey Hawkes and John F.
Seggar ; foreword by Russell L. Sturzebecker and Linda J. Carpenter.
      p.  cm.
    Includes bibliographical references and index.
    ISBN 0–313–30912–4 (alk. paper)
    1. Coaches (Athletics)—United States—Biography—Dictionaries.  2. Women coaches
(Athletics)—United States—Biography—Dictionaries.  I. Seggar, John F. A.  II. Title.
GV697.A1 H367   2000
796′.082′092273—dc21       99–088485
  [B]

British Library Cataloguing in Publication Data is available.

Library of Congress Catalog Card Number: 99–088485
ISBN: 0–313–30912–4

First published in 2000

Greenwood Press, 88 Post Road West, Westport, CT 06881
An imprint of Greenwood Publishing Group, Inc.
www.greenwood.com

Printed in the United States of America

The paper used in this book complies with the
Permanent Paper Standard issued by the National
Information Standards Organization (Z39.48–1984).

10 9 8 7 6 5 4 3 2 1

*Dedicated to all the little girls who just want to play,*
*for in children's play is found a microcosm of life.*

# CONTENTS

# FOREWORD

The changing role of women in both society and professional opportunities has profoundly affected the relationships between men and women.

The year 1998 marked the gathering in Seneca Falls, New York, of women's groups from across this nation to celebrate the 150th anniversary of women's rights. The original idea of holding a convention to consider women's rights was planned at the home of Jane Hunt attended by her sister-in-law Mary McClintock, by Quaker Minister Lucretia Mott, by her sister Martha C. Wright, and by a supporter, Elizabeth Cady Stanton. Four of the five women were Philadelphia Quakers who played roles in the business meetings of their Quaker church.

It appears that this session was an outgrowth of the Philadelphia Interracial Female Anti-slavery Society organized by Lucretia Mott and fellow Quakers in 1833. This group sponsored national conventions in 1837, 1838, and 1839.

A distinct parallelism is created by efforts of Dr. Hawkes and Dr. Seggar to identify the most talented role models of women sport coaches. Educators and student advisors as well as administrators recognize the vital necessity to have accessible the life stories of the successful women coaches who are the subjects of this volume.

An examination of their educational backgrounds, as well as their total experiences in their fields, marks their research efforts with a most successful effort.

This volume, with its myriad role-model women coaches across the United States, will motivate young women to follow in their footsteps.

This book represents the first of its kind to bridge the gap between women with the most successful coaching careers and their future replacements in the sport world of women.

It is hoped that the authors' efforts will inspire future writers to identify those women coaches who represent role models in the twenty-first and successive centuries.

Russell L. Sturzebecker
Professor Emeritus of Physical Education
West Chester State University
West Chester, Pennsylvania

For good or ill, the confusions and challenges of life and society find reflection in the microcosm of sport. Positive life lessons and healthy personal perspectives abound within that microcosm for those willing to reach for them.

The life lessons and personal perspectives gained by forty-two outstanding female coaches from the metaphoric laboratory of sport have been harvested through the perceptivity of the authors. Excellence and fortitude, seen and examined in the lives of these coaches, remove perceived barriers and strengthen our own resolve for crafting and nurturing such traits in our own lives and in our children's lives. Their harvest makes the pages of this book exceedingly rich reading. Enjoy the feast.

Linda J. Carpenter
Professor Emeritus of Physical Education
Brooklyn City College
Brooklyn, New York

# PREFACE

The social conventions of early- and mid-twentieth century America have sent implicit messages that women should not aspire to become athletic coaches. This message stopped many capable women from seeking coaching careers or even entertaining the idea of becoming coaches. However, during the last thirty years of the past century, in response to earlier exclusion, a cadre of capable women did succeed in becoming coaches. This book focuses on some of the women who ignored the negative messages and pursued opportunities.

Many of these women coaches were recruited and challenged to develop women's programs, and most often they were mentored to fill coaching positions vacated by high caliber male coaches. Those males, and other males associated with athletics, often started a chain of events that led to hiring selected women. These men saw the potential for future great female coaches. For other women, being hired as coaches was serendipitous: they were in the right places at the right times. When offered the challenge, they stepped forward and assumed the bid to coach either reluctantly or eagerly. Others were brought in to initiate a sport at an institution. In any case, the outcome was the same; these females have achieved excellence.

Most of these women did not plan to coach—they planed to teach. Committed to excellence, hard work, service, and—most especially—to youth, they are appreciative of those who had coached them and recognized their youthful potential. They feel obliged to give back a share of what they, as athletes, received.

These women have designed coaching programs in which athletes can be highly competitive. Realistic goals are integrated with hard work. The atmosphere created by their coaching combines firmness and respect with a good dose of consideration for the athletes and their expectations. Graduation and academic accomplishment head the list of goals for their team members. The coaches value education and had themselves been good students. In turn, they expect their athletes to achieve similar academic standards knowing that academic accomplishment contributes to athletic success as both are founded on hard work in an organized environment. They nurture and teach athletes that success is not instant nor elusive, but gradual and sustainable. Success is seen as a life process, not a one-time event.

Drawing on male role models and bolstered by a few female coaches, they created their own coaching paradigms. Many have been seasoned athletes and know what the path to the top requires. They took the upward steps with the finesse of rock climbers. The ascent was not simple. They experienced buffeting and bruising when lashed by winds of change. However, in their progress, they developed their own unique styles and erected lofty standards which stand as models for other coaches to match.

We have written this volume to give credit to nurturing coaches and leaders for the positive impacts they have had on young women of potential. By enhancing the lives of youth, they affect the present and the future. We want to share with the reader our view of the impact and importance of coaching and to see how women can:

- Rise above obstacles
- Seize opportunities and translate dreams into realities
- Plant new ideas even in rigid systems in order to cultivate new programs
- Harvest respect in a tradition-dominated profession without undermining celebrated programs or personalities
- Supersede limited budgets, spaces, and attitudes
- Excel at every level of coaching including the Olympic Games

It is our hope that the reader will gain a vision of what can be achieved by drawing upon one's own unique personal resources to uncover the distinct talents of others. We hope the reader will come to recognize and validate the inner power and value of women who lead. We also offer this book as a treatise on human excellence and its manifestation through the medium of sport. We want to encourage players and coaches to dream dreams and to work to make those dreams come true. Finally, we trust the reader will be encouraged by the accounts of the struggles of others who have taken on the awesome task of "giving-back."

The *National Directory of College Athletics* (Woman's Edition) provided us with a list of coaches of women's teams from which to select those to be included in this volume. From this list a group of twenty-five coaches was randomly selected to represent each of ten sports. Letters were mailed to 250 coaches asking them to indicate whom they considered to be the top five coaches in their respective sport. From the coaches' responses a list of names was compiled based on frequency of mention. Fifteen women were selected from this grouping and other women were added to this selection based on the fact that they had won a national title or had been a national team coach for the United States or had coached an Olympic team.

Since 1981, when the NCAA started sponsoring Women's National Championship, female coaches of women's teams have not won in tennis and volleyball. Jan Brogan and Ann Valentine (tennis) and Elaine Michaelis and Mary Wise (volleyball) were included because of their stellar accomplishments in their respective professions. Marynell Meadors was added because she had been the most successful woman coach in the first two years of the newly formed Women's National Basketball Association.

The original fifteen coaches selected for this volume were sent questionnaires soliciting information about their lives and coaching careers. In some cases the coaches responded with typed replies, others mailed voice tapes of answers and these were transcribed. John Seggar telephoned additional coaches and conducted taped telephone interviews, which were also transcribed.

A rough draft was constructed from the coaches's interviews. The rough draft was refined into a coaching biography with the various aspects of the development of a successful coaching career highlighted by subheading. Each biography includes many of the following major headings: Introduction, Personal Data, Formative Years, Sports History, Playing Career, Decision to Coach, Coaching, Philosophy of Coaching, Changes in Athletes, Challenges, Memorable Moments, Role Models/Mentors, Favorite Books and Movies, Hobbies, Life Beyond Athletics, Future Plans, and Recognitions and Awards Each biography concludes with a list of recognitions and achievements. The volume is alphabetically arranged by the last name of each coach.

The authors wish to express their appreciation to each coach portrayed within this volume. They inspire us to continue in our own quest for personal and professional excellence.

# ACKNOWLEDGMENTS

Our deepest appreciation is extended to a multitude of people without whose efforts this project would not have been possible.

To young women who aspire to compete at any level, whether or not they make the team. And to the millions of young girls and young women, and their coaches, who devote untold hours of work and who travel innumerable miles to compete, to recruit, and to represent their sports and often their countries.

To Donna Lopiano of the Women's Sports Foundation, for her continuing efforts to create gender-equitable opportunities for women in sport.

To Russ Sturzebecker, Linda Carpenter, and Vivian Acosta, for their continuing interest, support, encouragement, and professional expertise in behalf of women's sport.

To the Department of Physical Education and the Department of Sociology at Brigham Young University, for their support. And most especially to Rachel Orme, Stacey Gardner, Teresa Kearney, Kelly Dayley, and Maggie Shibla for their assistance and expertise in preparing this manuscript, and John Burton for his artistic assistance. We wish to thank the Greenwood Publishing Group staff. Most especially we thank Emily Birch for sharing our vision. And we acknowledge and appreciate the expertise of Betty Pessagno and Dolores Abbott.

To the forty-two coaches who were so gracious and patient while allowing us to intrude upon their busy worlds in season, out of season, in their offices, in their homes, and on the road in hotels.

And, finally, to our families and friends who have been constant, encouraging, and interested in us and the success of this project.

# INTRODUCTION

While women in the United States competed in sport as early as the 1880s, it was not until the Association of Intercollegiate Athletics for Women was organized in 1971 and the passage of Title IX of the Educational Amendments Act of 1972 that money began to flow to women's athletics. In this book we look at some of the significant accomplishments in women's sport in the last thirty years. As we begin a new the century, women are reaping benefits accrued from earlier days; yet they have not escaped many of the day-to-day vexations and problems.

The World Cup has taught us there are now 7.8 million young women competing in soccer in the United States alone. Approximately 650,000 tickets were sold to World Cup competitions. No fewer than 90,000 fans filled the stadium at the Rose Bowl in Pasadena, California, in July 1999 to watch the championship game between China and the United States. Certainly this signals a new era of competitive sport for women in America, if not in the world. Entering the new millennium there should be no lack of role models or opportunities for athletic young girls and women.

West Chester State University and the Philadelphia area (with its Quaker Society and its Catholic Youth Organization) have had a profound impact on women's sport by providing a philosophy, professional training, leadership opportunities and competitive structures. Certainly, this area of the country has led the way in encouraging and supporting young women's competition and has provided mentors to give young people vision to their potential.

It should be noted there is not just one path to success; different routes often bring similar results. As women's sport becomes more institutionalized and routinized, the avenue to coaching a female team will become less and less varied. As the caliber of women's performances improve, and media attention is drawn to the various sports, audiences will increase; as these increases ensue, so will the opportunities for young women to compete professionally increase, providing more possibilities for women to coach professional teams.

It also follows that as better-skilled women gain competitive prominence, more men will move into the coaching ranks of women's sport. In some sports men will likely dominate leadership positions. At this point in time, a woman coach has yet to win a national championship in swimming, volleyball, or soccer. A question remains: "Will we see the day when women coach men's teams, as does Terry Crawford at St. Luis Obispo, or will men's sport continue to remain a male domain?"

With the inauguration of the WNBA All-Stars game, it was interesting and exhilarating to listen to two competent women commentators call the game. Perhaps this also signals a bright future for women broadcasters, and it may engender a greater audience appeal.

The featured coaches in this volume have become visible through excellence. Their coaching artistry is a rich tapestry of strands abundant in corresponding characteristics. The end of each chapter attests to these characteristics as notable and similar.

The strands of similarity assert that few of the coaches planned a career in coaching; indeed, most were in the right place at an opportune time, and their adventurous natures and deep-seated values prompted them to accept a challenge. All of these women encountered obstacles punctuated with the hurdles of space, budgets, and limited attitudes. These annoyances were temporary inconveniences and trivial in contrast to the brilliance of a national championship or an Olympic medal. Perhaps such hurdles nurture the impulse to achieve higher standards personally and professionally. They keep their focus and forge their own sense of place without bowing to the pressures of a well-knit male establishment.

These female coaches identify as  role model combinations of one or more coaches, and, if not bound by personal relationships, some cite nationally successful coaches as role models. Many simply acknowledge their parents as having been the first and foremost of their role models.

Most of the coaches lament the athlete's shift toward entitlement and a soft attitude toward hard work. However, their stellar records indicate that they demand more physically and mentally from their athletes. They establish a mind set that poor performance is unacceptable and must be replaced with work skills and good study habits. Although human behavior changes little, values and attitudes do not maintain the same permanence. Most of the coaches express dismay at the lack of continuity and permanence in values in the present generation of athletes. They encourage their young competitors to shoot for the top of their game, and, in the process, they have fun and become winners. They hope that these values will transfer into other areas of their lives.

The achievement of the coaches profiled in this volume is phenomenal when viewed collectively. They have developed national champions, conference champions, All Americans, Olympians, Pan American Games champions, World University champions, and World Cup champions. Combine these awards with the special recognitions assigned to each of the coaches, add those who have been named Olympic coaches, and the numbers are impressive in any circle of professional attainment.

Such a collage of coaching accomplishments does not automatically transpire. They are founded in simple hard work, good preparation poised in simple schemes precisely executed and nurtured in a solid organization within a professional, businesslike atmosphere. These are the properties of excellence. They breed dreams and spawn the drive to realize them, and they seal the warmth for their athletes in an atmosphere that precipitates a large measure of respect in return for their efforts. It is evident that these coaches are mentors and teachers of young women.

This volume represents a very small selection of coaches from the hundreds, even thousands, of coaches who on a daily basis teach and coach our young women.

# LIST OF ABBREVIATIONS

| | |
|---|---|
| AAU | Amateur Athletic Union |
| ABL | American Basketball League |
| ACAA | Atlantic Coast Athletic Association |
| ACC | Atlantic Coast Conference |
| AIAW | Association of Intercollegiate Athletic Women |
| AMF | Sport Manufacturing Company |
| AP Polls | Associated Press Polls |
| ASU | Arizona State University |
| AVCA | American Volleyball Coaches Association |
| BYU | Brigham Young University |
| Cal-Poly | California State Polytechnic |
| CYO | Catholic Youth Organization |
| DGWS | Division of Girls and Women's Sport |
| ECAC | East Coast Athletic Conference |
| ESANDA | (name of a company in Australia) |
| GPA | Grade Point Average |

| | |
|---|---|
| HCAC | High Country Athletic Conference |
| IAC | Intermountain Athletic Conference |
| ICCWPE | Intermountain Conference of Collegiate Women in Physical Education |
| ISU | Illinois State University |
| ITA | Intercollegiate Tennis Association |
| JC | Junior College |
| JV | junior varsity |
| LA | Los Angeles |
| LPGA | Ladies Professional Golf Association |
| MTSU | Middle Tennessee State University |
| MVP | most valuable player |
| NCAA | National Collegiate Athletic Association |
| NCSU | North Carolina State University |
| NJCAA | National Junior College Athletic Association |
| NOPAC | Northern Pacific Athletic Conference |
| NORCAL | Northern California Athletic Conference |
| NWIT | National Women's International Tournament |
| PAC 10 | Pacific Athletic Conference |
| PCAA | Pacific Coast Athletic Association |
| Penn State | Pennsylvania State University |
| Prop-48 | Proposition 48 |
| SEC | South Eastern Athletic Conference |
| SWC | South West Conference |
| UAHPER | Utah Association for Health, Physical Education, and Recreation |
| UC | University of California |
| UCLA | University of California, Los Angeles |
| UMass | University of Massachusetts |
| UNC | University of North Carolina |
| UNH | University of New Hampshire |
| USC | University of South Carolina |
| USFHA | United States Field Hockey Association |
| USOC | United States Olympic Committee |
| USTA | United States Tennis Association |
| USWLA | United States Women's Lacrosse Association |

| | |
|---|---|
| WAC | Western Athletic Conference |
| WAIAW | Western Association of Intercollegiate Athletic Women |
| WBCA | Women's Basketball Coaches Association |
| WIAW | Western Intercollegiate Association of Women |
| Wilson/ITA | Wilson Inc. and Intercollegiate Tennis Association |
| WNBA | Women's National Basketball Association |

Photo courtesy of Old Dominion
University

# BETH ANDERS
*Field Hockey—Old Dominion*

## INTRODUCTION

Admired by colleagues as one of the most respected athletes and coaches in the game, Beth Anders' liaison with field hockey began at her mother's side. Alice Anders, mother, athlete, and field hockey competitor, took her two children to her competitions. Beth and her brother Stanley ran the sidelines keeping up with their mother on the field. To the children it was play, but to the spectators watching the chase it was good humor. The Anders family spent quality time together in athletic activities. This was natural as both parents were excellent athletes. Beth's sporting memories are centered around her nuclear family. Her father played with them in the evenings, and he often arose at 5 A.M. just to take Beth golfing or to play tennis; weekends were garnished with family golf and other games. The Anders children never simply watched their parents participate—they were an important inclusion in their parents' games and activities.

## PERSONAL DATA

*Born*: November 13, 1951, Norristown, Pennsylvania

*Father*: Stanley Anders, Jr.

*Father's Occupation*: Controller for ALCOA

*Mother*: Alice Monroe

*Mother's Occupation*: Housewife, window dresser, and Montgomery Hospital Volunteer

*Sibling*: Stanley Schultz Anders III

*Alma Mater*: Ursinus College—B.S., Physical Education, 1973

## FORMATIVE YEARS

Although Beth's nuclear family provided the frame for childhood play, the fact that she was raised in a neighborhood populated with a batch of game-minded children helped to sustain an interest in sport. In this environment she learned the games of childhood.

## SPORTS HISTORY

From grade school through high school Beth participated in every available sport. She competed in basketball, softball, lacrosse, squash, tennis, and golf. Her actual competitive start began in the sixth grade with Little Lassie Field Hockey. She also spent time watching her brother compete and practice. In high school her brother transferred to a private school and her parents were going to transfer Beth too. The transfer never occurred because the lacrosse and field hockey coach, Libby Williams, got wind of the move and without Beth's knowledge dashed to the Anders' home to talk with Beth's parents. When Williams left Beth's home, Stanley and Alice Anders were convinced that Beth should remain at Plymouth Whitemarsh High School. Although convinced, Beth's parents left the decision to Beth, allowing her the power to direct her own life. Her decisions were always fully supported by both parents. Although Beth made the decision, Libby Williams had persuaded them that Beth had great athletic ability and would receive excellent coaching. Libby Williams' estimation of Beth's abilities proved prophetic: Beth never lost a game on any team she played for while attending Plymouth Whitemarsh.

When it was time for higher education, Anders selected Ursinus College because of coach Eleanor Snell. She was also impressed with the players and the fine sports tradition they had established at the beautiful 160–acre campus. While studying to become a physical education and health teacher, Beth managed to find time to compete in field hockey, lacrosse, softball, basketball, and squash.

## PLAYING CAREER

It would be difficult for any one of Beth's contemporaries to match her brilliant competitive career or her stellar coaching record. The playing career, started in grade school, continued into high school where she played field hockey, lacrosse, and basketball. None of these teams ever lost a game. Her excellent athletic abilities prompted Coach Libby Williams to say, "Beth was excellent in everything she did." Beth would later remark, "I didn't think I was anything special in high school."

At Ursinus College Beth became one of the finest athletes that ever competed at the school. She was a nationally ranked tennis player, a member of the National Collegiate Basketball Team, a four-year member of the All Conference Field Hockey Team, and in 1970 she became the National Intercollegiate Squash Champion. In addition she was an All American in squash and basketball.

By 1973 Beth Anders was listed in the top thirty of her graduating class. After graduation she competed with the Ursinus Alumni and Brandywine Association teams. Other post-graduate competitions led to the following honors:

| | |
|---|---|
| 1969–1984 | USA 1st team—Field Hockey |
| 1971–1984 | Played on every World Cup Team |
| 1973 | All College honors |
| 1975–1980 | All World Team |
| 1979–1980 | Vice Captain National Team |
| 1980–1984 | Captain National Team |
| | Player of the Year each year |
| | Five years as captain of the team |
| | Scored most goals five years in a row |
| | Scored most goals in one game in the Olympics |
| | Played in over 100 international matches and scored over 100 goals |
| | Scored more goals than any player in U.S. history |

Along with the foregoing honors, Beth played on the Presidents' XI All World Team. Her selection was prestigious as it eclipsed the boundaries of her own country, linking her with other world-class field hockey players. In addition, other honors extended the already lengthy roster of accomplishments:

| | |
|---|---|
| 1982 | The U.S. Olympic Committee designated her United States top field hockey athlete |
| 1984 | Co-captained the U.S. Olympic team to a bronze medal |
| | At age 33 she became a 14–year veteran on the national team (each of these years she was named high scorer) |
| | Competed in three world championships |
| 1985 | Named head coach of the U.S. National and Olympic teams. In naming Beth head coach, Judith Davidson, president of the USFHA, said, "Her playing ability is recognized worldwide and her coaching expertise emerged in her three consecutive National Collegiate championships (she now has seven National Championships)." |

## DECISION TO COACH

Beth's decision to coach was made in high school. Even as she became a top-notch competitor, it was her dream to be a teacher rather than a coach. When she did ponder teaching and coaching, her always-supportive parents advised her to do what she wanted to do but to make certain to be the best at whatever she chose to do.

Her first teaching job came on the heels of graduation from Ursinus College. That was in 1973. It was a one-year appointment to fill in for a teacher on maternity leave. The teacher on leave returned as promised, but the school retained Beth, too. Perhaps it was an interest in students that maintained her teaching position. That first year also provided her entry into coaching, as it all began that first year when she started a seventh- and eighth-grade field hockey program while coaching high school basketball and track. To Anders this was not work, it was getting paid for having fun. Perkiomen Valley High School was the next stop on her way to Old Dominion College in Norfolk, Virginia. She stayed at the high school from 1974 to 1980. In 1980 she and the other members of the United States Field Hockey Team were preparing to compete in the Moscow Olympics. Going to the Olympics meant she would have to leave school two weeks early. Leaving school early was not an option with the school superintendent. He required her to make a choice between the Olympics and her job. Saddened at the ultimatum, she chose what might be a once-in-a-lifetime opportunity—the Olympics—and left her teaching post. Ultimately, she was disappointed again. The United States boycotted the Moscow games, shattering her Olympic aspiration. Shortly after choosing to leave Perkiomen High School, the field hockey coaching position at Old Dominion became available. Anders was hired and is in her eighteenth year at Old Dominion. She went from fifth in the state to fifth in the nation, and in the following year she jumped from fifth in the nation to the final four and came in third in that competition. Within the next three years she recorded a national championship back to back.

## COACHING

In 1973 Beth began her teaching and coaching career at Perkiomen Valley High School. During the seven years at Perkiomen, Beth Anders' teams either won the league or placed second in six of the seven years. Her teams went to state championships twice and district playoffs three times. In 1979 Beth was hired at Old Dominion College where she coached until 1984 before becoming national coach for two years. She returned to Old Dominion in 1987 and has remained there. For further accomplishments see the records and recognition page. On the international level she coached the U.S. team in 1985 and from 1990 to 1993.

## PHILOSOPHY OF COACHING

The foundation for Anders' philosophy of coaching was forged incrementally through the eyes of a world class athlete, teacher, and coach. For example, in 1987 Anders felt that athletes must develop a personality of their own. In 1992 she emphasized fun, but she also realized that she was becoming more vocal and demanding about the importance of academics. Along with academics and fun she saw a necessity to focus on dedication and desire. By July of 1992 she said, "I am looking for attributes other than outstanding athletic ability." Drawing on experiential reserves, Coach Anders tailored her viewpoint to achieve personal success and guide athletes to perform well athletically and academically.

From this unique perspective, Anders recognizes that individuals must choose to excel. This notion compels her to recruit players for Old Dominion who have strengths other than athleticism and who have a strong desire to compete. Anders feels that developing athletes is a process and a journey; hence, she works to develop a whole person, not just an athlete. This requires her to listen, to converse, and to be fully present in the effort to understand each athlete's aspirations. Once she, as coach, understands the athlete, she is in a position to customize instruction to the needs of that athlete.

For Beth Anders coaching is not about winning a championship, but it is about winning every day and becoming one's best each day. Being one's best on a daily basis allows everything else to fall in line. Even after a win, Anders wants to know how the team can improve next time.

It is also important to Beth's coaching scheme to know athletes well enough to assess how they are thinking and feeling at any given moment so she can direct their focus more effectively in helping them to make correct decisions, which, in the end, affect the whole team and not just the individual.

Looking from her philosophical viewpoint, Beth Anders has relaized that a coach not only has to love the game, but she must have a passion for it. When you love the game and have fun and the athletes have fun, then a work ethic can be built on fun. Beth Anders fashions obstacles into challenges by keeping instruction simple and fundamental.

## CHANGES IN ATHLETES

Beth feels that today's women are extremely fortunate to have so many athletic opportunities. It is Beth's hope that athletes will come "to see more value in intrinsic rewards than in extrinsic rewards." She understands well that "the process far outweighs the end result."

## MEMORABLE MOMENTS

Taking Old Dominion from fifth in the state of Virginia to fifth in the nation during her first year of coaching was not only a giant step for Coach Anders, but a prediction of future performance. "Winning that first national championship was really something. Number one, you are exhausted because of all the work it takes. It was overwhelming to me to see the reaction of the players because they just worked so hard to get to that point. It was just thrilling. We won that championship because we pulled the goalie. We were three goals down at half time. I pulled the goalie. Just to see them fight to come back, it was exhausting but very satisfying. I was very happy for them."

The roar of the crowd in the Los Angeles Coliseum during the 1984 Olympics was a never-to-be-forgotten sound for Beth Anders and the American field hockey team: "Going to the Olympics as part of the United States Field Hockey Team in 1984 I thought, 'This game is fun.' When we were there it was like Disneyland to me. I thought, this is the greatest thing going. It's not that the games aren't pressure, but you don't feel it. It's just so much fun. You're out there representing your country. I'll never forget the feeling of walking through the tunnel at the Los Angeles Coliseum and just hearing the roar. It was really something. You can still hear it at times. Actually getting out there and finishing third. It was a short period of time, but it was one of the greatest." Beth Anders, whose strong penalty corner was clocked at 90 mph, nearly single-handedly lifted the U.S. team to victory. She scored eight of her team's nine goals in its five-game performance for an Olympic record that still stands today.

## ROLE MODELS/MENTORS

*Alice and Stanley Anders*—Beth cites her parents as "the best of her mentors." They taught her the value of play and nurtured their children with love wrapped in quality time.

*Ms. Callahan*—Ms. Callahan was Beth's fourth-grade teacher. Ms. Callahan laid a positive foundation for Beth to attend to school work. She did not allow her to get away with things that could have later impeded her academic success. "She just got a lot out of me," says Beth.

*Mr. Brown*—Fifth-grade teacher Mr. Brown was a man who was gentle and kind and had an interest in sports. His classes were challenging and fun. Learning in an atmosphere that is fun has been a characterizing trait of Beth Anders' coaching.

*Libby Williams*—Libby Williams' sense of humor, combined with her demanding personality, sent a message that she cared deeply for everyone she taught. Libby had that "special something" that made students want to be their best. She took the time to teach and to discipline each person, and that demonstrated that she really cared about each individual. Students knew how deeply she cared, even though she never said it. It was Libby Williams who provided the pattern for Beth's coaching style.

*Eleanor Snell*—Eleanor Snell, women's coach at Ursinus College, insisted that athletes act, compete, and carry themselves in a way that showed class. She knew how to inspire athletes. For example, Beth vividly remembers the day she didn't run back after a practice drill and all Eleanor said as Beth went by was,

"A good athlete runs back." Beth wanted to be good and so that was all Coach Snell needed to say. Coach Snell knew to say the right thing at the right time, and most often her silent manner inspired athletes to excel.

*Marge Watson*—Marge Watson, a college coach, was the kind of person students could talk with freely. "She understood my frustrations, when I was down, what I needed to do, and how I needed to do it. She understood my stubbornness and even the times when I was scared about competing." This woman never doubted or stopped believing in Beth.

## FAVORITE BOOKS AND MOVIES

Beth reads a lot of biographies and other nonfiction books. She especially enjoys John Feinstein's books and Walt Disney films.

## HOBBIES

One should not be surprised to know that Beth enjoys any athletic activity. She also enjoys, along with reading, working jigsaw puzzles and creating stained-glass objects.

## FUTURE PLANS

When asked about her plans for the future, Beth responded, "It's like somebody said, 'Well, how can you ever stop playing?' I said, 'I think I'll know when I have to when I am ready. Right now I am just really enjoying what I am doing and hope I can keep going. I am not afraid of the future, but I don't think about what is next because I feel I am doing what I want to do right now. The thing I love to do is teach. The day that I can't come in and look forward to it, then I've got to leave. We all have tired days, that is pretty human, but I still want to come in. It is just something that I've chosen and I love. I really like it."

Beth recently completed a book to be published by Human Kinetics, *Steps to Success—Field Hockey*.

## RECOGNITIONS AND ACHIEVEMENTS

### Accomplishments as a Player

- All American Squash 1970 National Champion
- All American in Basketball (1973) Kodak National Women's Basketball Team
- Member of U.S. Field Hockey Team for 14 years, Captain for 5 years
- Member of the U.S. Lacrosse Team
- Holder of Olympic Scoring Record, 8 goals in 5 games, 1984
- Two-time Olympian and Team Captain, 1980, 1984 (bronze medal)
- Four-time All-College Field Hockey and Lacrosse at Ursinus College
- Scored over 100 goals in international play

- Led U.S. team five years in a row in most goals scored
- All-World All-Star Team, 1975, 1980
- Olympic Committee Sportswoman of the Year, 1980, 1981
- Amateur Olympic Athlete of the Year (Field Hockey), 1984
- Philadelphia Sportswriters Amateur Athlete of the Year, 1984
- ESANDA Trophy—MVP International Tournament, 1984
- American Cup USA Winner

### Coaching Recognitions in Division I

- Coach of the Year (Virginia), 1984
- Colonial Athletic Conference Champions—7 times
- Conference Coach of the Year, 1991, 1992, 1997, 1998
- Eight National Championships: 1982, 1983, 1984, 1988, 1990, 1991, 1992, 1998
- Overall Record 348–47–7 (.856)
- Winningest coach in history of U.S. collegiate field hockey
- National Coach of the Year, 1999
- Only coach to qualify for every NCAA championship tournament
- Only coach to reach 11 final fours
- First coach in NCAA Division I to win 300 games
- Most consecutive wins in a row: 66 over 4 seasons

### National Coaching Assignments

- U.S. Team, 1985, 1990–1993
- Pan Am Games Bronze Medal, 1991
- Produced 13 National Team players and 9 Olympians

### Other Recognitions

- Ursinus College Hall of Fame, 1988
- United States Field Hockey Association Hall of Fame, 1989
- Pennsylvania Sports Hall of Fame, 1999
- Coached the USA's successful qualification for the World Cup, 1994

Photo courtesy of University of
California, Los Angeles

# SHARRON BACKUS

## Softball—University of California, Los Angeles

### INTRODUCTION

The Sharron Backus story is cloaked in excellence, and it all began during her growing-up years in a neighborhood enclave of ten boys. The boys became her buddies and inspired her to hone her sports skills. Endowed with an insatiable desire to excel, young Backus thrived on shooting basketball hoops and pounding baseballs against a block wall in her backyard.

### PERSONAL DATA

*Born*:  Orange, California, 1946

*Father*:  Clarence Backus

*Father's Occupation*:  Pilot and flight engineer

*Mother*:  Idalea Roy

*Mother's Occupation*:  Homemaker

*Sibling*:  Linda

*Alma Mater*:  California State University, Fullerton—B.S., Physical Education, 1966

## FORMATIVE YEARS

The Backus family was closely knit. They taught their children to believe in God, work hard, keep their word, and live as good Christians. They supported their daughters and fortified them with love and trust; in return they expected responsible behavior. These footings formed values that laid the foundation for Sharron's remarkable career and assured her the opportunity to burnish the skills of a superb athlete.

## PLAYING CAREER

The incremental climb to athletic success began at age 6 and ultimately garnered for Sharron a host of athletic honors. At 13, she notified the coach of the Gold Sox Triple A softball team that she was trying out for the team. Triple A players were two years older and larger than Backus. Coach Margo Davis thought Sharron wanted to try out for one of the younger teams, but Sharron quickly informed Margo that it was for the Triple A team she intended to play. Sharron got her chance to try out. Impressed by Sharron's throwing and batting skills, Coach Davis signed her up and positioned her in left field. This began a three-year stint with the Whittier Gold Sox.

On their first road trip, the Gold Sox soundly defeated the Phoenix Ramblers in the first game of a double header. In the second game Sharron was switched to shortstop. After that game the Rambler coach told Davis that Sharron was a shortstop and "it will be a major oversight not to play her in that position." Davis, an astute coach, agreed that shortstop was the perfect position for Sharron to sport her talents. This change sent Backus on another road trip, which eventually led to her being honored five times as an All-American shortstop!

In the fifteenth inning of the national playoffs, Backus lined a base hit tying the game for the Gold Sox. Finally, after 19 innings, the Gold Sox mustered the edge to win the game and the championship. Three thousand spectators viewed the event and ABC-TV was on hand to televise its first National Softball Championship. This was an extraordinary experience for a fifteen year-old.

Returning to high school as a celebrated athlete, Sharron still found the time to compete in softball, basketball, golf, volleyball, swimming, field hockey, and track and field. In fact, along with a special recognition in swimming, Sharron was named Anaheim High School's Girl of the Year.

In 1964 Margo Davis lost Backus to Frank Cirelli and his Orange Lionettes. Backus, now a freshman at Fullerton College, continued to compete in established leagues because Cal State at Fullerton did not offer women's athletics. Under the able coaching of Frank Cirelli, Sharron was named All American in 1964 and 1965, and the Orange Lionettes garnered the 1965 ASA National Championship.

By the time Backus stepped to the helm as UCLA Softball Coach (1975), she had played on seven national championship teams, had been honored five times as an All American, and the Brakettes had just won their fifth consecutive National ASA championship (1971–1975). The only thing lacking in this rich competitive background was a softball coaching experience.

After signing on as coach at UCLA, the Connecticut Falcons contracted with Sharron to compete for their Eastern Division professional team in the summer seasons. After competing for two seasons with the Falcons, Sharron was named starting shortstop for the Eastern Division All-Star Team; they had won two world championships. At the age of 32, Sharron Backus retired from competition to devote full attention to her UCLA coaching career.

## DECISION TO COACH

After earning a degree in physical education and art design from California State College, Fullerton, Sharron began teaching at Western High School in Anaheim, California. During summer recesses she competed for the Raybestos Brakettes. The Brakettes chalked up five back-to-back national championships, and Sharron was twice named All American.

In the mid-seventies, Judy Holland, Women's Athletic Director at UCLA, began restructuring women's athletics at the university. Shortly thereafter, Backus was hired and designated women's softball coach. Sharron was delighted with the appointment, but felt she just happened to be in the right place at the right time. As a high school physical educator she had coached everything but softball, so her background as softball athlete to softball coach at a major university was an easy transition. To become a coach seemed a natural progression rather than the result of a major decision.

## COACHING

The Backus coaching challenge was realized with ease and enjoyment. She believes athletics represents a microcosm of life that offers youth an avenue to become one's best. Athletics also allows the coach to focus on assisting youth to achieve excellence in a "classy way." Authentic and unscathed by personal success and recognition, Backus has remained true to her convictions. Often criticized for this stance, she continues to be unpretentious, authentic, and focused while dealing with gender issues and other equally disquieting dilemmas.

Although Sharron has been influenced by coaches such as Ralph Raymond, Margo Davis, and **Billie Moore** and players like Joan Joyce, Donna Lopiano, Brenda Riley, Irene Shea, Joyce Compton, Snooky Mulder, Kathy Stillwell, Mikey Davis, Carol Spanks, and many others, she has never looked to a particular person to "emulate or copy." Rather, she has integrated many admirable qualities from these fine players and coaches into a distinctive Backus style and philosophy. She found it natural to follow the lead of Margo and Ralph, because their styles resonated well with her own value system and coaching style.

Sharron's youthful passion for sport has transformed into a mature recognition that how one wins is more important than winning. Backus surrounds herself with players and coaches who believe in her system. A case in point is co-head coach Sue Enquist who alerts Backus to changes in athletes and assists her to adapt to student needs. Backus has used Sue's ability to communicate with athletes, thus lessening many of her own coaching pressures and allowing her to better focus in certain areas. The system dictates that athletes play hard, play fair, and play with contentment. Backus has a belief that these qualities start in the classroom, move through practice, and extend to the playing field and competition. Keeping up with the technology available to softball is important to Backus as she believes this will give athletes an advantage. For example, video assessment of each athlete is combined with any unique training tool that is available. The mainstay in the UCLA system is skill analysis, of which Backus is an expert.

Coach Backus' goal is to create an attitude that will not permit athletes to be satisfied until the final out on the final day. She regularly looks for that special something to do just a little better, quicker, stronger, and faster than anyone else. She is an athlete-friendly coach who understands the necessity of creating good team relationships. This time-intensive process is planned and organized with the same intensity and care as preparing daily practice exercises.

The first three years of Sharron's tenure at UCLA were challenging because she was still an active competitor, yet she led the Bruins to two conference championships and a 44–20 win-loss record. In 1978 she turned all of her energies to coaching, compiled a 31–3 record, and orchestrated UCLA's first national championship (AIAW). The following year (1979) the NCAA began sponsoring national championships for softball. Since that time, UCLA has captured seven of the sixteen NCAA–sponsored championships while claiming five second places and two third places.

UCLA collared the 1978 AIAW Championship when they defeated Northern Colorado in the finals. In the 1979 NCAA–sponsored tournament, UCLA took second. In 1982 the Bruins garnered their first NCAA title. In 1983 the Bruins slipped to third place, but by 1984 they steamed to a season record of 45–6–1, taking both the conference and the national championships. Sharron was voted NCAA Coach of the Year for the second time. In 1985 the Bruins captured the NCAA championship, netting three championships for UCLA in four years. They also seized the College World Series by defeating Nebraska, and Sharron was named NCAA Coach of the Year (for the third time) and inducted into the American Softball Association Hall of Fame.

In 1987, after a bleak 1986, the UCLA Bruins started a seven-year run in which they either won the national championship or took second. In 1987 they placed second, and in 1988, 1989, and 1990 they seized back-to-back NCAA national championships.

Sharron's fifth NCAA championship came in 1989, and by 1990 the Bruins wondered if their success would ever end. In an unprecedented third consecutive NCAA championship, the Bruins beat Fresno 2–0 for the third straight year. That year the Bruins set a school record with 62 wins, and Backus was again voted NCAA Coach of the Year. In the 1991 championship, the Bruins lost to Arizona 5–1 in the finals, and Coach Backus received the honor of being inducted into a second hall of fame: the National Softball Collegiate Association Hall of Fame. In 1992 UCLA racked up their fourth national title in five years. The 54–2 record was the NCAA's best overall record (.964). The following year (1993), the Bruins compiled another great season record of 50–5. This year Sharron was inducted into the Women's Sports Foundation Hall of Fame.

## PHILOSOPHY OF COACHING

Preparing her Bruins for the season required Sharron and Sue, her co-coach, to establish a schedule for the year. Fall was devoted to off-season physical development. As the competitive season approached, the attention was focused on the mind and the body, executions, proper technique, and constant repetition. Backus feels that constant repetitions are important, because in competition ten out of ten is not enough, fifty out of fifty is the goal. In the fall of the year, an extra heavy emphasis was placed on the athletes' academic lives. In winter there was a shift of focus and by spring, when competition was to begin, the main focus turned to a total commitment to the program, to team positions, and to the team. The coaching staff and others closely associated with the team became sensitively attuned to the athletes and their needs. Programs became individualized to the athlete, and team goals were incorporated to direct individual efforts.

Sharron's journey to coaching excellence was born of hard work. Like other women coaches, she had to learn coping skills. Clarence Backus, Sharron's father, passed away at a critical time in her career; dealing with his passing, and the unwarranted stereotypes related to all phases of athletics, has been difficult. Great changes have occurred from the time she started to compete in the sixties until now. For example, now it is socially acceptable for a woman to sweat; in the sixties it was not.

Backus has been challenged to keep pace with change while maintaining an appropriate focus. Endorsements, contracts, coaching national teams, professional player contracts, and women's issues have been tempting distractions. When possible, Sharron has tried to avoid these so she could expend her energy on conducting a superior softball program. "Hopefully," Sharron says, "I will be rewarded for what we put on the field." Although she has been told that she needs to be more vocal and to express herself on professional issues, it is not her nature to do so. She claims to be "neither a women's libber nor a doormat."

Backus credits the UCLA administration for providing her and the softball organization excellent support. They continue to provide the emotional and the financial enhancement necessary to facilitate growth and improvement.

She recruits outstanding athletes who are willing to work hard to build an enviable tradition. In short, Sharron Backus is very satisfied coaching softball at UCLA.

Nineteen years of coaching, ten conference championships, seven second places, nine national championships, five second places, and three third places collectively disclose one segment of Coach Sharron Backus' coaching career. Another piece of the segment names Backus seven times PAC Coach of the Year, four times NCAA Coach of the Year, and for a finale she has been recognized with three hall of fame inductions. Without a doubt, Sharron Backus is clearly one of the best and one of the most accomplished women to ever coach the game of softball. In response to this claim, Sharron quotes the familiar Newtonian adage, "If I have achieved anything, it is only because I have stood on the shoulders of giants!" Surely she has assumed that stature in years of hard work.

## MEMORABLE MOMENTS

When asked to comment on one memorable moment of her excellent career, Backus said, "The winning of course; winning that first National Championship when I never knew what to expect. Winning a national championship a few times and transferring that into ways and means whereby kids can hang on to that first experience until they can taste it themselves and then, once they know what it takes and how sweet it is, then it just kind of perpetuates itself and so the coach just stays positive and encourages them to keep doing those kinds of things again."

Each championship has been different for her. Each had highs and lows. The unexpected win was the sweetest, and the excitement of back-to-back championships iced the cake. Such accomplishments were difficult, but the challenge was the joyful part.

Diplomatically declining to choose a favorite team, Backus feels each team had a special value or quality. She cites as especially notable watching athletes turn into "super people," even though they may not have had super qualities when they started to compete. These satisfactions have brought a sense of coaching fulfillment.

## RECOGNITIONS AND ACHIEVEMENTS

### Accomplishments as a Player

- Eastern Division All Stars
- All American, 1964, 1965
- Player on seven national championship teams
- Numerous all-state, regional, national, and international all-star teams

### Coaching Recognitions in Division I

- Conference Championships: 1983, 1984, 1986, 1988, 1989, 1990, 1991, 1993
- Conference Coach of the Year: 1982, 1984, 1985, 1987, 1990, 1992, 1993, 1995
- National Coach of the Year: 1982, 1984, 1985, 1992
- Nine national championships: AIAW, 1978; NCAA, 1982, 1984, 1985, 1988, 1989, 1990, 1992, 1995
- Overall record 847–167–3 (.834) NCAA Division I
- Overall 910–187–3 (.827)
- Professional Team Orlando Wahoos, World Champions, 1998

### National Coaching Assignment

- Pan Am Games assistant, 1983

### Other Recognitions

- Women's Sports Foundation Hall of Fame, 1993
- NSCA Hall of Fame, 1991
- American Softball Association Hall of Fame, 1985
- NCAA Softball Committee, 1982–1993
- Pan Am Selection Committee

Photo courtesy of University of
California, Berkeley

# JAN BROGAN

*Tennis—University of California, Berkeley*

## INTRODUCTION

Unlike many elite tennis players, Jan Brogan did not begin at an early age to hold a tennis racket or to take private club lessons. Jan began to play tennis when she was 15 years old, but by the time she entered her senior year in high school, she had achieved a meteoric rise and a national ranking. Encouraged by this degree of competitive success, she decided, much to the chagrin of her parents, to play professional tennis and postpone entering college. Jan's non-traditional entry into the world of tennis delayed, but did not handicap, her successful achievement as a fierce competitor and a top coach. Brogan's feisty climb to become a nationally ranked tennis player began in a city recreation league and continued at Ygnacio High School in Concord, California.

## PERSONAL DATA

*Born*: Concord, California, 1952
*Father*: Arnold Brogan
*Father's Occupation:* Postal Carrier
*Mother*: Wanda Lee Brogan
*Mother's Occupation*: Homemaker/Apartment Manager

*Siblings:* Sandy, Steven, and Laura

*Alma Maters:* DeAnza Junior College/San Jose State—B.S., Physical Education, 1978; John F. Kennedy University—M.S., Sport Psychology, 1998

## FORMATIVE YEARS

Jan was the second of the Brogans' four children. The family moved twice while living in Concord and eventually established themselves in the Peach Place neighborhood. The Peach Place cul-de-sac was a favorite playground and became Jan's arena for learning American childhood games. Boys were her playmates, and her ability to quickly learn skills gave her the opportunity to be involved in many sports.

## SPORTS HISTORY

A good student at Ygnacio Valley High School, Jan easily maintained a B average and was motivated to excel in athletics. In high school, she encountered change and challenges. First, she felt uncomfortable as a tomboy, so she changed to fit what she envisioned as her Ygnacio Valley High School image, and, secondly, she was switched to a more difficult academic track. Both situations called for new direction and new resolve. In junior high school she competed on the softball, basketball, and track teams. By the time she entered high school, she was drawn to tennis; however, it was a tennis class and an encouraging teacher, Mrs. Inez Gussey, that attracted her competitive nature and prompted her to engage in summer tournaments.

When school did not provide enough competitive sports for a young woman of Jan's talent and interest, Jan supplemented the schools' athletic offerings with neighborhood activities. Along with neighborhood happenings, family camping became another favorite outdoor activity. She especially enjoyed the opportunity to be with her father, grandparents, and cousins.

## PLAYING CAREER

Jan's parents understood her drive and her desire to excel, but they did not favor circuit competition as they felt that a college education would afford her a more secure future. Three years on the pro circuit somewhat satisfied Jan's competitive drive, and, much to the delight of her parents, she enrolled in DeAnza Junior College and found employment at the Los Gatos Racket Club. With no team for women at DeAnza, Jan tried out and earned a spot on the men's tennis team. She competed rather steadily in 4th singles and 3rd doubles positions. Once her degree at DeAnza was completed, she transferred to San Jose State and entered the school's physical education teacher preparation program. NCAA rules barred Jan from playing intercollegiate tennis because she was a teaching pro at the Blossom Hill Tennis Club. After completing student teaching in a high school physical education program, she felt she could better contribute to a collegiate program and applied for the position of head women's tennis coach at the University of California at Berkeley.

## DECISION TO COACH

In 1978 Jan became the Cal Women's Tennis Coach. To be head coach at Berkeley was a dream come true, but the $10,000 salary produced a low-grade nightmare. She would need to continue her Blossom Hill pro job to make ends meet. The necessity of working two jobs required a daily two-hour commute—not an easy entry into the new role of coach and the myriad associated responsibilities.

The impact of Title IX was felt in most college programs with an escalation in funds and leadership directed to women's sports; Berkeley was no exception. The tennis program needed direction and qualified leadership, and to provide both implied obligation and opportunity. Jan saw the leadership need, and this opportunity became, in her own words, "my career . . . and the greatest challenge of my life." Five years as a teaching pro and five years on the professional circuit prepared her to develop the fertile, untethered program into one of the premier collegiate programs in the United States.

The evolution took time. Some facilities were not up to par. She insisted that the tennis courts become regulation size, that the team be afforded the same priority in scheduling as the physical education classes and the men's team. Office space had to be created so she did not have to share with another coach, a secretary, a receptionist, or a photocopier. She had to have the physical facilities to compete in the recruiting wars with UCLA, USC, Stanford, and Arizona State. Amidst all of these inadequacies, she was saddled with administrators who were slow to respond to the needs of a floundering, fledgling tennis program. It was evident that developing a tennis powerhouse would be an uphill battle. These inconveniences did not dampen her spirit—they were only the temporary setbacks motivating her to excel.

Jan coached over 350 games at Berkeley and compiled a 71 percent win record. Her teams have been among the PAC 10 conference leaders, and she has been recognized as the NOPAC Coach of the Year five times, the PAC 10 Coach of the Year twice, the region Coach of the Year, and was named the 1989–1990 National Coach of the Year. With teams ranked in the top five NCAA for 11 of the past 12 years, Jan has demonstrated the ability to achieve success regardless of barriers that might have overwhelmed someone of lesser stature. Jan's method for building a high-level intercollegiate tennis program has been to aim for the top and inch ahead one step at a time. Evidence of the success of this operational plan is shown in the data table, which indicates the number of times her team has placed in the top ten in NCAA final rankings.

Believing that the drive to win or achieve excellence has to come from within, Jan has stressed throughout her career that developing the talents she believes God gives to all is what will determine one's success. Coaching in a structure which arbitrarily assigns the genders certain attributes has required Jan to coach and teach that attributes for achieving athletic success are gender free. She believes that male or female can overcome, if necessary, prior socialization and conditioning and develop behaviors and attitudes requisite for success. She has consistently taught her tennis players that, "Someone may have more experience than you technically, but no one should be better or stronger or last longer than you. Give your best effort and never beat yourself." This motto, coupled with her strong belief in sport psychology and strength training, has helped implant in her athletes the will to win. Her respect for sport psychology motivated her to become a marathon runner in an attempt to assist her in understanding endurance and also be attuned and be willing to do what she asks of her athletes.

Jan recognizes that sexism exists at Berkeley and in the sport of tennis. In spite of this condition, she feels that "One must face the reality of sexism in any form and deal with it in the most appropriate manner." For Jan, that usually means facing the reality that some people never change, and others change slowly, but change itself takes a long time.

## PHILOSOPHY OF COACHING

Jan believes that to have a good program, it must be balanced overall. To Jane this means there must be a demanding physical conditioning program and a practical mental preparation program, along with sound technical development and tactical strategies. With these components in place, she schedules tough competition that will demand her athletes to perform at their best. The Cal Tennis team records prove that her approach works.

Jan feels that it is necessary to move the athlete through the developmental stages from dependence to independence to interdependence. In order to do this, she has to be adept at switching from the role of coach to the roles of surrogate parent and mentor with the explicit goal of encouraging greater self-reliance. Her team-building approach requires the synergism of persons capable of interdependence. For Jan, the bottom line of her contribution is to nurture human beings, with tennis as the vehicle to accomplishing this goal.

Describing herself as "eager to gain the edge," Jan has, to this end, become knowledgeable in the psychology and sociology of sport and in the strength and conditioning aspects of athletics. Believing in the importance of showing a good example, she has entered 10Ks and marathons to demonstrate her belief and to take on new personal challenges. Jan obtained a master's degree in sport psychology to facilitate the practical application of psychology to tennis. Constantly learning and infusing these principles into her coaching have facilitated her becoming a strong force in women's tennis.

Goal-directed from youth, Jan's personal philosophy is manifested in the conduct of Cal's tennis program. A calculated risk-taker, Jan uses risk-taking to create new opportunities. A dauntless spirit impels her to manage obstacles and to create opportunities out of challenges. Pressing ahead, regardless of the obstacles or the challenges, has become her signature for excellence. Verbalizing this characteristic she says, "I believe if there is an obstacle, you must find a way to transform it!" This belief, which long ago gave her the courage to try out for the DeAnza College Men's Tennis Team, motivated her in her struggle to get regulation tennis courts, to improve weight rooms and office space, and tackle the task of renewing and redirecting Cal's tennis program. Her experience has shown that tenacity reaps rewards and dogged determination surmounts obstacles. Perhaps Jan Brogan's coaching philosophy is best summed up by the Latin motto, "*carpe diem*" or "seize the day." This conviction has served her well in creating Berkeley's enviable Women's Tennis Program.

## MEMORABLE MOMENTS

Jan notes her most memorable moments were when Lisa Albano became a finalist in the 1992 NCAA Singles Championship and when Amanda Augustus and Amy Jensen became NCAA Doubles Champions in 1988–Berkeley's first NCAA title.

## ROLE MODELS/MENTORS

As her success in coaching has grown, Jan has been quick to credit the contribution of Dick Overstreet, pro-coach at Diablo Country Club. Overstreet recognized the enthusiasm and raw talent of young Jan. Two other tennis pros, Dick Skeen and Mary Hill, also taught her their certain specialties that helped to influence her game and her career.

Mary Hill, a great coach and one of the few women pros in Sacramento, assisted Jan and is credited with giving her the greatest encouragement and help with her game. Jan spent her weekends driving to Sacramento to learn from Mary. Until her meeting with Hill, the young athlete had been coached mostly by men.

Jan also cites, as role models, *Martina Navratilova, Billie Jean King, Gloria Steinem, Martin Luther King, Jackie Robinson*, and *Albert Einstein*.

## FAVORITE BOOKS AND AUTHORS

The *Seat of the Soul* by Gary Zukov, *Tougher Training for Sport* by James Loetter, and the *Collective Works of Rumi*, edited by Coleman Barks.

## HOBBIES

Playing tennis and working out are still favorite hobbies for Jan. She also likes gardening, house remodeling, backpacking, and reading and writing poetry.

## RECOGNITIONS AND ACHIEVEMENTS

### Coaching Recognitions in Division I

- Seven Non–PAC Conference Championships: 1981, 1982, 1983, 1984, 1985, 1986, 1987
- Non–PAC Coach of the Year, 1981, 1982, 1983, 1984, 1985, 1986
- PAC Coach of the Year, 1987, 1992, 1994
- Northwest Region Coach of the Year, 1988, 1991, 1993
- Wilson/ITA Coach of the Year, 1990
- Produced 43 All Americans
- Sixteen NCAA Top Ten Finalists

### National Coaching Assignments

- World University Games, Japan, 1995
- USTA National Teams, 1985–1990
- U.S. Team to French Open, 1985

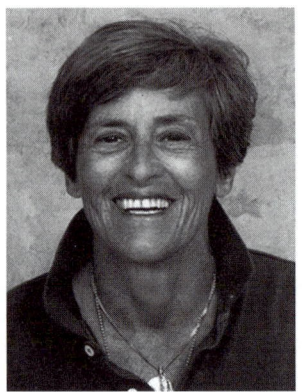

Photo courtesy of University
of Miami

# LELA CANNON
## *Golf—University of Miami*

### INTRODUCTION

For Lela Cannon "take me out to the ball game" meant going to Yankee Stadium with her father and watching baseball from his box. On one hand, Lela's interest in sports offset her father William Weinstein's desire for his firstborn to have been a boy. On the other hand, her mother had hoped her firstborn to be a girl who played with dolls. Charlotte got her girl, but Lela was more interested in playing games with the neighborhood boys than in playing house with dolls. Lela's early experiences translated into a lifelong interest in sports.

Lela Cannon could well be labeled a "late bloomer": she took up golf at the age of thirty-two. She honed her nascent talent in what started out as a one-year assignment and turned it into a seventeen-year professional challenge.

### PERSONAL DATA

> *Born*:  June 23, 1938, New Haven, Connecticut
> *Father*:  William Weinstein
> *Father's Occupation*:  Commercial building construction
> *Mother*:  Charlotte Solomon
> *Mother's Occupation*:  Homemaker

*Siblings*: Eileen and Richard

*Husband*: Anthony (deceased)

*Children*: Marc and Melissa; grandchildren, William and Katie

*Alma Maters*: Leslie College; Southern Connecticut State University—B.S., 1961

## FORMATIVE YEARS

Lela Cannon's early sporting experiences took place in summer camps. During camp she learned a variety of sport skills and discovered her athletic talent. Sports programs at Sheridan Junior High, in Westville, Connecticut, encouraged her to further develop softball and basketball skills. At camp Chippewah in New Hampshire she learned a lot about tennis and softball. The camp was inhabited by 200 youths—50 percent of which were boys. These elements created an exciting environment for discovery and personal development.

Cannon's higher education took place at Leslie College in Cambridge, Massachusetts. While there Lela met and married her husband, Anthony. Her son, Marc, was born in 1962, and Melissa, her daughter, was born in 1965.

## PLAYING CAREER

In 1970, at the age of 32, Lela took up golf and became a fine amateur golfer in the state of Connecticut. Later she became a member of the Connecticut State Golf Association; this membership required a player to have a handicap of sixteen or less. Married and raising two children placed a limit on the opportunities for her to develop an extensive early playing career.

## DECISION TO COACH

When the Cannon children were involved in swimming on the Woodbridge, Connecticut, age-group swimming teams, Lela involved herself as a volunteer coach. Then in 1983, when her children were grown, she tagged along with them to Miami, where they were attending college. When the University of Miami officials learned of her golf expertise, she was asked to coach the University of Miami Golf Team. Responding to the invitation to coach, she said she would coach for a year. She is now entering her seventeenth year as golf coach.

Lela's success as a golf coach became evident as she led her 1984 squad to a national championship. That same year she was named head coach of the U.S. All Star Team that competed against Japan.

## PHILOSOPHY OF COACHING

The Cannon philosophy of coaching is rather simple: "Stay focused and don't get over excited, take one shot at a time and one day at a time. The team that gets along together and bonds will generate, from within, their own motivation and determination to excel."

Lela's belief that athletes sense the coach, and so the coach must stay relaxed and focused, is basic to having fun and teaching that the world won't come to an end after a bad round. This philosophy works well for Cannon as she has observed the practicality of these beliefs. She also believes that an athlete must be extremely competitive, have inner strength, and want the win more than anything else. Cannon feels that a coach must show strength by being open to change and by finding the time to listen to each team member; coaching golf requires the coach to attune herself to each individual so she knows exactly what will work for each team member.

Five rules are required for teams coached by Cannon: (1) no drinking; (2) act like a lady, happy or unhappy, and respect yourself, the golf course, and the school you represent; (3) don't miss classes; (4) don't miss practice without a good reason; and (5) handle losing in the same manner you handle winning.

To date, Cannon's biggest coaching obstacle has been not having a campus facility to "call home." This causes an ever-present and time-consuming need to find times and practice space on off-campus sites. She feels it would also help her program if the city of Miami were to get better press.

## CHANGES IN ATHLETES

In Cannon's opinion, the American Junior Golf Association tournaments make superstars of young athletes before they are real superstars. She feels that these early recognitions put young golfers on pedestals before they mature as individuals or as athletes.

## MEMORABLE MOMENTS

Lela remembers winning the national championship in 1984 in a seven-shot, come-from-behind situation as an extraordinary experience. The team had won numerous tournaments that year, so they affirmed the fact that they had the ability to take the big one. It was also a memorable moment for her to be chosen the head coach of the U.S. All-Star Team that competed against Japan. Going to Japan and meeting the United States ambassador was also thrilling for Coach Lela Cannon.

## ROLE MODELS/MENTORS

*Mrs. Quinn*—Mrs. Quinn was a sixth-grade teacher. From her Lela learned one could do anything if the desire was great enough.

*Mrs. Dwyer*—Mrs. Dwyer was a physical education teacher. This teacher gave Lela encouragement in softball and basketball.

*Earl Stewart*—Mr. Stewart was Golf Coach at Southern Methodist University. He taught that the coach is responsible to the team and should not feel obligated to socialize with other coaches while on the road. He also believed that trusting and respecting athletes prompts athletes to extend the same treatment to the coach.

## FAVORITE BOOKS AND AUTHORS

Lela has read all of John Grisham's books. Her favorites are *The Client* and *A Time to Kill*.

## HOBBIES

Spending time with grandchildren and exercising top Lela's list of hobbies.

## FAVORITE MOVIE

*Chariots of Fire*

## FUTURE PLANS

Lela plans to coach for several more years. In addition she plans to play competitive golf.

## RECOGNITIONS AND ACHIEVEMENTS

### Coaching Recognitions in Division I

- State Championships: 1984, 1988, 1993
- National Coach of the Year, 1984, 1992
- National Championship, 1983–1984
- Eight All Americans and four Academic All Americans
- Five NCAA Championship appearances

### National Coaching Assignment

- U.S. vs. Japan, 1993

### Other Accomplishment

- Initiated into Iron Arrow Society, 1998

Photo courtesy of University of
Texas, Austin

# JODY CONRADT

*Basketball Coach and Athletic Director—
University of Texas, Austin*

## INTRODUCTION

While Jody Conradt was en route to becoming a basketball coach, she defied
her own beliefs about coaching. Coached only by men, Conradt never even
entertained the idea that she, too, was capable of coaching. In fact, she did not
even believe that women could coach. A woman of talent and energy, Coach
Conradt rose to the rank of fourth on the NCAA's roster of active Division I
men's and women's winningest basketball coaches.

## PERSONAL DATA

*Born*: Goldthwaite, Texas, May 13, 1941

*Father*: Charles Conradt (deceased)

*Father's Occupation*: Credit officer

*Mother*: Ann Conradt

*Mother's Occupation*: Homemaker

*Sibling*: Mike Conradt

*Alma Mater*: Baylor University—B.S., Physical Education, 1963;
M.S., 1969

## FORMATIVE YEARS

The Conradts nurtured their daughter with a              of athletic exposure and opportunity. Charles Conradt, a semi-p              player, took his
family on the Sunday circuit to watch his games, and              idt played softball in a highly competitive league. It was not until J              d Baylor University that she discovered her own incomparable a              age. She had
been reared by athletic parents and she had attended a              re everyone
played on a team and where girls' sports were afforded i              portance as
boys' sports. This realization helped her appreciate that              ch athletic
background unmatched by that of any of her peers.

## PLAYING CAREER

Jody, a native Texan and the first of two children, was born to Charles and
Ann Conradt in Goldthwaite, Texas. The small community was noted for its
school-related activities, but most especially, its athletic programs. Destined to
be a winner, Jody was consumed at an early age with an insatiable desire to do
her best athletically and academically. This drive to excel pervaded all aspects of
her life and proved to be well worth the time and effort invested. School
achievements included Jody's being high school class valedictorian, a
40-point-per-game high school basketball prepster, a student council member, and a participant in school literary events. Conradt describes those growing up years as "relatively uneventful," but the "uneventful" proved to be seed
and cultivation for the blooming of a brilliant career.

## SPORTS HISTORY

Enrolling at Baylor University for academic reasons, Jody intended to major in history and become a teacher. In choosing Baylor she bypassed trying to
earn a basketball scholarship at Wayland Baptist, reasoning that a degree from
Baylor University would be more impressive. At Baylor, Jody soon found involvement in sport through the intramural program. The women's basketball
team was composed of physical education students. Not wanting to major in
physical education, she resisted the coach's enticements to join the team until
the coach's urging finally persuaded her to change majors. Conradt graduated
from Baylor University in 1963 with a bachelor of science degree in physical
education.

Not long after graduation, Superintendent M. L. Rice of the Waco Midway
School District, who was also a successful basketball coach, persuaded Jody to
accept a job as his assistant coach. She accepted the job with little confidence in
her ability to coach. Rice carefully mentored her on the how-to's of discipline,
task completion, and skill development. After Rice retired, Conradt was offered the head coaching position, but at the same time Baylor University extended an offer to assist in coaching their extramural basketball team. She
chose Baylor, coaching for one year and earning a master's degree. From

Baylor she moved to Sam Houston State College (1970–1973) and the University of Texas, Arlington (1973–1976), until finally accepting the monumental challenge of coaching at the University of Texas at Austin in 1976.

Thus began the Jody Conradt era at the University of Texas. This was her first full-time coaching post. Conradt teamed efforts with Donna Lopiano, the newly appointed women's athletic director, and they directed their strength toward creating a national power in women's basketball. Shackled with a limited budget and six tuition scholarships, Jody quickly energized the program with several elite recruits. Like a refurbished house, the program improvements and the new leadership began to attract more outstanding athletes. Their quick success inspired Lopiano and Conradt to unfold an exclusive Lady Longhorn basketball schedule and a season ticket package. This brave step was an effort to gain their own cadre of fans separate from the men's team. The start was slow, but they mustered a loyal group of spectators and established a six-year record of having more fans, on average, than any other women's basketball program in the country (1985–1991).

Conradt is endowed with stability, energy, and creative talent. She approaches her job with a sense of balance and a sense of humor. She is willing to test new ideas, can unlock player talent, and is adept at attracting fans and friends. These qualities are fundamental to her ability to take on the dual roles of coach and women's athletic director (she assumed the latter role in May of 1992). With the help of a support staff, she accomplishes it all with the decorum of a "Goodwill Ambassador" and the skill of a CEO—a Herculean task by any trendsetter's standard.

## ROLE MODELS/MENTORS

The acumen required to assume the dual role of coach and athletic director could well have been honed in those early years of watching her own parents juggle their sports careers around childrearing and work schedules. Jody had also competed in junior high for Coach Ray Akins, who pushed for her best, not allowing self-satisfaction to be the end product. (Akins' son, Marty, led UT's football team to a national title in 1970.) Jody had also assisted Coach Rice, who opened her eyes to envision herself in a way she had not thought possible, and Olga Fallen, who had mentored her at Baylor.

## CHALLENGES

Every coach's career has a unique set of hurdles or impediments. Reflecting on these obstacles, Coach Conradt claims that most of her hurdles have been self-imposed. Nonetheless, she has had to look beyond the doubters who said women's basketball would not sell, and she has had to overlook the hurt inflicted by those who attach a negative label to females associated with women's sport. She claims to have had few obstacles or down days primarily because she loves the profession and the persistent challenges. She loves working with team-oriented athletes who are motivated to be successful, and she continues to gain her greatest satisfaction from working with successful, highly motivated athletes.

## PHILOSOPHY OF COACHING

Jody Conradt's style of coaching is undergirded by appropriate lines of communication, a firm method of discipline, and the ability to create close-knit, goal-oriented teams. Although a sports psychologist is called in when needed, doing so is not a pre-scheduled part of her coaching scheme.

## MEMORABLE MOMENTS

Over the past years, Conradt remembers her disappointment when in the 1984–85 season her Lady Longhorns, clearly the best team in the country, did not win the NCAA title. The following year, however, they did win the NCAA title with a perfect 34–0 record, becoming the first Women's NCAA Division I team in history to go undefeated en route to the NCAA title. She also remembers the thrill that occurred on the day in 1997 when she and Donna Lopiano stood outside the Texas basketball arena and saw the "sold-out" sign. They had filled the arena for the 1997 NCAA Women's Final Four.

## HONORS AND AWARDS

Conradt has been honored three times as coach of the year and was named Southwest Conference Coach of the Year four different times. The Women's Basketball Coaches Association gave her its highest award: the Carol Eckman Award. She was also inducted into the Texas Women's Hall of Fame in 1986 and the International Women's Sports Hall of Fame (1995), the Naismith Memorial Basketball Hall of Fame (1998), and the Women's Basketball Hall of Fame (1999). In 1987 she was the head coach of the United States National Team and led the ball club to a gold medal in the Pan American Games. In 1991 the National Association for Girls' and Women's Sports lauded her with the Guiding Woman in Sport Award, and in 1992 the NCAA recognized her contribution to basketball during the tenth anniversary of the basketball championship in 1992.

In 1995 the University of Texas, Austin, Women's Athletics Department reached the 20–year mark. At this point the program had an accumulated record of 20 national championships in sports ranging from swimming, tennis, volleyball, and basketball to track and field. Under Conradt's tenure as women's athletic director, Texas has earned four additional NCAA titles in women's track and field. All of the women's sports teams have been successful. Women's athletics is robust and visible. They are successful, and they have the records and the credentials to document that women can build a sports dynasty in a male-dominated cosmos.

Jody Conradt has demonstrated that although one does not always start with a grand plan, a penchant for hard work and the love of a good challenge can harvest an abundant crop. Athletic prosperity at the University of Texas was founded on empowering all athletic personnel to believe in themselves and their ability to accomplish their jobs. Each staff member is expected to have an ironclad work ethic with a commitment to set goals, follow goals, and reach goals. To do less would be to abandon the leadership legacy of coach and athletic director Jody Conradt.

## RECOGNITIONS AND ACHIEVEMENTS

### Coaching Recognition in Division I

- Conference Championships: 1982–1983, 1984, 1985, 1986, 1987, 1988, 1989, 1990, 1993
- Conference Coach of the Year, 1984, 1985, 1987, 1988
- National Coach of the Year: AIAW, 1979–1980; NCAA, 1983–1984, 1985–1986
- Eleven Top Ten finalists in AP polls at Texas
- Straight wins against conference opponents: 183
- Winningest Woman Coach in Division I in terms of wins active
- Nineteen All Americans
- Four Olympians, thirteen Olympic trialists

### National Coaching

- Pan Am Games, Head Coach, Gold Medal, 1987

### Other Accomplishments

- Texas Women's Hall of Fame, 1986
- Carol Eckman Award, 1987
- Guiding Women in Sport Award, 1991
- Texas Sports Hall of Fame, 1998
- Naismith Memorial Basketball Hall of Fame, 1998
- Women's Basketball Hall of Fame, 1999

Photo courtesy of California State
Polytechnic College

# TERRY CRAWFORD

*Track and Field—USA Olympics; Track—California
State Polytechnic College, San Luis Obispo*

## INTRODUCTION

When, on September 15, 1988, Terry Crawford walked into the Seoul Olympic stadium as head coach of women's track and field for the United States of America, this former USA top-ranked 800-meter runner and University of Texas head track coach felt as if she were living a dream come true. Filled with emotion, she was unable to contain the tears that coursed down her face. This memorable moment was the ultimate weigh station on a journey begun at a high school field day.

## PERSONAL DATA

*Born*: Greenville, Texas, February 21, 1948

*Father*: Daniel Hull

*Father's Occupation*: Manager, Pet Milk

*Mother*: Lucille Conway Hull

*Mother's Occupation*: Homemaker

*Sibling*: Judy

*Husband*: Mike Crawford

*Alma Mater*: University of Tennessee—B.S., 1970; M.S., 1972

## FORMATIVE YEARS

Terry was the Hulls' second daughter. A tight-knit and encouraging family, the Hulls gave their children support without pushing, exemplified the merits of their Methodist faith, and taught the values of personal morality, hard work, and how to make wise decisions.

A busy, independent child and a natural athlete, Terry ventured out with the neighborhood kids and competed in their football, basketball, and baseball games. She played clarinet in the school band, directed the intramural program, and proved to be a high-achieving, goal-oriented student. The 1960s were lean years for girls' interscholastic sports nationwide, but Greenville substituted for this lack with high school intramurals and field days.

## SPORTS HISTORY

Talent and a passion to run competitively led Terry to develop a close association with coach Ed Temple and the famous Tennessee State Tiger Belles' Track Team. Temple had developed a number of Olympians such as Wilma Rudolph and Wyel Matias. This accomplished squad of black women showered the lone white runner with camaradarie and mentorship. After a brief but successful running career, Terry's competitive journey ended in 1972, when an injury squelched her Olympic dream.

Although Terry discovered her love for track at the high school's annual field day, it was a former Greenville high school runner who recognized her endowment for running and encouraged her to test that talent in competition. Running goals coupled with a desire to become a teacher prompted Terry to enroll at the University of Tennessee in Knoxville to pursue both goals. When she entered Tennessee, the school was just initiating a women's track and field team at the same time a local track club was starting a team for women called the Tiger Belles. The Tiger Belles club featured outstanding women like Madeline Manning, Martha Watson, and Estelle Basterville. These women facilitated Terry's passage into the competitive track sphere. This bit of good fortune formed an important link that would lead to Crawford's later accomplishments.

During her stay at the University of Tennessee, classmate Mike Crawford became her off-track investment. Mike played junior college baseball and transferred to the University of Tennessee to concentrate on academic work. Shortly after her graduation, Mike and Terry married. This was in 1970.

After graduation Terry enlisted Roger Gumm, a former University of Kentucky 800–meter man, to be her personal coach. The fine record she established at the university, where she specialized in the 800–meter, qualified her for a position on the national team from 1969 to 1971. Next came membership on the U.S. Pan American Games team. From there she soared to be one of the top-ranked 800–meter runners in the United States. Amidst these remarkable achievements, Terry never lost the memory of the thrill of competing in the first AIAW Intercollegiate Track and Field Championships. Nor did she forget the deep appreciation she felt for the people who believed in her enough to extend their support. These successes opened new competitive opportunities plus the chance to complete a master's degree. Her dreams had come true!

Success and opportunity present challenges and disappointments. Crawford's hopes to be an Olympic competitor were dashed prior to the trials. A 1972 disc injury and a serious hamstring pull made it impossible for her to compete. These injuries forced retirement and thus ended an illustrious track career. Crawford completed her master's degree and began teaching at Knox County High School, where she organized a girls' track team. During that year she was invited to join the University of Tennessee's Physical Education faculty and take charge of the year-old women's track and field program. Title IX was flexing its legislative muscle in favor of women's athletics, so the University of Tennessee instituted track to help establish a strong women's athletics program to compliment a budding national caliber program for men.

## COACHING

In the fall of 1973, at 24 years of age, Terry Crawford donned the head coach's cap and began to engineer the University of Tennessee's track and field program. Over the next 11 years Tennessee's track and field program was transformed into one of the United States' premier track and field ensembles. It was exhilarating for Crawford as she melded personal experience and knowledge with the spirit of a pioneer.

Terry quickly taught her crucible of high-held principles to eager athletes. Fundamental to all else, each athlete had to understand that sacrifice and devotion were required to achieve one's best—this was the basis for excellence. In 1980, the lady Vols showed their principled commitment by winning the AIAW National Championship. It was their first national championship; it was a team effort. In praise of this accomplishment, Crawford lauded them as a "wonderful group of young women who had fun and enjoyed each other's association." To explain her own professional experience and feelings she stated, "One of the things I've always said about my job is that I have been able to accomplish the things I have because it's been fun for me. I've never looked at coaching as a job; the fact I was able to earn a paycheck for what I did was just a bonus for me."

In 1982 and 1984, Terry's lady Vols were runners-up in the NCAA championships behind UCLA (1982) and Florida State (1984). Thus Terry Crawford became the most successful female track coach of an NCAA women's track team. At the Los Angeles Olympic Games in 1984, Terry was there to witness her renowned runner, Benita Fitzgerald, win gold in the 100-meter hurdles. She described the opportunity to witness the event as a "tear jerker and a great moment." For Crawford, words could not adequately portray the rapture of watching Benita cross the finish line first and mount the victory stand.

That year, 1984, was a year of achievement climaxed by an offer to accept the position as head coach for women at the University of Texas. Crawford readily accepted the post for two reasons. First, the University of Texas was the flagship of progress in supporting women's athletics—this excited her. Second, building another top-notch team was an irresistible challenge. Recruiting western runners to Tennessee had been difficult. Texas was better located, which would enhance recruiting possibilities from all sections of the country. Terry always found the challenge of a new journey more enjoyable than the end result, and, because the University of Texas was progressive and highly competitive, it offered new opportunities for her to learn and to grow personally and professionally.

This change compelled Terry to leave Knoxville. Mike's insurance business was doing well, so Mike and Terry opted for a commuter marriage. Terry spent the next nine years coaching at the University of Texas. During these nine years her teams won five national championships. In 1986, her team won the cross-country and the indoor and the outdoor NCAA championships. They won the NCAA indoor title again in 1988 and 1990.

In 1988 Terry was named head coach of the USA Women's Track and Field Team, who would compete in the Seoul Olympic Games. The team was made up of 49 women, including such well known running celebrities as Evelyn Ashford, Gail Devers, Florence Griffith Joyner, Jackie Joyner Kersey, Mary Decker Slaney, and Gwen Torrance. In addition, Terry coached three of her own athletes, Joetta Clark (800m), LaVonna Martin (100m hurdles), and Delissa Walton Floyd (800). She also coached Patti Sue Plumer (3000m) whose coach was unable to attend the games. Terry describes her feelings at Seoul: "When I walked into the Olympic stadium in Seoul, Korea, in 1988 as head coach of the United States Women's Olympic Track and Field team, it really made me feel complete in what I had accomplished as a coach. I had met all of my personal goals."

After nine years and another incredible success story at Texas, Terry was stirred to search for the next journey. Maintaining a top-level program while keeping it at the top of the ladder set the stage to consider a new challenge. A reminiscing Crawford claimed she had reached all of her professional goals. She had been the 1988 head Olympic coach, one of her athletes had won a gold medal, and several athletes had set American and world records. Looking ahead, she began to think about what else she wanted to accomplish in the sport and realized she had never had the opportunity to coach men.

After taking Sandy Richards to the 1992 Olympics in Barcelona (Sandy took seventh in the 400 meters), Terry moved to San Luis Obispo to become with Bruce Johnson the co-director of a combined men's and women's track program at Cal-Poly. Their mandate was to remodel a Division II track and field program into a Division I program. So, with a new spin to her challenge, she has moved on to another structuring journey. Aspiring to raise a top-notch

Division I team for men and women has renewed her excitement for life and track.

## CHALLENGES

One of the most discouraging moments in Crawford's life occurred when she suffered an injury prior to the 1972 Olympic trials. She was heavily favored to make the team, and this important life goal was never accomplished. That injury led to her retirement as a runner. The injury, the discouragement, the depression, and the disappointment were turned into determination and stick-to-itiveness. This coaching dictum helped her fashion a proper-perspective plan. She uses this tool to understand and advise athletes when they experience their own sets of adversity, and she feels this helps them to place their lives in proper perspective.

Terry feels fortunate to have coached at two universities that were committed to excellence in women's athletics. She looks at obstacles as learning opportunities, at hindsight as a safeguard against future mistakes, and she feels that sport encircles her in a professional environment filled with stimulating top-notch professionals.

## PHILOSOPHY OF COACHING

A philosophical tenet of Crawford's coaching belief is the concept that individuals are the team, and the team will come together if each athlete prepares to achieve full potential. If the individual does well, it is then reflected in the performance of the entire team. Terry aspires to instill athletes with the idea that they are individual sport athletes and must concentrate on self-performance, and that by so doing they will control the team's performance. The core of her philosophy is for people to attain their full ability, and she gears and guides her efforts into facilitating each athlete to reach his or her potential. She tries to look at the total athlete and help each to realize that being a track and field athlete is not just being in the sport, but is a lifestyle. An athlete must not walk off the practice field or the competitive field and become somebody else; being an athlete is a twenty-four-hour-a-day commitment. It's not like putting a hat on and taking it off. This is the philosophy Terry feels has been the cornerstone of her success as a runner and a coach, and she attributes to this belief the success her athletes have had.

In regard to mental preparation for competition, she claims what an athlete does daily is founded on being a good student of one's event. Being confident and feeling prepared physically and mentally grounds an athlete's competitive competence. To do that, one has to be able to analyze day-to-day accomplishments. She tries to teach her athletes ways to manage their mental make-up, to prepare positively by learning ways to cope with stress, to mentally process what's happening to them as athletes in competition, and to analyze their strategy which may require collecting research and doing some real competitive homework. This approach is a vital requisite to an athlete's competition. She talks to athletes about these event strategies each day prior to integrating them into each practice session. The reasons for doing anything are always explained to the athletes so that their mental edge is being toned along with their physical preparation. While she does not use extensive bio-feedback or psychological talks or sessions with her athletes, she understands these processes and has created a simplified version of mental preparation for athletes to grasp, regardless of their competitive level.

For Terry, the coach must be a bit fearful in order to keep the mental edge. This means fear of mistakes, or fear that someone is doing a better job of coaching. This keeps the coach searching and on the edge. Her goal in coaching is to realize that she never gets to the point that she is past learning.

## ROLE MODELS/MENTORS

While Crawford doesn't have one mentor she looks to, she feels she has colleagues with whom to share ideas, and she engages them in an ongoing dialogue. She always seeks out those who are more successful than she, and either picks their brains or becomes a close observer of how they prepare their athletes, the techniques they use, their knowledge of the sport, and where they obtain that knowledge.

## CHANGES IN ATHLETES

Over the 24 years Crawford has been coaching she has seen a lot of changes in athletes that reflect changes inflicted upon society. These changes are entangled in the demands of dealing with the stresses of family life and work. One of the more distasteful changes Terry has observed is that athletes are more demanding of what they expect of college programs and that these demands are in disproportion to what they feel they should give back. This is a sad note for Coach Crawford because she always felt being on a team was a special privilege. She feels that athletics is a game of merit and that a person's hard work and efforts are what bring rewards, whether they be scholarship money, equipment, recognition, or special privileges. Today's athletes come with distorted views of what their worth is or what value they are going to be versus what they are going to receive. These changes are a reflection of what she sees happening in the larger society. To adjust to these times is difficult but necessary, and the programs get rearranged to accommodate such attitudes.

Looking back Terry thinks, "One of the factors that has made me successful in the coaching profession and made my career as pleasant as it has been—and I have been satisfied over 85 percent of the time—is that I've really been accepted in the male structure of the coaching ranks. I've worked at being non-confrontational and have been non-combative with my male counterparts. I have gained their respect for my actions. I have looked at them just as a colleague going about doing what we do in coaching. We put in the effort, the work, and pursue the same goals."

Stan Huntsman coached with Terry at Tennessee and Texas for about fifteen years. He was skilled at the implementation of a philosophy to produce a winning program. Huntsman was instrumental in Crawford's understanding the phenomenon of applying a philosophical stance. Occasionally, there are coaches that feel threatened, especially the younger male coaches. Some of these are merely jealous and resentful of female coaches because they feel slighted when administrators seek female coaches to coach female teams. There is no way we can increase the number of women coaches unless special efforts are made to encourage our young female athletes, who are coming out of sports into coaching opportunities.

Terry feels very fortunate she got into coaching because she was one of the few women coaches. She was successful and worked diligently to show her commitment to the coaching profession and to demonstrate the talent she has.

## FUTURE PLANS

Terry's immediate goals are first, to plot a personal life of balance and happiness that extends to all aspects of life, not just the professional dimension. Secondly, she hopes to have success in building the Cal-Poly team into a top-ten program for both men and women. Planning to coach for at least another ten years, Crawford believes ten years will give her time to construct a program that will attract top athletes to Cal-Poly to pursue their athletic aspirations. When Cal-Poly moved to Division I in track competition and changed conference alignments from the American West to the Big West Conference, Crawford was named head track and field and cross country coach for both the men's and the women's teams. This happened in 1997 and thus made her the only woman to hold such a position in the United States. In December of 1996, Terry Crawford was given the distinctive honor of being inducted into the U.S. Track and Field Hall of Fame.

## RECOGNITIONS AND ACHIEVEMENTS

### Accomplishments as a Player

- Member of National Track Team, 1969–1971 (800 members)
- Member of Pan Am Team

### Coaching Recognitions in Division I

- Eight Indoor Conference Championships, SWC, 1985–1992
- Eight Cross Country Conference Championships, SWC, 1985–1992
- Ten Outdoor Conference Championships: 3 SEC, 1981, 1982, 1983; and 7 SWC
- Fourteen Top-Ten Finalists

- National AIAW Championship, 1981
- National Championship Indoor, 1986
- National Championship Cross Country, 1986
- National Championship Outdoor, 1986

## National Coaching Assignment

- Head Track and Field Coach for Women, 1988 Olympic Games

Photo courtesy of University of
Minnesota

# JUDITH DAVIDSON

*Athletic Director—California State College
at Sacramento*

## INTRODUCTION

A side light of Judith Davidson's heritage is that her great great uncle helped overthrow the Russian Czar. It is possible that this strand of ancestry advanced Judith's historical interests to earn a doctorate in sport history. It is amusing that a history instructor once exclaimed, upon learning Judith was going to become a physical education teacher, "What a waste of a good student!" The "good student" was not wasted—Judith shines as a scholar, a celebrated coach, and an athletic director.

## PERSONAL DATA

> *Born*: November 7, 1944, New York City, New York
>
> *Father*: James Davidson
>
> *Father's Occupation*: Distribution manager for Universal International Films
>
> *Mother*: Miriam Karensky (grand niece of Alexander Karensky)
>
> *Mother's Occupation*: Executive secretary
>
> *Sibling*: Joel Davidson, younger brother

*Alma Maters*: University of New Hampshire—B.S., 1966; Boston University—M.Ed., 1973; University of Massachusetts—Ph.D., 1983

## FORMATIVE YEARS

Change was the constant in the young life of Judith Davidson. Frequent moves helped Judith to become both adaptable and restless. The family lived in Brooklyn, Yonkers, Maryland, and southern New Jersey; her father's job transfers required these moves. In six years Judith attended five different schools. While living in Yonkers two male cousins became her constant buddies in active games. Most often the games were either stick ball or punch ball. This period of activity was focused around her immediate family. Judith's father took the time to teach her to catch and throw and to ride a bicycle. The influence of her father at this early age, no doubt, helped to sustain her intense interest in sport. Sport was important to Davidson's growing-up years, but Judith was also exposed to cultural events. A trip as a young adult to the Boston Gardens flower show turned into a lifelong love for flowers and gardening.

Looking back on these years, Judith remembers them with fondness and feels blessed to have grown to adulthood in the quintessential nuclear family: two parents, two kids, and a life nurtured by a caring father and mother in a positive world environment filled with attainable dreams for an even better future.

## SPORTS HISTORY

By the time Judith left Yonkers she had played on a softball team. Before softball, her play consisted of unorganized children's games. The tenth grade was her first time for participation in an organized team sport, and the sport was field hockey. For her, playing on an organized team at Lenape High School was "a terrific experience." Before becoming a member of the team, Davidson knew nothing about the game; in fact, she recalls hearing about field hockey but never having seen a field hockey stick. When she saw a young girl holding a field hockey stick, she asked the girl, "Is that a field hockey stick?" The girl answered, "Well, what do you think?" Davidson replied, "I don't know. I've never seen one before." Surely it would have been hard for Judith Davidson to have imagined that one day she would come to love the game of field hockey, win a national championship, and become president of the USFHA.

Davidson also played softball and basketball at Levittown High School. However, it was through her efforts that the school even offered the two team sports, as they offered nothing for girls until Judith created the awareness for the school to start girls' sports. Documentation exists verifying that because of the agitation and single-handed efforts of Judith Davidson, a basketball team was organized her junior year, and softball and field hockey teams were organized during her senior year of high school. These organizational efforts of young Judith were to become trademarks of her dogged determination to improve competitive opportunities for young women in high school and university settings.

The 1960s were not a favorable time for women who desired to compete in sports. Knowing such opportunities were limited, and recognizing that competing in field hockey had become very important to Judith, it was important to find a school where she could compete. Competition on the field hockey, lacrosse, and basketball teams at the University of New Hampshire captured her sporting spirit enough to further the adventure. At New Hampshire she was goal keeper and was consistently selected as all-tournament goal keeper, played on several All-Tournament teams and on a USFHA sectional team. Along with school competition, she played for coach Joan Stone and the New Hampshire Field Hockey Club. In England she played on the first team at Chelsea College, University of Sussex, in Eastbourne, England.

## COACHING

After graduating from the University of New Hampshire, Davidson spent a year in England studying movement education and playing field hockey. Returning to the United States she taught at Newton High School in Newton, Massachusetts. For the next seven years she taught physical education and coached field hockey, basketball, and softball. Concurrently with teaching and coaching, she completed a master's degree at Boston University. While at Boston University, she was enrolled in an educational statistics class where students were expected to present their research paper to the class. After Judith presented her paper, "An Analysis of Public Attitudes on Women in Sport," she received a standing ovation.

The desire for further education sent Judith to the University of Massachusetts on an athletic assistantship to coach field hockey and to work on a doctorate degree. Two weeks before the field hockey season began, the head coach left, so Judith was invited to coach the team for "a few weeks." A few weeks actually turned into a two-year assignment as head coach, because the former coach did not return. During that time, Judith coached and completed all of the necessary course work for a Ph.D. She even took a team to the AIAW National Championship playoffs during the second year.

Energetic and productive, Judith had the profile of one ready to grasp an opportunity for a future in coaching. Accordingly, during her second year at Massachusetts, she was offered the head field hockey coaching position at the University of Iowa. Christine Grant made the offer, but Davidson refused, intent on completing her degree. Grant sweetened the deal, making it possible for her to become field hockey coach, assistant professor, and with the opportunity to teach sport history. They even gave her an immediate second semester leave of absence to take her comprehensive exams. After ten years at Iowa, Judith Davidson's record was impressive.

The Iowa years were flavored with various successes including becoming the most winning coach in the history of Iowa (185–51–16 or .734) and the Big Ten. Her teams appeared in ten NCAA post-season tournaments, attended three national championships, and several individuals played on the national team and competed in the Olympic Games.

Sandwiched between these feats, Judith was asked to coach in the National Sports Festival and the National Junior Olympics. This was 1985. The next year she coached in the National Olympic Festival. For several years Davidson had awakened at 3 or 4 A.M. wondering, "What am I going to do with the rest of my life? . . . I had never planned to become a career coach." So it was natural that she took a long shot and interviewed for the position of Athletic Director at Central Connecticut State University. She was hired. Coming from one of the top universities in the country and having academic credentials played in her favor. The next seven years were spent at Central, where she worked to improve athletic relationships with the faculty. The following year she reestablished at the University of Minnesota, then by August of 1996 she made a another change to California State College, Sacramento.

## DECISION TO COACH

Judith Davidson prepared for a physical education teaching career and surrendered to coaching through administrative invitation. Success, love of the game, and energetic young athletes have lengthened her stay in this professional avenue.

## PHILOSOPHY OF COACHING

Although Davidson believes a coach should compete to win, her focus is not on winning championships, but on being excellent in executing every aspect of the game. Judith stresses fundamentals much like a conductor might emphasize playing the individual notes correctly before the concerto can take shape. Hence, a tremendous amount of time is funneled into stressing fundamentals.

Davidson does not believe in the coach as a cheerleader shouting from the side lines general encouragements or abusive language. What she does subscribe to is giving athletes specific feedback that will change behavior rather than yelling out abusive comments that intimidate athletes into changing play. In this respect it appears that the Davidson coaching style focuses on helping athletes to understand how good they can become, and then providing an instructional environment to secure individual excellence. Judith feels that she can do this if the athletes are receptive to her help in developing their own abilities.

In a nutshell, Judith Davidson explains her personal philosophy this way: "If I have to go to work at McDonald's, I'll end up owning it." She asserted this take-charge attitude as a high school student when she agitated the administration to get girls sports in her school.

## CHALLENGES

Judith noted that faculty and administrators were sometimes impediments to her ability to develop programs to their potential or for her to reach her own potential. She remembers two situations where university presidents said they wanted a strong program but refused to fund the programs. She also commented on a high school physics teacher who did not want females to enroll in his physics class, but she ignored the message and enrolled anyway.

As an athletic director, it is easy for Judith to detect the part limited financial resources have played in women's sports. This problem previously curtailed expansion and halted the stature and image of university women's sport. To continue to improve, she feels that women's teams, like men's, must win consistently and must develop a strong community following. She believes that Sacramento "is hungry" for teams that win consistently, both men's and women's.

## CHANGES IN ATHLETES

Judith feels many changes have occurred in women's athletics, but all of the changes are not especially good. She feels that too much money is spent on high profile athletic programs, especially in the area of recruiting, and that much of this expenditure is unnecessary. The "give me entitlement" attitude, and a lessened commitment to athletics and working hard, limits the number of athletes who stay with a sport through college. Finally, Davidson does not buy the concept that the coach should be an all-powerful authority figure, even though she feels it generally appears that athletes have less respect for authority than in former times.

## MEMORABLE MOMENTS

Coming in as an NCAA runner up in 1984 was a real highlight for Davidson, because it put the team on the winning track. After several losses in a row, they met Northwestern in the regional finals and beat them, going on to the final four, and taking second place. This was a remarkable accomplishment.

The year before winning the NCAA National Championship (1985), Davidson's team was the finest in the country. They played their arch rival Northwestern University and had some of the best competition Judith had seen. The most thrilling game was in the NCAA Regional Finals when they played two overtimes and a triple tiebreaker. A number of players from that superb team made the national team and the Olympic team. Unfortunately, Judith's team lost, but it was a superb game even though they did not win.

The next year was a rebuilding year where 50 percent of the team were freshmen, and winning the national championship during this rebuilding year was clearly unexpected.

Extremely satisfying to Davidson is to realize that many former players are now still in the game, still giving back through coaching. Many of these women coach at universities like Duke, Virginia, and Northwestern, and many of these women played for the national team and competed in the Olympics. This collage of successful young women has left Judith with a sense of pride.

Certainly Judith Davidson will not forget her eight years as president of the United States Field Hockey Association, an organization for women. During her presidency, the United States Olympic Committee mandated that the men's and women's field hockey associations merge into one organization. Through Judith's leadership, the men's organization was absorbed into the women's association. Her action preserved the only sports organization for women that is governed by women. Males are seated on the board of directors, but a woman is still president of the organization.

## ROLE MODELS/MENTORS

*Doris Slick*—Doris Slick was a high school biology teacher. Doris awakened Judith to the joy of biological sciences. Her classes were demanding, fair, and set with high standards. Working to meet these standards alerted Davidson to the reality that it took a mix of hard work and focus to reach high standards. After this class, Judith had a pattern for everything she did.

*Mary Lattanzi*—Mary Lattanzi was a high school physical education teacher. Mary took 17–year-old Judith to play for her adult club team. This experience taught Judith she had athletic potential as a field hockey goal keeper. "Something Mary did for me which has pretty much been my life's mantra was when she told me, 'Judith, make them prove you wrong!' "

*Ruth Murray*—Ruth Murray was a college instructor who taught movement education. Ruth kindled Judith's interest in movement education and facilitated her pursuing a year of study at Chelsea College in Eastbourne, England. This experience was significant because it had a profound effect on Judith's teaching and coaching styles.

*Milton Cantor*—Milton was Judith's graduate school history professor. His influence had a profound effect on Judith's thought. "[Milton] forced me to be intellectually precise in the way in which he demanded rigorous thinking and research. These skills I have found indispensable throughout my career."

*Christine Grant*—Christine was Director of Women's Athletics at the University of Iowa. Christine was a key person in leading the movement for women's intercollegiate sport. Judith learned many leadership skills from this woman, and the value of being guided by a strong philosophical position.

*Parents*—"Miriam Ruth Karensky and James Harrold Davidson probably didn't really understand exactly what it was that I was doing or why their daughter was so driven to participate in sports. Nevertheless they were always supportive and wanted to make sure that I was happy. My father attended more of my early athletic contests than my mother, and I think it pleased him that I was adept at sports. I know he was very proud when I was elected president of the United States Field Hockey Association just before he died. It was one of the last things he ever said to me, and I can see him in his hospital bed as I stood there next to him holding his hand."

## FAVORITE BOOKS

The *Power Broker* by Robert Karo, the biography of Robert Moses who was the commissioner of parks in New York City.

## LIFE BEYOND ATHLETICS

Judith Davidson is intensely interested in history and is a voracious reader. In addition, she enjoys all athletics and is an avid gardener—an interest generated from early experiences at flower shows.

## FAVORITE MOVIES

Judith prefers live theater to cinema. *Carousel* ranks as her favorite because it is fanciful and expresses the universal longing for the someone whom we have lost to return.

## FUTURE PLANS

Travel to places like China, Scandinavia, and Alaska are part of Judith's future plans.

## RECOGNITIONS AND ACHIEVEMENTS

### Coaching Recognitions in Division I

- Seven Conference Championships, Big Ten: 1980, 1981, 1982, 1983, 1984, 1986, 1987
- Conference Coach of the Year, Big Ten: 1983, 1984, 1987
- National Indoor Championship, 1984
- Runner-up Outdoor, 1984
- National Champions, 1986
- Final Four, 1987
- Produced seven Olympians
- Thirty-seven All Americans
- Winningest Coach in Iowa History, 175–45–14

### National Coaching Assignment

- Olympic Festival Coach, 1985, 1986

### Other Accomplishments

- Vice President United States Field Hockey Association, 1981–1983
- USFHA President Elect, 1983–1985
- USFHA President, 1984–1988
- USFHA President, 1988–1992
- USFHA President, 1992–1995
- Member, International Federation of Hockey, 1987–1992

Photo courtesy of Yale University

# MARISA DIDIO
*Field Hockey—Yale University*

## INTRODUCTION

Two older brothers must have inspired Marisa Didio to love the sporting life. A childhood filled with street hockey, inventive childhood games, and the unconditional support of Marisa's parents in regard to her athletic decisions set the stage for a competitive venture as athlete and coach.

## PERSONAL DATA

*Born*:  August 28, 1956, Lynnfield, Massachusetts

*Father*:  John Didio

*Father's Occupation*:  President, Candy Co. and owner of the New England Oyster House

*Mother*:  Jacqueline Williams

*Mother's Occupation*:  Homemaker

*Siblings*:  Kenneth Burnham and John Didio, Jr.

*Alma Mater*:  University of New Hampshire—B.S., Physical Education, 1978

## FORMATIVE YEARS

Marisa grew up in rural Lynnfield, Massachusetts, in an area named Sherwood Forest. The family home was about a mile down a dirt road dotted with a few homes. Marisa describes the area as "a kid's neighborhood." The place was continually growing in homes and children. Play was a favorite pastime and the children played and played. Their play included creative activities such as building forts and engaging in all sorts of sport games. At the age of six Marisa was swimming competitively across a pool, and when her brothers played games, she played too, including football.

## SPORTS HISTORY

Summer swimming programs for Marisa began at an early age. By the time she was nine, she was swimming on an AAU team. In middle school the physical education classes were the only sports available. Junior high offered so few sports that many of the athletic girls turned to cheerleading to fill their energetic needs. Along with swimming, Marisa competed in field hockey and softball. After her sophomore year she decided to focus on field hockey. This was an easy transition as she had spent years playing street hockey with her brothers.

Before high school graduation, Marisa traveled to several small schools to investigate possibilities for higher education. The University of New Hampshire held the most interest because she was exposed to the school through her brother, who attended, and his friend, who played ice hockey there. From them she learned about the school, and that prompted her to seek schooling there. So she entered the University of New Hampshire's College of Health Studies and selected classes leading to a degree in physical education. Several days after entering school she found they had a field hockey team. She joined the team and was coached by Welsh woman Jean Rillings. Marisa played field hockey throughout her college experience, and she competed in lacrosse from her sophomore year until graduation.

After completing a high school student-teaching experience, Marisa realized she was not interested in teaching high school. She wanted to coach at the collegiate level or work in a YWCA or other fitness-related institutions.

## DECISION TO COACH

After graduation in 1978 Marisa was invited by Jean Rillings to be her assistant field hockey coach. Then, in the spring of 1979, she became an assistant to **Pam Hixon,** who was the head lacrosse coach at the University of Massachusetts. In the fall of that year, she took her coaching skills to Tufts University, a small Division III liberal arts school. One of Marisa's high school English teachers who taught part time at Tufts informed her of the opening and recommended her to Athletic Director Rocky Carzo. Not really wanting to leave the University of Massachusetts, she almost avoided the opportunity at Tufts.

After interviewing, she was hired. That started 22-year-old Marisa's first chance as head coach.

Tufts had not performed very well for several years previous to Marisa's tenure. She coached both lacrosse and field hockey and exposed them to the winning business. Three and a half years later, in the spring of 1983, Rillings, head coach at New Hampshire, resigned and approached Marisa to test her interest. By now the NCAA had taken over women's sports and new opportunities were on the horizon. Marisa accepted the invitation at UNH and spent the next six years posting an 84–25–9 field hockey record. The team advanced to the NCAA tournament each of those years. In 1985 Marisa's New Hampshire team won the National Lacrosse Championship and then, with most of the same athletes, took second in the NCAA field hockey championships the following year (1986). Of those UNH teams, the most successful was the 1986 squad who finished 17–3 before advancing to the final NCAA game. They lost 2–1 in a double overtime to the University of Iowa. **Judith Davidson** was the Iowa coach.

Marisa's teams had quite a few crossover athletes between field hockey and lacrosse. In those days training was different than at present. The team would play field hockey from 6–8 A.M., attend classes, and then practice lacrosse from 8–10 P.M. The athletes were unbelievable. The work ethic the athletes had made it possible to accomplish what they did in 1985 and 1986. In 1988 Marisa took a year's leave to assist Baldwin Castling, a Dutch coach for the U.S. Olympic Team.

Returning to UNH after the Olympic experience, Marisa worked to sharpen UNH back into the competitive shape necessary for NCAA tournament play. Soon she felt she had done all she could do at UNH given facility limitations and budget constraints. The athletes had gone beyond the limitations. Other schools had been catching up to New Hampshire. Knowing it would take more to maintain a top program, Marisa stopped coaching lacrosse after the national championship in 1985 and focused on field hockey. Coaches and athletes started specializing more, and crossovers were becoming less typical.

In spring of 1990 Northwestern University called. Marisa had competed against Northwestern in some tournament situations and was somewhat familiar with their programs and their potential. She had coached some Northwestern athletes at the Olympic sports festivals in Minnesota. She heard the coach had resigned, and she knew the athletes who were returning to Northwestern. That fact precipitated thoughts about opportunity and another challenge. Northwestern would be a challenge as it was in a different region of the country and it was in the Big Ten Conference. She also knew great changes were on the threshold for women's sports—it seemed the right time to make a move. Her father had recently passed away and moving to another region of the country offered a challenge to start again in a new environment to see if success would come again.

Different playing surfaces, a new geographic location, and the Big Ten Conference were all appealing. Marisa coached at Northwestern from 1990 to 1994. She delivered a 60–31–5 overall record, entered four NCAA national tournaments, produced twelve All Americans, and was voted the Big Ten Coach of the Year. Marisa was involved with the national Olympic team for 1996 and served as a coach for the U.S. Field Hockey Association development camps. Yale University hired Marisa as a consultant to review the Yale program and to make recommendations. In 1997 they hired her to implement the recommendations. In Marisa's first year they won eight games, including five of the last six. In her second season at Yale (1998), the team went 15–4 and won the ECAC Conference.

## ROLE MODELS/MENTORS

*Bob Roland*—He was Marisa's swimming coach from the time she was 5 years old until she was 16. Roland was an Ice Hockey Coach and a top-notch motivator. He had a limited setting in which to work, but he was very creative in using charts, tasks, and competition to keep each athlete swimming.

*Jean Rillings*—This demanding, tough, disciplined woman, an expert in educational gymnastics, was creative in teaching various physical activities. She explored new ways to bring field hockey to a more sophisticated level. "She was a woman ahead of her time," says Marisa.

*Pam Hixon*—Marisa feels Pam is an outstanding woman who is a positive role model and that learning from her was "refreshing."

*Dotty Zenaty*—Dotty taught with students as her first consideration. This Springfield College teacher was honest and never had a hidden agenda.

*William Rodan*—Rodan was the Lynnfield High School Football Coach and history teacher. He also coached Marisa's brother, Kenny. Rodan taught Marisa to "work hard and do it the right way."

## PHILOSOPHY OF COACHING

Each of Marisa's role models made an important contribution to her philosophical stance. She interwove their beliefs with her own, combining consistency, hard work, learning, and assuming responsibility as key concepts. "Knowing why you are doing what you are doing and how you are going to do it" is another important underlying theme. Didio believes athletes must define what they want to accomplish even though the definition may vary from year to year. According to Didio the idea is to "have athletes progressively define who they are, what they represent, and what they want to represent. What they want to accomplish and how they are going to make that happen!" After going through this process, she asks each athlete to make a written statement. They post the statements so everyone can read them on a regular basis.

## CHALLENGES

During the years Marisa coached without adequate facilities or finances, she discovered creativity as one way to solve problems. However, the constant tension from unrealized dreams absorbed vital coaching energy. Each coaching change from Tufts to New Hampshire to Northwestern and finally to Yale provided different challenges and learning situations where the ability to adapt and create became a necessity. Moving brought many challenges, especially when she was hired to rebuild a struggling program.

The building process was a challenge she enjoyed; even though it required energy, it was satisfying to see the incremental progress. The next challenge for her was to maintain a successful program; maintaining a program imposes a pressure different than that of building—both are stressful.

Marisa feels that coaching women's sports, especially field hockey and lacrosse, requires one to convince others that you are doing something that is worth doing. In addition, the coach must convince decision makers to examine fairness issues, particularly in respect to the athlete. She feels these issues will be around for a long time. Each time Marisa moved, she moved to situations where she could develop and foster strong programs. In some areas, those affiliated with higher-prestige sports do not treat women in less-prestige sports fairly.

Marisa coaches because she has a passion for the game. Field hockey is a sport in which she could have an impact. She relishes the opportunity to impact, to influence teams to adopt better values, athletic skills, and lives in general. In her opinion there is not a better profession or a better forum in which such on opportunity can occur. Marisa realized this powerful tool when she took the break from college coaching to work with the national team in the 1995–1996 season. That's the reason she returned to coach college athletes.

## CHANGES IN ATHLETES

Didio feels that present-day athletes seek discipline and structure, and it is the coach's responsibility to educate athletes to meet the overall demands progressively. She feels many of today's athletes have lost the joy of playing a sport for its own sake.

Marisa views sport as an extension of the college educational community experience. Yale does not offer athletic scholarships, and Marisa is glad to be in an environment where athletes play because they want to. Yale women make the choice to have athletics be part of their student experience. Making such a choice also means athletes find it easy to walk away and not see themselves through all of the struggles associated with athletic performance.

## LIFE BEYOND ATHLETICS

Marisa says she likes to wine and dine. She loves piano bars and listening to music, along with live theater and the movies. She loves to run, golf, work out, and she reads a wide variety of books when time permits.

## MEMORABLE MOMENTS

When asked about memorable moments, Marisa reports that she thinks in terms of the total process and not specific moments or events. Her special moments are when athletes call or return to talk over old times. She loves to share in news about their families, their marriages, and their babies. She values these times as memorable.

## RECOGNITIONS AND ACHIEVEMENTS

### Accomplishments as a Player

- National Field Hockey Team, 1978–1980
- National Lacrosse Team, 1978

### Coaching Recognitions in Division I

- Conference Championship Big Ten, 1994
- Conference Championship ECAC, 1988
- Conference Coach of the Year, 1982 NESCAC
- Conference Coach of the Year, 1994 Big Ten
- Regional Midwest Coach of the Year, 1993
- National Coach of the Year Lacrosse Division I, 1995
- National Championship Field Hockey, 1985
- National Championship Lacrosse, 1985
- NCAA Runner-up Field Hockey, 1986
- Produced 12 All Americans at Northwestern University

### National Coaching Assignments

- Olympic Festivals, Bronze 1989, Silver 1990, Gold 1991
- Assisted Olympic Coach, 1988, 1996
- Coached many of the USFHA developmental champions

### Other Accomplishment

- University of New Hampshire Hall of Fame

Photo courtesy of University of
California, Fullerton

# JUDITH GARMAN
*Softball—University of California, Fullerton*

## INTRODUCTION

The daughter of an athletic mother and a clergyman father, Judi Garman played out her childhood fantasies on baseball diamonds and athletic fields in Canada. If play is the work of childhood, then Judi masterfully extended her play into adult work.

Born in Pennsylvania and reared in western Canada, Judi, along with her sister Lorraine, learned sporting skills under their athletic mother's tutelage. Later, as the young athletes joined teams, their mother lent support by attending each of their competitive events. Garman's father held puritanical views of leisure and work. His father had passed on before he was born, so he had worked hard from a very young age. He dubbed sport participation "a poor use of time." But when he recognized that his daughters would participate regardless, he encouraged them to excel in one sport rather than become a "jack of all trades." Judi capitalized on softball, and Lorraine matured into a professional golfer.

## PERSONAL DATA

*Born*: March 27, 1944, Harrisburg, Pennsylvania

*Father*: John Garman

*Father's Occupation*: Minister, Brethren in Christ Church

*Mother*: Ruth Ulery

*Mother's Occupation*: Minister's Wife

*Siblings*: Lorraine, Henry, and Bruce

*Alma Maters*: University of Saskatchewan, Canada—B.S., Physical Education, 1966; University of California, Santa Barbara—M.S., Physical Education, 1969

## FORMATIVE YEARS

Judi Garman's beginnings were in the mountain community of Iron Springs, Pennsylvania. Her minister father was then transferred to Canada for a two-year assignment and fell in love with Saskatchewan where he received subsequent assignments and eventually made permanent residence. Remaining in Canada was especially good for the Garman girls because the western Canadians used the European model of sports participation, and that provided lots of opportunities for girls.

On their farm outside the little town of Kindersley, Judi, for her first year of school, attended a one-room schoolhouse for grades one through eight. The place resembled the one in the Little House on the Prairie stories. She attended school by horse and carriage, and in the winter a sleigh replaced the carriage. Then they moved to the town of 1500, where Judi attended a regular school. When first Canadian snows fell, the youngsters played hockey until the spring thaw, then they took up baseball. Without the distraction of a television set, play filled their days from morning to evening. Using childhood ingenuity, they built their own baseball diamond on the prairie and even started a prairie fire trying to burn the infield off. Their diamond survived with the help of fire trucks, and the finished field featured a sunken dugout with benches. This carefully crafted diamond provided hours of playing time for the two girls and their male friends. They even structured teams with playing contracts.

Typical vacations took the family on to Pennsylvania or Ohio for church conferences. The church picnics were especially great fun as they were spiced with lots of softball games, races, and other competitions. The family came to enjoy fishing, too, as a special family activity.

## SPORTS HISTORY

By her ninth year, Judi Garman was playing on her first organized team. It was little league baseball, but her career was cut short when the team went to regionals—she was released for being a girl. Judi and her sister were the only girls playing among the clan of boys. The prairie baseball teams eventually dissolved because the boys' parents insisted, over their sons' objections, that they join the town's little league baseball team. The only thing the boys liked better about their new league was the fact they had official uniforms.

From the prairie baseball teams, two of the childhood playmates designed careers. Wayne Morgan heads European scouting for the Toronto Blue Jays, and Judi Garman is head softball coach at Cal State–Fullerton. Judi's trip to the top did not occur overnight. She attributes her success as a coach and a builder to her father's early struggle to support his family. The reverend Garman's first ministerial assignment in Canada paid him $75 a month. This was not adequate to support a family of six, so he developed creative ways to generate the money necessary to sustain his family. His example taught Judi valuable lessons in pioneering that would transfer nicely to her own successful career.

In junior high school, Judi and Lorraine were invited to play on a women's softball team. The older women watched out for them as they traveled all over Saskatchewan. High school began at a small Mennonite boarding school that did not have a gym or a physical education program. The family moved to Saskatoon when she was a senior in high school, and Judi insisted on transferring to a school that had a physical education program and a gymnasium. There she played badminton, golf, and basketball. This move also enabled Garman to play softball for a women's team in Saskatoon. The team became the Canadian Champions and competed in the World Championships. This first introduction to high-caliber competition made a great impression on Judi. She also played on a top Canadian basketball team. Although she sat the bench a good deal of the time on the basketball team, she did take careful note of the coaches and their coaching styles. It was her dream to be a physical education teacher, drive a red sports car, and live in a big city. In addition, it was her dream to become the female version of John Wooden. Therefore she read everything that could be found on John Wooden.

Impressed by the strong physical education program at the University of Saskatchewan, Judi enrolled there to complete a degree. Softball was not available at the university because of the long snow season, so basketball became her competitive sport. This was another learning experience in coaching that prompted Garman to keep a card file on every drill and each important comment the coach made. This was a rich training forum for one eager to learn.

Judi's master's degree was earned from the University of California, Santa Barbara. This degree was in physical education with an emphasis in sports psychology. Job seeking after graduation showed a scarcity of opportunity until a position became available at Westmont College. In her first two years at Westmont, she coached volleyball, basketball, tennis, and softball. Her stay was not long because financial cutbacks forced the school to eliminate her position. Meanwhile, after mailing a multitude of applications, she received an offer to coach softball and one other sport at Golden West College. Fred Owens, chair of the physical education department, offered her the job. He was motivated because one of his six daughters wanted to play softball, but the only thing available to her was a recreation league with worn-out equipment. At the time of Judi's hire, the Golden West softball team was one year old and had a 0–30 record. The softball team's record changed drastically when Judi came aboard. Under her leadership the team became one of the best in the country. She coached them to four consecutive national championships.

Learning from her father, John Garman, who melded about thirty different jobs with his ministerial duties during her growing years, Judi has applied his innovative methods for facilities and equipment fund raisers. His enterprising efforts to raise money led to the construction of three church houses and support for his family, thereby providing a perfect example for Judi's own building projects. At Cal State, Fullerton, she has raised over $750,000 to benefit women's sport.

Garman remained at Golden West from 1972 to 1979. Those years were filled with coaching responsibilities: she coached basketball (1973–1976), cross country (1977–1979), and softball (1972–1979). The softball team not only won an unprecedented four consecutive national championships, they compiled a 211–40 record. Twenty-one of her softball players received scholarships to four-year institutions. Due to these outstanding feats, the California Community College named Garman to their hall of fame.

After Judi's stay at Golden West, she joined the coaching staff at Cal-State, Fullerton, as a full-time softball coach. On March 7, 1996, she won her one thousandth game. That game was against Long Beach State. Now she is the nation's winningest active coach; her record is 1089–383–4 (.740). Her first 211 victories were tallied while coaching at Golden West Junior College (1972–1979). In 1993, she was inducted into the National Softball Coaches Association Hall of Fame.

## MEMORABLE MOMENTS

Garman finds it difficult to identify just one extraordinary moment because she has enjoyed so many wonderful memories. However, winning the Division I national championship was satisfying because some critics believed that winning at a junior college did not mean one could win in big-time competition. The most emotional of her memories was when she asked her best friend why she was crying after winning the big one, and she responded, "I know how many years and how much hard work you have devoted to getting there."

## PHILOSOPHY OF COACHING

Garman uses softball as a vehicle for an educational enrichment opportunity. In addition to teaching her athletes to be competitive on the field, she wants players to learn as they experience new places. Road trips conveniently expose students to new places and other cultures. Consequently, athletes are given opportunities to tour and to participate in activities they might not have otherwise. Garman's squads have toured a prison, snorkeled in Hawaii, camped in the mountains, and taken the Pearl Harbor cruise. One team competed in Sweden, another in Australia and New Zealand. Resting in a hotel before and after competitions is not her idea of a good educational experience. This aspect of her philosophy was reinforced by an athlete who wrote a letter explaining that she could not remember the scores of their games, but that Garman had provided her with experiences she would never forget. The educational opportunity for athletes is a foundational cornerstone in Judi Garman's coaching philosophy.

## CHALLENGES

Raising money in unique ways is a Garman trade secret for building facilities and conducting other events she deems important. At Golden West College she was instrumental in constructing two beautiful softball fields with lights and snack bars. Not claiming to have done it all on her own, she did get the city to help in the lighting project. Just as Garman was surrounded with ideal coaching conditions, she left to assume the head softball coach position at Cal State, Fullerton.

Fortune was with Garman that first year at Fullerton; a College World Series pitcher was dropped in her lap. Pam Edde had pitched her team to a fifth-place finish in the College World Series but left the school she pitched for after the series. Edde stayed out of school for a year and selected Cal State, Fullerton, to finish her college career. This piece of prosperity, along with Garman's coaching credentials, placed Fullerton ninth in the nation in preseason polls.

Cal State was not all peaches and cream, however. The school was without softball facilities, so the team was forced to practice and compete on four different softball fields in surrounding areas. Determined to build a field on campus, Judi found an old orange grove with trees so embedded in the ground that no one could figure how to get them out. Naturally, Judi Garman found a way. She contacted the Army Core of Engineers to dynamite them out. When the core of engineers rolled in with their equipment, the university became nervous about liability issues, and suddenly they found a way to get the trees removed. Two softball fields with lights now stand in the former orange grove. Boyfriends of the women's softball team built a $20,000 press box for $3,000 after trying to get the university to do the project. The work does get done, but often it is the coach's ingenuity that has created the work force.

## CHANGES IN ATHLETES

Present challenges converge around how athletes have changed. Generally Garman and her associates believe that California athletes are difficult and different from the ordinary breed of athletes. She also feels too many athletes have the "what's-in-it-for-me" attitude. In addition, she finds that parents can be the most trying part of coaching. Earlier, the parents went to the athletic director; now they start with the university president and work their way down. Nonetheless, she feels, "The real reward comes in later years with the calls and cards from former athletes thanking you for the difference you and athletics have made in their lives."

## FAVORITE BOOKS AND AUTHORS

Garman's reading time is limited to softball books.

## FAVORITE MOVIES

Garman especially enjoys musicals and live experimental theater. *Phantom of the Opera* and *Evita* are her favorites.

## LIFE BEYOND ATHLETICS

Traveling and skiing occupy Judi's vacation time. Conducting workshops in Italy gives her the opportunity to travel. She also has a family business in Canada that produces moccasins.

## FUTURE PLANS

At the right time she will retire and spend time traveling, golfing, and skiing.

## RECOGNITIONS AND ACHIEVEMENTS

### Accomplishments as a Player

- Played on Canadian National Championships Team Saskatoon Imperial, 1969, 1970
- Canadian National Team, 1970
- Canadian All-Star Outfielder, 1969

### Coaching Recognitions

- Big West Conference Championship: 1993
- PCAA Conference Championships: 1986, 1987
- WCAA Conference Championships: 1981, 1982, 1983, 1984, 1985
- Seven Regional Championships: 1981, 1982, 1983, 1985, 1986, 1987, 1995
- JC National Championships: 1975, 1976, 1977, 1978 at Golden West
- Qualified for post-season play seventeen consecutive years: 1980 to 1996
- Winningest active coach and all-time Division I 913–376 (.708)
- All-time record 1124–416 (.729)

### National Coaching Assignments

- Pan Am Team Coaching Staff, 1979
- More than 16 National Team players

- Runner-up College World Series, 1981, 1983, 1985
- Three Honda Broderick Award Winners (Nation's Top Collegiate Softball Player)
- National Championship, 1986

## Other Accomplishments

- California Community College Hall of Fame, 1992
- National Softball Coaches Hall of Fame, 1993
- Women of Excellence in Sports, Orange County, 1995
- President of National Softball Coaches Association, 1990–1991

Photo courtesy of University
of Virginia

# LAUREN GREGG

## *Soccer—National Team*

## INTRODUCTION

Former University of Virginia Women's Soccer Coach, Lauren Gregg has always been among the first. She explains, "I have ridden the crest of the first wave of soccer. Being part of the first is one of the most unique aspects of my career as a player and as a coach." At the age of sixteen she joined Wellesley High School's (Wellesley, MA) first varsity soccer team. The Wellesley beginning activated a brilliant string of firsts for this exceptional athlete and coach.

Head USA Women's Soccer Coach Tony DiCicco said, "Lauren Gregg has been the epitome of an assistant coach. She has the soccer savvy of a head coach, the loyalty and persistence to get the job done, and the knowledge of coaching women that is an invaluable resource." Anson Dorrance, her long-time soccer mentor, was the person who encouraged Lauren to coach. He has a strong belief that women should coach women, and he teaches that one should give back when opportunity presents itself.

## PERSONAL DATA

*Birth*: Rochester, Minnesota, July 20, 1960

*Father*: James Alan Gregg

*Father's Occupation*: Physician

*Mother*: Veronica Anne (Ronnie) Nowick

*Mother's Occupation*: Publishing

*Siblings*: Kathy, John, Jim, and David

*Alma Maters*: University of North Carolina—B.S., Psychology (High Honors), 1983; Harvard University—M.Ed., 1985

## FORMATIVE YEARS

The Gregg family moved to Massachusetts when Lauren was ten. Lauren's parents imbued their young family with a love for learning and the notion that one should endeavor to do well in school and life. It was always assumed that they would go to college and attend a professional school, if necessary, to achieve their goals. As Lauren's parents allowed her to choose where to invest her energies, she plotted out her time between academic and athletic pursuits. For Lauren there were never enough hours in the day as her love for soccer always commanded a sizable chunk of time.

## SPORTS HISTORY

Although this high-spirited young woman was attracted to athletics at an early age, the opportunity to play organized soccer did not arrive until her fourteenth year. In high school she competed in swimming and lettered in four sports: basketball, softball, field hockey, and soccer. When soccer was offered, she jumped at the opportunity to compete and dropped field hockey to devote her time to the sport that had become her passion.

## PLAYING CAREER

After high school graduation, Lauren faced the fact that there were few intercollegiate soccer programs for women. Furthermore, she was not encouraged by her high school advisors to select a college based solely on its having an intercollegiate soccer team. Thus her collegiate days began on a challenging note because Lehigh University's women's soccer team only had club status. To fulfill this great need to compete in a highly organized and competitive soccer program, she soon tried out for the men's junior varsity soccer team and made the team. This shift implied she had abandoned the women's club because she felt herself too good. In time both teams realized that Lauren was simply interested in playing highly skilled, competitive soccer. For the next two years she played junior varsity soccer on the men's team and varsity basketball and lacrosse with the women.

After two years with the men's team, Lauren still yearned to play women's soccer. Prompted by this desire, she sought acceptance at Harvard University and was admitted on a one-year visiting student status. Lauren describes the Harvard experience as "heaven on a daily basis." At last she was able to compete with other women who were skilled and serious about high-level competition. She was extremely happy with this opportunity, but it was not without its tensions. Her sheer love of the game was often misinterpreted by teammates who did not share her same competitive drive.

Lauren possessed a compelling desire to improve daily. She treasured each practice session and competition, knowing the year would end all too soon. The end came with Harvard taking third place at the first unofficial national championships at Colorado College. For Lauren Gregg this held all the splendor of a dream. The Harvard experience had delivered all she had sought. Inspired by academic and athletic success, she lobbied for just one more year at Harvard. Her attempt was foiled as the admissions dean felt that circumventing the school's policy would set an unwanted precedence. This decision sent her in search of another school to meet her high academic standards and her athletic expectations. Two schools looked appealing: the University of Massachussets and the University of North Carolina. North Carolina won as she already had established a reputation there by scoring three goals when Harvard defeated UNC 5–3 at the national championship. The University of North Carolina's coach Anson Dorrance, knew a good athlete when he saw one and was pleased when he heard Lauren was considering transferring there.

After carefully exploring the strength of UNC's academic programs, Gregg felt that maybe she could have it all over again there. In the fall of 1981, Lauren Gregg enrolled at UNC and participated in North Carolina's winning of the *first* AIAW National Championship. This prestigious win brought another of Gregg's dreams to reality as she chalked up two more firsts to her burgeoning list and found a bonus in Coach Anson Dorrance as a mentor. The following year, 1982, UNC won the *first* NCAA National Championship. This win affixed another first to Gregg's expanding roster of precedents.

Lauren graduated from UNC with high honors, was voted ACC's top female student athlete, received the Marie James post-graduate scholarship, and returned the following year as a graduate assistant to Coach Dorrance. With summer's arrival, Gregg tallied another first when she was selected for the first U.S. Olympic Festival Team. Competing on two teams, the United States National Team and the Seattle Cozars—consumed a lion's share of Lauren's time during the 1986–1988 seasons.

## DECISION TO COACH

Returning to Harvard, this time as a graduate, Lauren enrolled in the master of education program specializing in counseling and consulting psychology. At the same time, she served as an assistant coach with the women's soccer team and continued to compete on the national team. A year and a half later, Bruce Arena, the men's soccer coach at the University of Virginia, invited her to apply for the coaching position at Virginia. This was unexpected because she had never considered a coaching career.

The opportunity to coach was appealing; it would provide a mechanism to give back to the game that had captured her heart. With the intention of paying back those wonderful years of athletic engagement, Lauren went to Virginia to interview. It was love at first sight. She liked the school, the location, the academic emphasis, and the opportunity to develop an excellent women's soccer program. Gregg accepted the job offer and went to the University of Virginia in the summer of 1986. In assuming this position, she established herself as the first woman to coach soccer at the University of Virginia. Medical school had always been in her plans; now it was on hold. The decision was tough, but the opportunity was attractive and one that could not be disregarded.

## COACHING

Lauren's coaching career started in 1986. Within five short years she developed a highly regarded soccer program. This was accomplished with just a couple of recruiting classes. Her Virginia team was nationally ranked, and even ranked number one for a period. In 1989 she was asked to serve as the top assistant in the women's national team program. By 1991 she took her team to the NCAA Final Four and was selected NCAA Coach of the Year.

In the spring of 1992, Lauren confronted a different foe. An injury compounded by a chronic ailment left her with a fractured back. This was to become the most difficult time in her life and would take over two years to bring under control. The back fracture created extreme pain, limited mobility, and brought neurological complications that impinged on every spectrum of coaching and her life in general. For two months she was hospitalized with patients who had suffered strokes and severe spinal injuries. These days were difficult because she was uncomfortable with the doctors' prognosis of the amount of time expected for recovery, and she was among patients whose injuries were much different. Knowing she would recover, the experience became a test of patience, of will, and of hope. The recovery time continued well beyond her expectations. When released from the hospital, she spent the next three months at home in bed and the following year confined to a wheelchair.

Lauren's injury occurred in the early spring and caused her to miss most of the 1992 summer office work and recruiting. In August she was still limited to a wheelchair, experiencing constant pain, and unable to undergo the necessary physical therapy. These conditions brought her mother to her bedside to provide the care that only a mother can. Her mother, Ronnie Gregg, stayed for five months and enabled her daughter to keep the prospect of coaching alive. Without her help and sacrifice, Lauren would have been unable to coach that season.

As fall approached, Lauren was uncertain she could fulfill her responsibilities as coach. "Logistically I knew I had no idea what coaching would entail. It required a decision and a commitment that was tantamount to traveling down a dark tunnel, where every step was on untrodden ground. I kept going by believing in myself and what I knew I could do. This was a scary time for me. My moment of decision came late one night after receiving a telephone call from one of my players. She had heard I wasn't going to coach and was extremely upset. She said one thing that hit home. 'Lauren, we want you to coach us.' I replied, 'Even if that means coaching you from a wheelchair?' She paused and replied, 'We would want you in whatever capacity. Having some of you would be better than none at all!'" After that phone call, Lauren told her mother she had to continue to coach and asked her mother to stay and help her resume her responsibilities. Together, they embarked on a journey. This was to be a first that she had not sought.

Physical limitations were one hurdle, but the next hurdle was an administrative one. The administration did not support Gregg's decision initially and feared future injury. They felt that if she were to be injured getting in and out of a golf cart going to and from practice, the university would be liable. Lauren knew they cared about her. At this juncture Dean Lampkin, the UVa's advocate for disabled faculty and students, teamed up with Gregg to champion her cause. She informed Lauren of her rights, and they worked together to make it possible for Lauren to continue coaching.

Still confined to a wheelchair, unable to be barred from coaching, and being evaluated at every move, Gregg began the 1992 season with a plan for getting to daily practice. A golf cart solved this problem, but it was just the beginning of a two-year series of similar obstacles. At first, she envisioned coaching only at home games. However, when the road contests were in sight, Lauren knew she must go. Her mother and team members stepped forward to provide the assistance she needed while traveling to the various competitions. The university purchased a scooter which she used to transport herself on trips and at home. Cast in the role of a handicapped person, she entered a new dimension of life and of understanding. Her brief glimpse of the constraints and judgments imposed on many persons for their entire lives left her with a heart-felt admiration for such individuals.

The illness had sapped her independence and mobility; the wheelchair offered a limited adaptation for both; but neither inconvenience had robbed her of the knowledge of the game of soccer and how to coach it. That fall the University of Virginia went undefeated in regional play and completed the season ranked fifth in the nation. Gregg's team was invited to their sixth consecutive play-off appearance. She credited the players for making the season successful as they were the ones most directly affected by her disability. The support, love, and belief of a dedicated team helped carry Lauren Gregg through times when she didn't know if she could make it through another day.

Although Gregg was able to control her destiny on the field, she could not control others' reactions to her disability. How would recruits assess her capacity to coach from the restraints of a wheelchair? Some experiences showed that society responds negatively to a person in a wheelchair: "Because I could not walk, I was often treated as if I had lost my mental faculties, too." Such conditions could not be controlled. Yet, she felt a duty to educate and to change these perceptions. For instance, she believed her inability to walk would be overcome. This reality required her to be courageous and confident. With this self-imposed mandate, she mustered the fortitude to openly project her confidence. As a result, she excelled as a recruiter. Gregg summarized recruiting that year in this way: "The kids we recruited were strong individuals that were willing to take a risk, or so it may have been perceived." Indeed the risk takers added a valuable dimension to an already capable team.

Happily, several years have passed since her injury, and Lauren is able to walk and participate in sports and activities. Progress has been slow, but a full recovery is expected. In June of 1994 she resumed her position as one of the coaches of the United States National Team.

In 1996 she resigned her position at Virginia to become a full-time coach with the national squad and won the gold medal at the Olympics. After the games she was appointed to be the head coach of the Under 21 National Team and led them in 1997 to the Nordic Cup Championship, which is the unofficial world championship for that age group. Throughout 1998 through July of 1999 she was involved in preparing the United States Soccer Team to win the World Cup playing against China in the final game. In this game, they played before over 91,000 spectators in the Rose Bowl in California.

When asked how she has remained committed to the coaching profession through such a tremendously physically and mentally challenging time, Gregg stated, "It is a rewarding yet difficult profession for a woman. One that requires tremendous personal commitment and many choices. I had the advantage of entering the profession at a relatively young age. So many other things that I want for my life still remain as viable options for the future."

Well educated in fields unrelated to coaching, Lauren has felt others often view her coaching as trivial or temporary. Her master's degree in education is often wrongly assumed to be in physical education, which she claims is unfairly perceived with a certain stigma. She has had to work to change her own views. These attitudes have motivated Lauren to become a true educator and use her coaching role as a vehicle to dismiss false impressions that many assume naively.

In her own words Lauren says, "I had a passion for the game, and its demand was so complete that it was at the exclusion of many other aspects of my life. During my first few years as a coach at Virginia, I was only part time. To increase my income, I found an evening job as a patient representative in a hospital emergency room. Five nights a week, I would run off the field, change, eat, and go to the hospital until midnight or so." This job allowed Lauren a better balance in her life than what would transpire over the next several years as she sculpted a life as a coach with national repute.

The consuming first love of a sport called soccer heads Gregg's roster of firsts. Her passionate drive to excel will be etched in silent memory by those who shared her "gutsy" performances as an athlete and as a coach.

## MEMORABLE MOMENTS

In 1991 two things happened to Lauren. Her collegiate team was ranked number one, which is significant because only ten teams have ever been ranked at the number-one spot. Her team made it to the NCAA Final Four. She, however, had to be in China with the national team as they were participating in the World Cup for the first time ever in women's soccer. The USA won the first ever world championship by defeating Norway 2–1. It was such a successful competition that Lauren believes it established that women's soccer needed to be considered for the 1996 Olympic Games.

In 1996 the U.S. team (Lauren was one of the coaches) won the first-ever gold medal. After the 1995 loss to Norway in the semi-finals of the World Cup, the team said that they would do whatever it took to be successful in the Olympics. This success was a dream come true for Lauren who had had an Olympic dream since her younger years.

Probably the most significant, and certainly most fresh in her memory, was the 1999 World Cup. It was a landmark event. Over 650,000 tickets were sold for the tournament and over 91,000 attended the final in the Rose Bowl in Pasadena, California. It is estimated that approximately 40 million watched the event on the ABC television network. It was a landmark soccer event and recorded the largest audience ever to watch a women's sporting event. It received one of the highest television ratings for the semi-final on ESPN.

## ROLE MODELS/MENTORS

*Veronica "Ronnie" Gregg*—Lauren's mother has given so much of herself to assist Lauren throughout her career as both a player and a coach. Ronnie encourages Lauren to live a life in which anything is possible. Ronnie, a bright, intelligent woman, loves to read and learn, and Lauren says her mother has passed this passion on to her. "Ronnie" is seldom in the limelight but is always supportive. Most recently she helped Lauren by editing Lauren's recently published book, *The Champion Within*.

*Anson Dorrance*—Anson Dorrance had a considerable impact on Lauren because he stressed the importance, to all his players, of giving back to the sport. He continually stressed remembering where they had come from in their sport and who had made it possible and that, for the sport to continue to grow, players had to give back by coaching, refereeing, organizing, etc., for the upcoming generation. Had he not done this, Lauren may not have become a coach.

*Linda Bunker*—Linda Bunker is the dean of education at the University of Virginia. Linda brought sport into the academic setting. Everyone wanted to take her classes. Linda became severely disabled with cancer but continued making significant contributions. She teaches that you have to live life every day. She always has a smile on her face. She is always very positive. She is a visionary and a leader. Linda makes a difference in the lives of everyone who knows her. She has a passion for life.

## CHANGES IN ATHLETES

There is no doubt, according to Lauren, that when compared to the athletes of fifteen years ago, today's competitors are much more athletic. At the national level there has been a layering process where team members have become better and better. They are "very lean machines." There is greater acceptance of women athletes now, and they are basically rid of many of the stigmas that were attached to women in sport. They are intelligent, athletic, and feminine, too. Present-day athletes are proud of their sculptured bodies and about being women. They have moved the role of women in sport into a new era. They fight harder to maintain their individuality and, on the national squad, they have a cultural dynamic of what's best for the team; they downplay the singling out that periodically occurs because of media attention to certain individuals by thinking "We're a team."

## LIFE BEYOND ATHLETICS

Lauren loves to write and has just had her book, *The Champion Within: Training for Excellence*, published by JTC Sports. Lauren enjoys photography, particularly documentary photography, and she likes to read philosophical novels and stories that teach. Bicycling, walking, and hitting tennis balls are also part of her leisure routine.

## RECOGNITIONS AND ACHIEVEMENTS

### Accomplishments as a Player

- All-Conference Atlantic Athletic Conference (ACC), 1980, 1981, 1982
- All-Region, 1980, 1981, 1982
- All American, 1980, 1981
- National Team, 1986–1989
- Olympic Festival East Team, 1985
- Olympic Festival South Team Captain, 1986
- National Champion UNC Team Captaim, 1981 (AIAW)
- National Champion UNC Team Captain, 1982 (NCAA)
- National Challenge Cup, 1986, 1987, 1989

### Coaching Recognition in Division I

- ACC Coach of the Year, 1990
- South Region Regional Coach of the Year, 1991
- National Soccer Coaches Association Coach of the Year, 1991

- Team Ranked in Top 20, 1986–1995
- Final Four, 1991

### National Coaching Assignments

- Olympic Festival, 1990
- World Cup Team Assistant, 1989–present
- World University Games, 1993
- Goodwill Games, Gold Medal, 1998
- Olympic Team Assistant, Gold Medal, 1996
- World Cup Champions, 1991, 1999
- National Under-21 Team Head Coach, 1995–present
- Nordic Cup Champions, 1997, 1999

### Other Accomplishments

- First woman to serve as an assistant coach for any U.S. soccer team
- First woman to serve as head coach for the under 20's national team, 1996–present
- Craig Fielder Memorial Award for Courage in the Face of Adversity, 1993
- Spokesperson for Smoke Free Kids Campaign
- Committee for Soccer in the Streets
- Committee for Soccer for the Challenged
- Author of the book, *The Champion Within: Training for Excellence*

Photo courtesy of University
of Illinois

# THERESA GRENTZ

*Basketball—University of Illinois*

## INTRODUCTION

Head coach Theresa Grentz coaches one of the premier basketball teams in the country. Theresa Grentz grew from an admired basketball player to an acclaimed coach. The game has been good to Theresa. The Shank family basketball court was where Theresa met her husband Karl. They were both kids—he was the paperboy from down the street who joined her and the neighborhood boys playing basketball on the Shank's home-fashioned court. Since those childhood days, Theresa amassed myriad honors as a basketball player, and now she is a much-honored coach. The honor she deems most important, however, is that of wife to Karl Grentz and mother to sons Karl and Kevin.

## PERSONAL DATA

*Born*:  March 24, 1952, Spangler, Pennsylvania

*Father*:  John Shank

*Father's Occupation*:  Selector for A.P. Corporation

*Mother*:  Christina Shank

*Mother's Occupation*:  Registered Nurse

*Siblings*: Michael, Donna, Charles, and Anthony

*Husband*: Karl Grentz

*Children*: Karl and Kevin

*Alma Mater*: Immaculata College—B.S., Biology, 1974

## FORMATIVE YEARS

Theresa grew up in a Philadelphia row house in a working-class district. She attended Catholic schools where, at the time, playing on the school courts was not acceptable for girls. Energetic and athletic, Theresa convinced her father to make their driveway into a basketball court. Shanks' basketball court attracted the neighborhood boys and, of course, Karl Grentz, her future husband. The neighborhood kids also played baseball, spit ball, half-ball, and wall ball. In the ninth grade Theresa attended Cardinal O'Hara High School, where she started an illustrious basketball career.

## PLAYING CAREER

Grentz began her sports career playing on the seventh grade Catholic Youth League basketball team. She was in the sixth grade at the time. In high school she played softball and volleyball along with basketball. At Cardinal O'Hara High School, she scored more than twelve hundred points and led her team to three consecutive Philadelphia Catholic and City League Championships. Although she decided not to play college basketball, she changed her mind when she entered Immaculata College and became a standout player. During those four years her teammates were **Marianne Stanley**, now coach at UC Berkeley, and Renie Portland, now coaching at Penn State. Their team won three remarkable AIAW national championships from 1972 to 1974 playing for Coach **Cathy Rush**. Named an All American for three consecutive years, Grentz was also named Collegiate AMF Player of the Year in 1974.

## COACHING

Grentz graduated from Immaculata College in May of 1974 and married in June. Her plans were to use her biology and chemistry background to shape a career in medical research. These plans changed when the St. Joseph University's basketball coach, Ellen Ryan's field hockey team, which she coached for the Country Day School in Philadelphia, was involved in an automobile accident. While her team recuperated, Ryan took a sabbatical, and Theresa was contacted to coach basketball at St. Joseph's in her absence. Theresa took the job and led the team to a winning season. Ryan did not return after the first year, and Grentz coached the team to an 18–3 season. At the end of that year she was offered a job at Rutgers University. She accepted the offer and became the *first* full-time head women's basketball coach in the nation. She coached at Rutgers for 19 years and compiled an outstanding record of 434–150 (.740), including nine consecutive NCAA tournament appearances from 1986 to 1994. Fourteen of her teams won at least 20 games a year. In 1982 her team won the AIAW national championship. From 1981 to 1994 she coached the Junior National Team (1981), the Maccabe Team (1981), the World University Games Team (1990), and the U.S. Olympic Team (1992). Hired by the University of Illinois in 1995, she led the Fighting Illini to a 24–8 season in 1997, and a post-season NCAA tournament appearance to the Sweet Sixteen.

## MEMORABLE MOMENTS

Looking back and comparing teams is not typical for Theresa Grentz. Nevertheless, she does remember those teams that were outstanding, namely, the 1982 and 1987 teams at Rutgers and the 1997 team at Illinois. She describes each team as selfless and totally dedicated. Even though all teams have distractions, these teams were so focused they did not allow the distractions to impede their achievement of their goals. This modest woman did not acknowledge any of her achievements as moments to remember.

## PHILOSOPHY OF COACHING

According to Grentz, "You have got to be yourself and allow players to know who you are." Grentz also endorses the belief that it is the coach's job to communicate to athletes the importance of what they are doing and how the coach wants it to be done. She feels that athletes' ability to be prepared and to do the best possible job is based on a core of accountability, responsibility to student athletes, trustworthiness, and courtesy. Athletes must understand that they will be criticized. They must also understand they have to be loyal, and they must want to win. Winning gets attention!

## ROLE MODELS/MENTORS

*John Shank*—Theresa's father taught her never to quit!
*Christina Shank*—Theresa's mother taught her to find a way!
*Maryanne Nespoli*—This high school coach was an excellent communicator and one who cared a great deal about her players.

## CHANGES IN ATHLETES

Grentz feels that parents and families have changed; parents can be extremely demanding. The fact that two-parent families are atypical has had a great impact on young women. If young students have not learned obedience, discipline, integrity, and honesty from their parents, it will be impossible to teach these qualities in four years.

## LIFE BEYOND ATHLETICS

Karl, Theresa's husband, attended Wynder College in Pennsylvania. He is a National Account Manager for Xerox. With their two children, Karl, 19, and Kevin, 11, they form a close-knit family. They are protective of their time together. Their favorite vacations include Disney World and cruises.

Since becoming Head Coach at Illinois in 1995, Theresa has spoken at more than 500 civic organizations and functions. It is apparent that one so successful is in great demand to motivate and share experiences with others who are interested in excellence.

## FAVORITE BOOKS

*Mother Teresa: A Simple Path* and *Military Leadership: In Pursuit of Excellence* are Theresa's favorite books.

## RECOGNITIONS AND ACHIEVEMENTS

### Accomplishments as a Player

- All American, 1972, 1973, 1974
- Played on National Team against Australia, 1974
- Earned a Silver Medal in World Games, 1973
- Played on National Championship Team, Immaculata, 1974

### Coaching Recognition in Division I

- Conference Championships, Atlantic 10 Conference, 1986, 1987
- Conference Championship, Big Ten, 1997–1998
- Conference Coach of the Year, Atlantic 10, 1987, 1988, 1992, 1993
- Conference Coach of the Year, Big Ten, 1996–1997
- Regional Coach of the Year, District II, 1987–1988, 1992–1993
- Regional Coach of the Year, District IV, 1996–1997
- Kodak All American, 1 Academic All American, 1 National Team Player

### National Coaching Assignments

- World University Games, 1989
- Goodwill Games Gold Medal, 1990
- Olympic Games, Bronze Medal, 1992
- Maccobiah Games, Silver Medal, 1981
- Jones Cup, Gold Medal, 1985

## Other Accomplishments

- Nike Hall of Fame, 1992
- Cardinal O'Hara High School Hall of Fame, 1996
- Member of Olympic Committee
- Founding Member of Women's Basketball Coaches Association
- President WBCA
- Second fastest coach to reach 400 victories
- Seventh overall winningest active coach

Photo courtesy of University
of North Carolina

# SYLVIA HATCHELL

*Basketball—University of North Carolina*

## INTRODUCTION

If playground balls could communicate, Sylvia Hatchell's would spin tales of a young girl's childhood adventures. They would report resting in a box next to her bed each night. They would speak of Sylvia's insatiable love for games and the hours she devoted to bouncing and hitting them to her younger brothers. The basketball could describe the intrigue of watching Sylvia and her pals carefully removing a window to gain entry into a locked gymnasium. Another would recount the relief of resting in its bedside carton after being pounded against the side of a wall for hour upon hour. The balls would unanimously proclaim that Sylvia never neglected any of them.

Well, balls don't speak, but Sylvia Hatchell's early fascination with games and balls helped change her from an ardent competitor to a highly honored basketball coach. And now, years later, ball games still dominate her life. Sylvia even married a basketball coach. Both are head basketball coaches at two different institutions.

## PERSONAL DATA

*Born*: February 28, 1952, Gastonia, North Carolina

*Father*: Carroll Rhyne

*Father's Occupation*: Machinist for Amps, Inc.

*Mother*: Veda Shepard Rhyne

*Mother's Occupation*: Church Secretary

*Siblings*: Phyllis, Ralph, and Ron

*Husband*: Sammy Hatchell

*Husband's Occupation*: Basketball Coach

*Child*: Van

*Alma Mater*: Carson-Newman College—B.S., 1974; University of Tennessee—M.S., 1975

## FORMATIVE YEARS

Growing up in Gastonia, North Carolina, with parents who focused on the family provided Sylvia with a stable, happy childhood environment. Family trips and the extended family were favorite and basic components of Sylvia's early life. Her parents encouraged physical activity, and opportunities for sports participation were provided by neighborhood, church, and YMCA programs.

## SPORTS HISTORY

As a toddler, Sylvia had a fascination with balls, regardless of shape, color, or size. With a multitude of cousins, two younger brothers, a neighborhood of kids, school and church playgrounds, and the nearby YMCA, she had ample opportunity to play ball. When she was not playing football, basketball, or baseball, she shagged balls or watched the older kids play while waiting for an opportunity. Hanging around ball parks and gymnasiums acquainted her with coaches who allowed her to field practice balls or fill-in for an absent player.

Although competitive sport opportunities for girls were not offered at her high school, the YMCA and the city recreation department provided the basketball and softball for girls that the school withheld. It was not until college that Sylvia had the chance to play on a school team. However, the lack of competitive opportunities did not dampen Sylvia's interest in the world of sport. In fact, early in life she decided she wanted a career based on something in the world of sport and athletics.

## COACHING

Sylvia does not remember just when coaching became her career choice. What she does recall is thinking it would be nice to coach boys because it did not seem possible to coach females. Her coaching opportunity came while playing on the basketball team during her senior year at Carson-Newman College. She was asked to coach a school team of 7th- and 8th-grade girls. The girls were daughters of tobacco farmers in the small community of Talbott, Tennessee. Because the school played their games on nights when Sylvia did not compete, she accepted the job and scheduled practices around her own team practices. Hatchell emerged from this first coaching experience with a 16–4 record. The school was small, and they still played the old six-player girls' basketball. It was a wonderful experience for her; she loved the students and community. Now she was really hooked on becoming a coach.

After graduation, she headed to Tennessee for graduate work. In graduate school at the University of Tennessee, she developed a great friendship with the now well-respected basketball coach, Pat Head Summit. Pat had an assistantship to coach the University of Tennessee women's basketball team. She asked Sylvia to coach the JV team, and Sylvia gladly accepted. After running practice for the JV team, she stayed and helped with varsity practice; when she was not helping she just watched.

Her next coaching stop was Florence, South Carolina, at Francis Marion College. The team was young, less than two years old, providing an excellent opportunity to build a strong team. Working day and night, Sylvia recruited from the talented pool of local high school athletes. Her hard work paid off because she recruited top athletes, and the team continually improved to the point of winning the 1982 AIAW Division II National Championship. In 1986 her team won the NAIA Basketball Championship. According to Hatchell, those early teams were as good as present-day Division I teams.

Hatchell orchestrated an 11–year (273–80) winning record at Francis Marion. Her teams not only defeated Division II teams, they also defeated every Division I team they played. Basking in success, she knew she could only move up the coaching ranks by changing schools. In the meantime, she received recruitment calls from five different athletic directors, including Indiana, Texas A & M, Florida, and South Carolina. It had always been her dream to coach at the University of North Carolina. Eventually UNC called to schedule her for an interview. At the time, they were also interviewing four other coaches with Division I head coaching experience. When Sylvia was interviewed she merely stated, "I want the job!" Wanting the job meant she did not care about the salary or anything else. She was hired, and she experienced a tough, tough beginning because UNC, unlike other schools in the conference, did not have access to Prop 48 athletes. After four years, the conference passed a Prop 48 athletes' rule. With this change, she galloped from last in the conference to a national championship in three years.

As Sylvia surrounded herself with good assistants, her teams became consistent winners. Since 1991, with the exception of the 1995–1996 season, the UNC Tar Heels have won more than 20 games per year. The highlight came in 1994 when they won the national championship. This championship distinguished Sylvia Hatchell as the only coach to win NCAA, NAIA, and AIAW national championships. In addition to her collegiate efforts, she has been actively involved with the USA Basketball National teams. She was an assistant coach for the USA Basketball Goodwill Games, the World Games in 1986, and the Olympic Games in 1988. She was head coach for the R. William Jones Cup Team that went 8–0 in 1994 and the World University Games in 1995. In 1994 she was named National Coach of the Year by *USA Today* and *College Sports Magazine*.

## MEMORABLE MOMENTS

Winning three national championships, AIAW in 1982, NAIA in 1986, and the NCAA in 1994, has provided special memories for Hatchell. Not only has she won three national titles, but she also has been head coach of every basketball team that represents the United States except the Olympic team. For Hatchell, each of these accomplishments is memorable because the achievements come so few times in one's lifetime. She believes representing one's country conjures feelings that create a realization that "you are the best at that moment in the history of that sport!"

## PHILOSOPHY OF COACHING

Hatchell believes that most often people create their own opportunities. One does this by looking at a situation and then making something out of it. Hard work produces improvement over time. Going from last in the conference to national champions in three years was the result of hard work. "It comes from not giving up, from believing in what you are doing, from staying the course and hanging in there." Success for Sylvia is not just about winning, but she has the record (541–231) to verify the program is working.

Big on team work, Sylvia seldom talks individually with players. She likes to demonstrate to the team how the better players are so much better as a team than as individuals. The program is structured around a family-like atmosphere. The binding force of this atmosphere is built on extreme loyalty and trust. The athletes trust Sylvia, and she returns an extreme loyalty to them. In return, the same loyalty is expected of team members. When these values are combined with a work ethic, says Hatchell, "you are going to be winners."

## ROLE MODELS/MENTORS

*Carroll and Veda Rhyne*—Sylvia credits her parents for being tremendous examples and raising children in a very disciplined home without raising their voices. Their exemplary ways, and those of her grandparents, relayed to her strong messages of how to deal with challenging situations. They encouraged Sylvia "to be the best I could be at whatever I did."

*W. F. Woodall*—Pastor of Unity Baptist Church in Gastonia, North Carolina, Woodall was Sylvia's pastor from ages 9 to 19. Under Woodall's leadership, she watched his congregation grow from 150 church members to 850. She gleaned many insights while observing his "marvelous" ways of dealing with people.

In addition to her parents and Pastor Woodall, she has taken bits and pieces from coaches and other people she admires.

## LIFE BEYOND ATHLETICS

Sylvia Hatchell lives a full life. Time away from basketball is spent in family and church-related activities. Her husband and son occupy most of her spare time. She takes time to do things with her young son like attending movies and sporting events with him. The family also spends quality time at their beach home.

Otherwise, Sylvia participates with the women's group at church. This is enjoyable as some of the women know little about basketball and little about Sylvia's basketball accomplishments. She deems it as "sort of fun to have friends who just see you as who you are."

## FAVORITE BOOKS AND MOVIES

Although she enjoys reading, her favorite book is the Bible. Some of the other books she deems good are *Fried Green Tomatoes*, by Fannie Flagg, *The Magic of Teamwork*, by Pat Williams, general manager for the Orlando Magic, and *Mayburry Humor*, by Jennie Robertson, a friend of Sylvia's. Her all-time favorite movie is *The Sound of Music*.

## FUTURE PLANS

Presently, Sylvia is very happy coaching at the University of South Carolina and conducting a basketball camp program that attracts 4,000 youngsters. It is the largest in the country; her husband, Sammy, assists in this venture.

## RECOGNITIONS AND ACHIEVEMENTS

### Coaching Recognitions in Division I

- AMF Voit Championship Coach Award, 1986
- Three National Championships: NAIA 1982, AIAW 1986, NCAA 1994
- Regional Coach of the Year, NAIA, 1986
- National Coach of the Year, *College Sports Magazine*, 1994
- National Coach of the Year, *USA Today*, 1994
- ACC Coach of the Year, NAIA, 1986
- College Basketball Coach of the Year by Athletes International Ministries, 1995
- Four Conference Championships in the ACC: 1994, 1995, 1997, 1998

### National Coaching Assignments

- Olympic Festivals, South Assignment, 1982
- World Games, 1983, 1995 Gold Medal

- World Championships Assistant, 1986
- World University Games, Gold Medal, 1986
- Olympic Staff 1984, Gold Medal, 1988
- Team USA 1994, Jones Cup Gold Medal

## Other Accomplishments

- Francis Marion University Athletic Hall of Fame, 1993
- President of Women's Basketball Coaches Association, 1996–1997
- Carson-Newman Athletic Hall of Fame, 1999
- Over 500 career wins

Photo courtesy of University
of Massachusetts

# PAM HIXON

*Field Hockey/Lacrosse—University of Massachusetts*

## INTRODUCTION

Born with an ice hockey stick in her hand, or so it seemed, Pam Hixon got an early start in hockey on a nearby ice pond—her father saw to it. These childhood experiences fueled Pam's enthusiasm to earn a spot on an intercollegiate field hockey team years later. Today she uses the skills and strategies gained early in life in her role as a teacher and coach at the University of Massachusetts.

## PERSONAL DATA

>*Born*: June 30, 1951, Everett, Massachusetts
>
>*Father*: Phillip Dana Hixon
>
>*Father's Occupation*: Representative for Dennison Manufacturing Company
>
>*Mother*: Elaine Capone (Hixon)
>
>*Mother's Occupation*: Housewife and Executive Director for Public Housing
>
>*Siblings*: Charles, Jennifer
>
>*Alma Mater*: Springfield College—B.S., Physical Education, 1973

## FORMATIVE YEARS

Pam Hixon's youth was spent in Framingham, Massachusetts, in the same town her father spent his boyhood. Her father helped build their home. No children lived close to the Hixon home; it was considered an out-in-the-woods suburb. The neighborhood consisted of four homes on a long, tree-lined street. Pam's friends lived about a mile away, requiring Pam's mother to transport the children to places where they could play with other children. Framingham was a small community clothed in the friendliness of a place where everybody knows everybody in town.

Each summer the Hixons lounged at the beach and enjoyed their grandfather's summer home. At the seaside home Pam enjoyed swimming, kick-the-can, and associating with other children on the beach. The Hixon family still spends one week a year skiing in Colorado.

Attending the theater in Boston was a favorite part of the family's entertainment. The Hixons made sure their children had exposure to a broad range of activities, including cultural events. In addition to the immediate family Pam had close ties to all of her grandparents who lived close to them. One grandparent, Lilian Capone, is 93 and still lives an active, enjoyable life.

Pam's favorite activity in elementary school was to be outside and run. She remembers well two teachers, Mrs. Flagg, the second grade teacher, and Mrs. Hayes, the sixth grade teacher, for their contributions toward nurturing her competitive desire to learn, to improve, and to excel.

## SPORTS HISTORY

Pam's athletic genes come from her father. He played semi-pro hockey, competed for Boston University, and also coached the game. From her father, Mrs. Hayes, and Mrs. Flagg, Pam received early incentives to participate in athletics. She and her siblings started skating not long after they learned to walk. At the age of three years she owned an ice hockey stick and was competent enough to move around the skating rink. A nearby ice pond was convenient for play, and it attracted towns people and hockey-playing boys. Playing ice hockey gave Pam her first taste of competition. Ice hockey was a daily event during the winter months and most of her play was engaged with the boys on the pond. Pam was a regular with the boys because she had good game skills. From grade school to high school she was involved in ice hockey.

When Pam reached thirteen, her father took her hockey stick and told her not to play with the boys. He worried about her safety and felt it was time for her to participate in activities with high school girls. Pam has never forgotten the day the stick was taken from her. It was a devastating move, but it didn't stop the boys from hiding a stick under the ice house with an open invitation for her to join the play; of course, her father was not privy to their secret.

In high school Pam mingled with kids from other parts of town. Framingham had grown big enough to support two high schools. Pam attended South Framingham High School where the student body was over one thousand. She made friends all over town, and these friends were strong academically, ethnically diverse, and active in athletics and various student body affairs. It was a wonderful mix of friends, and she felt fortunate to have their friendships.

In her first year at South Framingham, Pam played basketball and softball. She was hesitant to try the unfamiliar, but she eventually played field hockey. Thus she became a three-sport high school athlete. The teams Pam played for did not take part in high school championships. They played a competitive schedule, but their schedules did not culminate in championships as high schools do today. High schools in the sixties and seventies did not offer many females a state championship tournament.

It was an unspoken expectation that Pam would go to college. She wanted to go, and her mother claims she was like a directed arrow from the day she was born. Goals and direction were the way Pam ordered life; she knew where she wanted to go, and she knew what she wanted to do, and she sensed how to make it happen. During the summer of her senior year in high school, her parents accompanied her to several college campuses. Springfield College, in Springfield, Massachusetts, was high on the list of choices. Pam wanted to be a physical educator, and Springfield offered an outstanding program with an outstanding reputation. She also looked at Skidmore and the University of Massachusetts. After looking at all three, Springfield was first on the list. In her view, there was no other place internationally or domestically where physical educators were so well prepared.

At Springfield College she earned a place on the varsity basketball team. Although she played field hockey, she did not excel but was good enough to play on the national team for ten years (1969 to 1979). During her sophomore year she competed on the lacrosse team. As graduation neared (1973) she accepted a teaching position at South High School in Newton, Massachusetts. It was her plan to teach several years before seeking further education.

## DECISION TO COACH

Hixon's experience on the National Squad in 1969 verified that she wanted to coach athletes at a high-skill level. She taught and coached field hockey, basketball, and softball for three years at Newton's South High. She started the softball team and enjoyed the challenge of starting from nothing and engineering a competitive team within three years.

Three years at Newton and a thirst for further education encouraged Pam to return to school and work for a master's degree. She acquired an assistantship and as an assistant coached field hockey, basketball, and softball. Near the end of the second year, a head coaching position for field hockey and lacrosse became available at the University of Massachusetts, and she took the job. She started in 1978.

Halfway through her junior year in college she had thought about what to do in life. "I have always wanted to do what I've liked. If I could do something where I had a lot of fun, and it was something I really liked, then I knew I would be happy in the work place."

Her always-supportive parents taught her, "Do what makes you happy within the structure of society, if you're a good person, and you are doing something that you like and you are happy, then you just run with it." They thought the decision to teach and coach was wonderful because she could earn a living doing what she thoroughly enjoyed. Her family has always followed her activities. In fact, this is something they do for each other; they reinforce each other by supporting their personal interests.

At one point in 1978, UMass had been on a rollercoaster ride. The field hockey and lacrosse teams had done fairly well, but scholarship money had been cut back. It didn't detract too much, because good athletes came to the university because of its strong academic programs. They had a lot of in-state kids playing on the field hockey team. Lacrosse was relatively new, but the athletes were teachable enough to bring the lacrosse team into national prominence. The same thing happened with field hockey; Pam just plugged along with outstanding athletes, taught them the game, and also elevated the field hockey program to national prominence. She has kept the tradition of national prominence going. Fifteen to twenty years ago, lacrosse was a catchall sport that pulled field hockey players, basketball players, and others to compete on the team. Presently, the practice of crossing over from sport to sport is rare.

Pam coached at UMass from 1978 to 1995 before taking a two-year leave to coach the Olympic field hockey team. She returned for the 1996 season. In April of 1997 Pam resigned from UMass to become the U.S. National Team coach on a full-time basis. All told, she has worked for the national team for four years. In 1994 the team was ranked eleventh in the world. According to Pam, **Beth Anders**, the previous coach, had established a good framework, and the team finished third in the World Cup, second in the Pan American Games, and fifth in the Olympics. Following the Olympics there was a large turnover in personnel. Young American athletes are not exposed to the same international experience as athletes in other countries. Our college game does not adequately prepare athletes for international competition. Because of her international coaching experiences, Pam believes she is a better match as a collegiate coach. She especially likes the college structure and atmosphere.

## MEMORABLE MOMENTS

The first year the NCAA offered championships for field hockey and lacrosse was 1981. This was a not-to-be-forgotten year. In the fall they played in the finals of the national championship and lost to Connecticut in a 4–1 game. Then, in the spring of 1982, the UMass team trounced Trenton State 9–6, winning the National Championship. It was a special year; the athletes were highly competitive—they were actually in "two championship games."

Pam contends her memorable moments were created by the athletes and her assistants. Speaking of the loss to Connecticut in the field hockey final, she said, "I couldn't think straight. Our team had gone undefeated all year, and it was the only loss that year. Even so, it was special, it was televised. The thrill of being part of the first televised game removed some pain from the loss. It was the largest crowd and audience we had ever played for."

For the second game, the core of players was the same so she had a championship-seasoned team. The approximately 50 percent overlap on the field hockey and lacrosse teams gave many athletes the opportunity to play in two championships—one in field hockey and one in lacrosse.

In 1984, Judy Strong, one of the University of Massachusetts' local athletes, was selected for the Olympic team. To see a team member win the bronze medal in the Los Angeles Olympics was a wonderful milestone for the athlete and for Pam.

The last memory of note happened to the last final-four University of Massachusetts team Pam coached. The year was 1993. She had three foreign athletes on the field, two from England and one from Canada. These young women had shared their knowledge and skills with the American athletes. Between the time the season started and the time it finished, the American athletes were vastly improved due to the foreign players. These women had improved in all areas of the game and were now giving more than the foreign athletes who had taught them so well.

## ROLE MODELS/MENTORS

*Mrs. Flagg and Mrs. Hayes*—Both teachers taught Pam how to be competitive and, in so doing, how to be one's best.

*Phillip Hixon*—Pam's dad had played collegiate and semi-pro ice hockey. He was a superb role model.

*Kitty Walker and Pat West*—These two high school coaches planted in Pam the idea that she must do her best. They encouraged hard work, team work, being responsible, and playing with heart regardless of the outcome. These women set the framework for being an athlete. They inspired her to become a teacher, a trainer, and a coach. Kitty and Pat directed her to a career in physical education and coaching.

*Dottie Zenaty*—Dottie was a teacher, coach, and mentor to Pam at Springfield College.

## PHILOSOPHY OF COACHING

To help athletes establish a work ethic is Pam's number one philosophical tenet. Being competitive in practice ranks as number two—"how you practice is how you play." Pam also believes it is as important for athletes to be good university citizens as it is for one to be a good citizen in a country. Both types of citizenship expectations are extremely important to Pam. She promotes the idea of performance on the field as only one aspect of the total person, and she feels that what one does outside the game sets a tone of respect for when the team "shows up on the field."

She encourages athletes to follow their dreams. "What's in their heart as a competitor should always be there. It's not about succeeding on the first try. It's about ultimately succeeding. As long as one wants to play and compete, one must keep at it until personal satisfaction has been reached."

## CHANGES IN ATHLETES

Pam claims publicity even for the "blue-chip" athletes had to be sought in the mid-eighties. The media didn't seek information; coaches had to go to the media. Recruiting is also very different from the early eighties: now athletes are called frequently, and they are heavily recruited. Earlier athletes came to a school because they liked the school and the program. The hype around an individual was really not that great. Personal identity was based on their own unique personality. These competitors had an identity much different than the identity of a lot of blue-chip athletes today.

It seems to Pam that the athletes recruit the coach. The roles are reversed. It changes how those athletes feel about coming to an institution. Every coach would like a team of stars, but it is impossible because everyone can't be a star. Players have to learn to be more self-less, and Pam believes it is a very difficult thing for the high school athletes to do today. The whole process of recruitment has tainted the role of coaches and athletes. For example, coaches are responsible for everything: academic support, nutritional services, and the unique needs of each individual. Coaches are doing so much for athletes that it has significantly reduced the amount of time actually spent coaching. Pam feels that this is unfortunate.

According to Pam, it took ten years for weight training to be viewed as "cool" for women athletes. Earlier the athletes participated in summer conditioning programs based on running and jumping to stay ready for fall competition. Pre-season programs also helped athletes to prepare for the season. In these times little information was available on nutrition or the academic part of school and competition. The athletes had to do much more for themselves. They even had to develop their own classroom survival skills. Women did not receive the benefits their male counterparts had in earlier years.

## LIFE BEYOND ATHLETICS

Pam has been busy operating White Mountain Sports, a camp for field hockey, for the past twenty years. She is beginning to add other camp activities relating to recruiting issues and a camp designed for different levels of field hockey athletes. Her ideas would expose more females to the opportunity to go to college and to seek scholarships. She is also considering doing the same kind of thing with other sports.

Along with her sports program, Pam plays golf and spends time skiing in Colorado. Reading mysteries and murder stories is a treasured pastime. Her favorite authors are Patricia Cornwall, Mary Higgins Clark, and Dick Francis. Francis writes about horses. Her favorite movie is *Cool Runnings*, which she laughs at during each viewing as it exposes the political implications behind team coaching.

## RECOGNITIONS AND ACHIEVEMENTS

### Accomplishment as a Player

- National Field Hockey Team, 1969–1979

### Coaching Recognitions in Division I

- Conference Coach of the Year, Atlantic 10: 1990, 1991, 1992, 1993, 1994, 1996
- Twice National Eastern Region Coach of the Year
- Collegiate Coach of the Year, Field Hockey, 1981
- Four Final-Four appearances: 1980, 1981, 1983, 1984—Lacrosse
- Four Final-Four appearances: 1981, 1983, 1987, 1992—Field Hockey
- National Championship, Lacrosse, 1982
- Eighteen First-Team All Americans
- Four Olympians and 19 National Team Members
- UMass Field Hockey 272–75–18; UMass Lacrosse 91–30–2

### National Coaching Assignments

- World University Games, 1990
- National Coaching Staff, 1981–1994
- Head Coach, Olympic Festivals: 1981, 1982, 1983, 1986, 1987, 1989, 1990
- Pan Am Games, Silver Medal, 1991
- World Cup, Bronze Medal, 1994
- Olympics Head Coach, 1996—Field Hockey
- World Cup, 1998

Photo courtesy of University of
Texas, Austin

# BEVERLY ANN KEARNEY

*Track and Field—University of Texas*

## INTRODUCTION

"They will be trained in head, hand, and heart: their heads to think, their hands to work, and their hearts to have faith." This lofty 1904 mission statement of the celebrated black educator Mary McLeod Bethune is still being realized 96 years later by another young, black educator who also chose to rise above and look beyond the institutions and insinuations of racism. She could not be shackled by the attitudes of those who desired to dampen her spirit. Coach Beverly Ann Kearney's indomitable reach for excellence would have brought contentment to her esteemed role model, the late Mary McLeod Bethune.

## PERSONAL DATA

*Born*: February 25, 1958, Mississippi

*Father*: Beverly Kearney, Jr.

*Father's Occupation*: Air Force

*Mother*: Bertha Booey Kearney

*Mother's Occupation*: Dry cleaner

*Siblings*: Alice Jefferson, Howard Adams, Ernestine Driggs, Cherry Buie, Gerettia Booey, and Derick

*Alma Maters*: Auburn University—B.A., Social Work, 1981; Indiana State University—M.S., 1983

## FORMATIVE YEARS

Beverly Ann Kearney was born in Mississippi, the sixth of seven children born to a military family. She still bears the scars of gender and racial bias and the loss of her mother who died while Bev was a teenager.

Admiration for her older sister, Gerettia, drew Bev to run track. She admired Gerettia's strong will, popular manners, talent, and the fact that she ran well enough to earn a scholarship to Auburn University. Gerettia, along with younger brother Derick, inspired Bev to pursue her ambition of earning a college degree with a track scholarship.

The early years posed difficult times as the family moved frequently due to her father's military career. Beverly was very shy and timid, but she mustered enough courage to run for junior high school class president. In a cruel turn of events, vote counters manipulated the election results and denied Bev the office she had rightly won. When the vote scandal was made public, the junior high school students organized a protest in favor of Bev. The protest caused Bev to be kicked out of school for inciting a riot. Ironically, some months later, the city of Monrovia, California, awarded her an Outstanding Citizen Citation.

## SPORTS HISTORY

By the time Bev entered high school, she had competed in age-group track programs in California and Nebraska. Upon the family's return to Florida, Bev eagerly joined Brandon High School's first girls' track team. Linda McQuay, organizer and coach of the team, showered young Kearney with the support and encouragement necessary to excel. Kearney, also a member of the school's first-ever girls' basketball team, was inspired by family and coaches to pursue a career in track as opposed to basketball.

The death of Bev's mother was a loss of immeasurable proportions for the high school senior. Like other family members, Bev was expected to leave home and establish independence at the age of eighteen. Without a mother, a home, the means to finance a college education, or other family members with the means of financial support, she felt lost. At this crossroads, Joan Falsone, track coach at Hillsborough Community College, offered her a much-needed athletic scholarship.

Bev's brother Derick financed his education through the use of Pell Grants and the income from his mother's social security benefits. "It was a difficult time," Kearney explains. Falsone understood their struggles and was as supportive as a coach could be under the circumstances.

Understanding Bev's deep desire for further education, Falsone assisted her in earning a track scholarship at Hillsborough Community College. When Bev entered college, Mrs. Falsone furnished the housing amenities that a mother would deem necessary for a daughter to begin school. Coach Falsone became a second mother to Bev and made certain that she understood that reduced circumstances need not undermine her success.

## DECISION TO COACH

Like other female athletes of this generation, Bev abandoned earlier career choices to join the emerging women's coaching profession. During her fifth year at Auburn, she was designated student assistant coach. In this position, Kearney came to understand why so many women athletes leave college without graduating. It was obvious to her that females and minorities are especially vulnerable to failure and are often unable to cope with student life because of lack of support in assisting them to demonstrate their academic abilities and the cultural differences in pre-college preparation. Kearney suspected that higher education administrators had never considered a system to target the specific needs of this special population of women. These realities remained foremost in Kearney's mind as she entered the coaching arena.

After graduating from Auburn University, Kearney moved to California where she became a health spa instructor and a publications coordinator. Neither position proved satisfying, so she accepted an assistantship to coach the men's and women's sprint teams and to work on her master's degree at Indiana State University. The move was wise; it planted the seed that quickly blossomed into an illustrious coaching career. However, the Kearney family was stunned at her decision to seek further education and thereby continue to struggle financially.

After a short stay at Indiana State, the University of Toledo snatched her up to be their assistant men's and women's sprint coach. Toledo's indoor facility appealed to Bev's warm-blooded nature, and before year's end she welcomed the opportunity to become Toledo's head women's track coach. Touting one of the country's best recruiting seasons at the University of Toledo, she even enticed a California state champion to join the roster of Ohio stand-outs.

Next, the University of Tennessee wooed Kearney for their top assistant track coach position. It was here that Beverly's brother Derick rejoined her to finish his education, graduating with honors from the school of business. At the University of Tennessee it became clear that Beverly Kearney had a special knack for the coaching profession. Her team maintained a top-five NCAA finish all three years as Bev coached several national champions and All Americans along the way. She was only 24 years old.

After a successful, eye-opening experience at Tennessee, the University of Florida solicited Bev for the head women's coaching position at their school. Eager to try her hand as head coach, Kearney applied and was offered the job.

By then 29 years old, Kearney became not only one of the first minority coaches at the University of Florida, but the youngest.

## MEMORABLE MOMENTS

In retrospect, Bev Kearney looks at her most memorable moment as the time she became head coach in Florida. Under Kearney's leadership, her Florida athletes garnered numerous national and conference championships, had a record number of athletes selected to the All Academic team, and during her five years there, earned six individual national titles.

In 1992—five years after Kearney had first joined the Florida staff—another outstanding institution came calling. When Beverly Kearney accepted the women's head coaching position at the University of Texas at Austin, there were few, if any, in the track community who had not heard of the dynamic young coach. Within two years Kearney had repositioned Texas at the top of the national standings. Under Kearney's guidance, track aficionados knew it was simply a matter of time before Texas claimed an NCAA title . . . or two.

Woven throughout Coach Kearney's win–loss register are the threads of stories depicting the struggles and triumphs of a person who does not believe in limitations. These stories run the gamut from the impossible to the inspirational. They tell how a young black woman rose to the top of her profession in record time by applying honest effort and hard work in a profession few minority women had dared pursue. They detail how she found a way to excel in her profession—despite the obstacles presented by those unwilling or unable to understand her motivation. They describe how, through perseverance and some tough learning experiences, she ultimately gained the respect of her peers.

The inspirational story tells how Beverly Kearney did not allow the cheap shots to deter her plans, nor did she permit the hostility that grips so many who face similar obstacles to ignite the flames of hate intended to undermine her efforts to succeed. The inspirational story also reveals the firm religious faith that has always been a part of Kearney's life and motivation. Kearney supplemented her deep-seated beliefs by drawing on the experience of role models like the Rev. Martin Luther King, Jr., Mary McLeod Bethune, Maya Angelou, and Oprah Winfrey. "I admire Oprah Winfrey because she has endured and has had to overcome so much in her life," Kearney says. Determined not to let these leaders down, she has emulated their finest qualities. Quiet and unrelenting, Kearney continues to keep their memories and good works alive.

## PHILOSOPHY OF COACHING

Realizing today's youth live in a society where choices are riddled by drugs and violence, Coach Kearney enfolds her team in reachable goals. She has also found great satisfaction in hearing from former athletes who have gone to widely varied careers including publicists, teachers, doctors, and politicians. They all have attributed Bev with making untold positive contributions to their careers and to their lives. Learning of the successes of former team members—in athletics and in their careers and personal lives—is one of, if not the most, treasured highlight of her coaching career. Bev believes athletics is a means to an end, and the end is education.

Kearney believes that each athlete must be taught to face the mental and physical challenges that are unavoidable in achieving excellence. The focus of Kearney's coaching philosophy is "to always give it your best, no matter what your best may be. Sometimes your best is first place or it could be sixth place. It's what you become because of those efforts that really counts. In the long run you will be successful." Kearney also points out that, "No one should ever desire more for you than you do for yourself. Some people may have more talent than you do, some may have more money, some may even have more opportunities than you do, but no one should have more heart than you, more drive or determination."

## ROLE MODELS/MENTORS

*Maya Angelou, Oprah Winfrey, Mary McLeod Bethune, the Rev. Martin Luther King, Jr., and Nelson Mandela*—Beverly supplements her deep-seated beliefs by drawing on the experiences of great leaders. These people were role models because each stood strong in the face of great adversity and succeeded in spite of life's circumstances; they possessed a vision of life and refused to let it go.

*Joan Falsone,* **Terry Crawford**, *Bobby Kersee, Barbara Jacket*, and most importantly *Ed Temple*, coach of the famous Tennessee State Tiger Belles—These men and women stand out among Bev's many sport-related role models.

Determined not to let these leaders down, Bev has emulated their finest qualities. Quiet and unrelenting, Bev Kearney continues to keep their memories, accomplishments, and contributions alive.

## FUTURE PLANS

What does the future hold for Beverly Kearney? "Sometimes I feel like a fish going upstream, going in the wrong direction, because I think by nature I may be too soft for the highly competitive level of this sport." However, she feels, "The Lord still has some things for me to accomplish in athletics. My goal remains the same. I want to be the best possible coach and role model for each of my student athletes." For now, Kearney is pleased with the impact she is having on the athletes she prepares for high-level competition. Who wouldn't be—with a consistently high-ranking NCAA team such as that of the University of Texas, which, during the last six seasons, has compiled four NCAA second-place finishes. In 1997 Bev was named co-national coach of the year. For the future Kearney has thoughts about entering the field of Christian psychological and academic counseling. Her close association with athletes in a minority academic setting has prepared her well for such a counseling alliance.

Beverly Kearney is a pioneer. She has carried on the fine tradition of Mary McLeod Bethune. It is her deepest desire to encourage black and female athletes to get into the coaching ranks and to help them understand that they can make a difference. Surely the example of Beverly Kearney will provide a fertile field for an upcoming generation of coaches.

## RECOGNITIONS AND ACHIEVEMENTS

### Accomplishments as a Player

- All-American NJCAA
- All-American AIAW
- Olympic Trialist, 1980
- Athlete of the Year, 1980

### Coaching Recognitions in Division I

- Three SEC Championships: 1990, Indoor 1992
- Eight SWC Conference Championships: 1993–1996, Indoor/Outdoor
- Five Big 12 Conference Championships: 1997 Indoor, 1998 and 1999 Indoor/Outdoor
- Conference Coach of the Year 15 times:
  Indoor: 1990, 1991, 1992, 1994, 1995, 1996, 1998, 1999
  Outdoor: 1989, 1990, 1992, 1993, 1997, 1998, 1999
- District VI Coach of the Year 7 times:
  Indoor: 1997, 1998, 1999
  Outdoor: 1993, 1994, 1996, 1998
- National Coach of the Year:
  Indoor: 1990, 1991, 1992, 1999
  Outdoor: 1992, 1997, 1998, 1999
- Five National Championships:
  Indoor: 1992, 1998, 1999
  Outdoor: 1998, 1999
- Twenty-four athletes earning 113 All-American Awards
- Produced 10 Olympians
- More than 25 athletes on the National Team

### National Coaching

- Olympic Festivals, 1983, 1987
- Goodwill Games

### Other Accomplishment

- President of Men and Women's Track and Field Coaches Association, 1996 (first woman to hold that position)

Photo courtesy of Harvard
University

# CAROLE KLEINFELDER
*Lacrosse—Harvard University*

## INTRODUCTION

Carole Kleinfelder's athletic start began at Archbishop Prendergast High School in Drexel Hill, Pennsylvania. Kleinfelder tried out for the high school varsity basketball team and made it. This was an accomplishment; in fact, it was an achievement for an incoming freshman to make any team with a freshman class of 1300. This accomplishment, and her participation in the Philadelphia Catholic League, started Carole's athletic dream.

Some coaches are consumed with the single passion of coaching. Carole Kleinfelder has two passions: one is for coaching and the other is for restoring old homes, which began with an interest in antiques.

## PERSONAL DATA

*Born*: September 29, 1943, Philadelphia, Pennsylvania

*Father*: Julius Kleinfelder

*Father's Occupation*: Regional sales manager for IT&T

*Mother*: Delores Bentzel

*Mother's Occupation*: Homemaker

*Siblings:* Mary Ellen and Richard

*Alma Mater:* West Chester State College—B.S., Physical Education, 1965

## FORMATIVE YEARS

Carole attended a Catholic school in a newly developed neighborhood in Springfield, Delaware County. The family moved from the inner city to an area with children—mostly boys. The children played wire ball, box ball, and kick the can, rode bicycles, sledded, and flipped baseball cards. The annual Kleinfelder family vacation was spent in Ocean City, New Jersey. Carole has continued with this family tradition.

## PLAYING CAREER

Carole started playing organized sports in the Catholic Youth Organization (CYO) basketball leagues as an elementary school student. She was encouraged by her coach and the nuns. The teachers were also very encouraging in her academic accomplishments.

Carole and her sister, Mary Ellen, joined the Recreational League at Springfield High School. In the ninth grade Carole went to Archbishop Prendergast High School and tried out for the varsity basketball team. There were 1300 students in the freshman class, and she was one of 664 students in the graduating class. It was the baby-boom era.

The Philadelphia Catholic league was the hot spot for women's basketball. Her parents were supportive of her and her sister's participation and on occasion they attended games. Carole's team won the league and, as a consequence of her visibility, a coach from Ursinus College asked her coach about the possibility of Carole going to Ursinus on a scholarship. Carole really wanted to go to Immaculata, but her father was Protestant and felt she needed a public education. He suggested West Chester State. Her sister was already enrolled at West Chester, so they attended together. After the first year, Carole began a major in physical education. She describes herself as "not the fastest or the strongest, but I could see the game." She knew she had the ability to teach and coach, and it came easily.

At West Chester Carole was exposed to new sports like field hockey and lacrosse. She tried out for lacrosse and became the JV goal keeper. The next year she made varsity. In addition, she played basketball for four years (lacrosse for three).

Carole had two great coaches at West Chester: Vonnie Gros for lacrosse and Lucy Kyvallos for basketball. Carole attended West Chester from 1961 to 1965. She advanced enough to play on the national team and also to coach the national team.

## DECISION TO COACH

Carole wanted to be an airline hostess until she realized she had a fear of flying. Her student-teaching experience lessened her desire to teach; nevertheless, she took a job at Finny High School in Detroit, Michigan, near to where her parents had recently relocated. This was the time of the Detroit riots. She describes that job as a wonderful experience. She liked the students, she felt appreciated for her contribution, and it turned into a positive experience. She coached the basketball team and led them to an undefeated season—prior to that time the team had not won a game in two years. The team had not really been coached before she took over. This first coaching experience was interesting for Carole—when halftime arrived, the team dispersed into the bleachers to visit with their friends. It was easy to see why they had not won a game; there was no focus, and they were not competitive. She learned, in this racially mixed city school, that it takes time to get results and, by lingering after school, she could teach kids to pay a price and be successful. At Finny, she also coached the field hockey team.

Carole taught at Finny for a year and a half before she got the bug to move back to Philadelphia. Philadelphia offered more competitive action, and she could also continue competing in lacrosse and AAU basketball.

In 1968 Carole taught at North Penn High School, a large rural school. She assisted with basketball, coached the field hockey team, and started a lacrosse program. She also coached gymnastics and softball. She stayed a year and a half before going to Radnor High School. This time she remained for five years (1970–1975). Radnor had four field hockey and lacrosse teams. They were a hotbed for those sports. She coached lacrosse and basketball and assisted with field hockey. Soon Radnor cut their commitment to girls' athletics; they dropped teams and stopped hiring women with strong coaching and teaching skills.

Title IX passed in 1972 and college teams began to improve the opportunities for women. While this was happening, Carole was involved in coaching the U.S. lacrosse team and had established herself as a competent coach. Brown University in Rhode Island was one of the schools intent on improving sport for women. Carole went to Brown to coach basketball and assist with field hockey. She also coached softball. After a year at Brown, Harvard recruited her to coach women's basketball and assist with field hockey and lacrosse. After two years at Harvard she was given the head coaching job for lacrosse. As women's sports grew, so did their competitive schedules; it became impossible to coach more than one sport, and Harvard asked her to step down as basketball coach.

## MEMORABLE MOMENTS

Carole claims, "I was a disaster as the national coach." In retrospect, she says she was way too young, and too immature for such a responsibility. Acknowledging that she learned from the experience, it was memorable but not a satisfying experience for her.

Carole remembers winning the first Ivy League Conference Championship as a great moment. It was extraordinary. "We had been building for that and it happened for us. We knew what we wanted to do and we did it." In her first year at Harvard she took the team on a spring-break tour to play West Chester and Ursinus; they soundly defeated Harvard. Within three years Harvard beat both of the teams, helping to soothe earlier wounds.

Harvard had a great year in 1987. The freshmen made an immediate impact. In 1989 they went all the way to the finals and were defeated by Penn State 7–6 coached by **Sue Scheetz**. The team was so upset at losing, they felt they had been denied. The team chemistry, the talent, and the leadership were outstanding. In 1990 the same group, less a goalkeeper and two mid-fielders, returned. Carole says she tried to stay away from talking about a national championship. They focused on winning the Ivy League Championship, a difficult task because it is such a competitive league. The team was driven and focused. It was a very, very competitive and intelligent team. This time the Harvard Crimson were not to be denied, they won the national title defeating the University of Maryland 8–7. (Two of the team members became doctors, one became a lawyer, and another chose a career in public service.)

Carole's teams have won 12 Ivy League Championships. Currently she has more wins than any other coach in women's lacrosse.

## ROLE MODELS/MENTORS

*Helen Frank*—Carole's first coach, Helen knew how to make everyone feel part of the team. She was highly competitive and loved the game of basketball.

*Vonnie Gros*—Vonnie Gros began coaching at West Chester State during Carole's junior year. Vonnie was an Olympic field hockey coach and an All-American lacrosse coach and field hockey player. She was well equipped to teach Carole a phenomenal amount about coaching both sports.

*Lucille Kyvallos*—It was Lucille Kyvallos who had a profound effect on Carole. Carole says she is probably the single most influential person in her development, both as a teacher and a coach. Carole admired Lucille Kyvallos' intelligence. She was balanced, and her interests went beyond basketball even though basketball was her passion. She loved history and was an avid reader. She had a very broad perspective. She was ahead of her time as a basketball coach. She had been a great player and loved the game enough to want to expose athletes to higher levels of the game. She took the girls to watch AAU games and exposed them to skills they had never seen. Athletes did not mess around with Lucille Kyvallos. She had a great personality and was a great teacher. She taught the majors class in coaching, and Carole learned from her what to look for in an athlete, how to put people on the court, and when to make adjustments.

Kyvallos came Carole's sophomore year: "When Carole arrived at West Chester, she made the varsity team as a starter. When Lucille Kyvallos came, half times had the guards in one room, the forwards in another. Boy was it different in terms of coaching. No one talked to each other. They listened to the coach. She got us equal time in the gym and there was no question she was going to get things done. She was not going to allow the women to feel like second class citizens and that came across to the team very clearly." Lucille Kyvallos taught Carole that basketball was more than a physical game. She challenged Carole and the team intellectually about the theoretical part of the game.

Carole also has great respect for John Wooden and Billie Jean King.

## PHILOSOPHY OF COACHING

At half time, Carole talks with her team in this way: "This is what I see. This is what this team is trying to do and this is what we need to do to counter. Or, this is what we need to do to fix it. Or, this is what we are doing well or what we are not doing well and this is what we must do to correct it." Carole believes in telling players to be patient. She had to yell a lot at non-competitive teams. But when the team gets competitive, the yelling diminishes. Carole deeply believes games must be won by the team and not by the mistakes of the other team. "You cannot count on the mistakes of others to be successful." She teaches teams to understand their strengths and use them. By the same token, she teaches the team to know where they are weak and learn to cover their weak spots. Trying not to play beyond oneself, supporting each other and working hard away from the ball are all key elements that combine to win. Winning usually happens based on what goes on away from the ball. Carole thinks it "a joy to work with her athletes."

## CHALLENGES

Dealing with the male structure has had its own set of challenges, especially as far as college facilities are concerned. It has been important to be courteous about practice distractions and to have a field good enough so teams will not refuse to come to one's home field to play.

Coaching the Ivy League has some special challenges—coaching females in particular. It took a while for Carole to convince women to be committed to the sport. Once they started to win, it happened. She had to teach them how to compete. Her players typically come from private preparatory schools. Eighty percent of the national championship teams had been at prep schools. Otherwise it is about 60 percent. Another obstacle is to have kids sit on the bench or to cut athletes from the team. At Harvard it is difficult because these women have been used to being the best.

It has also been difficult to teach athletes to respect themselves as athletes and to demand the same things the men receive. Getting facilities, uniforms, trainers, budgets, and office support have been all been part of Carole's uphill battle.

## CHANGES IN ATHLETES

To Carole's mind recruiting is out of hand, and the NCAA is missing the big picture as the heart of every sport is the players. Competing is not as much fun as it used to be. Carole thinks we have lost our perspective of what playing a sport is all about. Sports are meant to be fun, but parents put tremendous pressures on the kids. She believes playing should be a release, not more pressure. The academics are pressure enough.

The talent level has increased. Title IX forced the high schools and colleges to offer programs for females and to improve coaching. As a result athletes are more fit and more committed. Now it is acceptable for a woman to be an athlete and work out in the weight room.

## LIFE BEYOND ATHLETICS

Carole likes to read *The Wall Street Journal*. She dabbles in the stock market. She likes to read biographies and enjoys music and French cooking. She runs sports camps and renovates houses. She also has a penchant for antiques. Most of all she enjoys time spent with family and friends.

## RECOGNITIONS AND ACHIEVEMENTS

### Accomplishment as a Player

- U.S. National Team, 1968–1971

### Coaching Recognitions in Division I

- Twelve Conference Championships, Ivy League: 1981–1985, 1987–1993
- National Championship, 1990
- Winningest Collegiate Lacrosse Coach
- Produced 28 All Americans and 10 National Team Players
- National Coach of the Year, 1990

### Other Accomplishments

- President of United States Women's Lacrosse Association, 1992–1994
- Pennsylvania Hall of Fame as basketball player and lacrosse coach, 1996

Photo courtesy of University of
California, Los Angeles

# VALORIE KONDOS

*Gymnastics—University of California, Los Angeles*

## INTRODUCTION

By interlocking strands from the philosophical skeins of three highly respected mentors and weaving in her own common-sense values, Valorie Kondos has fashioned a unique coaching philosophy. The first strand was spun by Ingrid Carriker, a ballet teacher who greeted her students with a meticulous personal appearance in the era of the "unkept look." Students were impressed with the notion that she thought they were important enough for her to look her best. Another mentor, Nolan T'Santi, recognized that Valorie's Mediterranean dancing style, if connected to her piano background, would facilitate her understanding of the dynamics of musical phrasing. The third philosophical influence came from co-founder and director of the New York City Ballet, George Balanchine. The world-renowned dance choreographer inspired and taught that one must make dance look easy.

## PERSONAL DATA

*Born*:  August 20, 1959, Sacramento, California

*Father*:  Gregory Kondos

*Father's Occupation*:  Landscape painter

*Mother*: Rosie Thalas

*Mother's Occupation*: Homemaker

*Sibling*: Steven

*Husband*: Bobby Fields

*Alma Mater*: UCLA—B.S., History, 1987

## FORMATIVE YEARS

Valorie spent her first four years in Sacramento before the family moved to Greece where her father taught for a year at the American University. While there, Valorie visited her grandparents in their village. It was interesting for her to learn that her mother's father and her father's mother grew up in the same village and they both married people from other villages. After the year in Greece, they returned to Eldorado Hills, California—an out-of-the-way town between Sacramento and Lake Tahoe. Later the family moved to Shingle Springs, even more remote from the city.

The two Kondos siblings developed a marvelous friendship. Their different personalities blended well. Steven, left brained, analytical, scientifically inclined, "always had his nose in a book and was not at all gregarious." Valorie claims to have been "a loud-mouthed brat." She and Steven and their friends often joined together for parties and group activities.

Active and energetic, Valorie studied piano, ballet, and horseback riding. She was a Campfire Girl and describes herself as "a real tomboy" cavorting on the soccer field and the basketball floor with the neighborhood boys. A natural leader, she was also a good student who liked the process of studying, writing papers, and learning. Piano, ballet, and horseback riding lessons didn't allow much free time, but being so involved led to popularity. Her peers respected her dedicated and active life.

Because Valorie had a sway back problem, her parents enrolled her in ballet lessons hoping to correct the problem. Although she liked piano lessons and loved horseback riding, she had a dislike for ballet until she was about 12 years old and she became hooked on performing. The stage was great, but classes and rehearsals were still unappealing tasks.

In junior high school Valorie participated in basketball, track, and soccer. Going to UCLA to compete in athletics was a high school dream until her love for performing was transformed into concentrating on ballet. Instead of attending UCLA Valorie enrolled at Sacramento State College (Cal State at Sacramento). After one quarter she was dancing, so her parents advised her to concentrate on dance and to travel and return to college at a later time. So she went to New York City and took some unimpressive dance classes. However, she spent time with a friend who was a soloist in the New York City Ballet. After her dance lesson, she would go and watch the NYC ballet rehearsals. Each night she watched the performance from back stage. Here she could see the great George Balanchine standing behind the first wing. (George Balanchine was the Russian ballet master who had co-founded the company.)

To see the command he had of his dancers was phenomenal. He inspired people. He loved it when dancers would try so hard they would fall. If they jumped or turned in the air and ended up on the floor, he thought it was great because he knew they were pushing the limits of their potential. After New York, Valorie went to Washington, D.C., and danced for Capitol City Ballet Company and the Washington, D.C., Ballet Company. After four years Valorie concluded she no longer wanted such a dancing career and returned home to Sacramento. There she played the piano for a gymnastics club. One of the fourteen-year-old students, Trina Tinty, told Valorie UCLA was looking for a dance coach.

## DECISION TO COACH

That was all she needed to hear. Valorie flew to UCLA for an interview. The interview went well, but she remembers wishing it had been more thorough and intense. She got the job, but felt it was because of a strong résumé and not based on what they knew she could do. She was 22. Jerry Tomlinson needed a dance coach, but he really didn't understand what Valorie was all about. He explained "you don't really have to do much; they have had a ton of dance training so you just need to oversee them." The job included a full scholarship to attend UCLA and to be part of the athletic program. Valorie figured it was as close to the dream of coaching as she could get.

The first year posed some frustrations. One day an athlete mid-way through performing a beam routine stopped and said, "What do you do here?" This caused Valorie to question her role. Was just standing around watching enough? She didn't feel she was hired to just stand and look. When it came time to be rehired, she told Jerry Tomlinson she would stay, but she felt she had a gift to offer the program, and it went way beyond what she had been doing. She was interested in teaching movement quality, musicality, and how to feel confident in any circumstance. She wanted to coach and have the authority to coach and, if necessary, kick someone out of the gym. He responded by saying "go for it!" The next year Valorie came in a totally different person and coach. Jerry was very pleased. He thought what she was doing was great. He started to sing her praises and was thrilled to have hired her.

UCLA did not renew Tomlinson's contract in 1990, and Valorie and Scott Bull were named co-head coaches. In the five years of co-coaching, their team was nationally ranked in the top five four times. In 1995 Scott left UCLA, and Valorie became head coach. In the next four years UCLA finished fourth, second, first, and fifth. In 1996 and 1997 Valorie was voted National Coach of the Year. She has coached 26 athletes to 89 All-American honors. UCLA and Georgia are the only two teams to be advanced to the Super Six Team Finals every year since its inception in 1993. It is surprising to note Valorie has never competed in gymnastics. Her background was dance. She credits Jim

Stephenson, current co-head coach at the University of Minnesota, for teaching her gymnastic fundamentals.

## MEMORABLE MOMENTS

In the late 1980s (1987–1990), Kim Hamilton won three consecutive NCAA floor exercise titles. This makes her the only NCAA gymnast to have ever won three consecutive event titles. To Valorie this was exciting, but even more exciting was watching this gorgeous 5'6" African American perform. Valorie says she has never seen another gymnast move as well and with such an understanding of the music as Kim—"she truly brought out the artistic quality of the sport."

The year before UCLA won (1997) the National Title, nationals were held in Alabama. Fourteen thousand screaming fans were in the audience. UCLA was seeded ninth and they were doing what they always try to do—be the best they can be. While the Alabama and Georgia fans were fighting it out, the Bruins (UCLA) were focusing on good gymnastics and having a good time, and they ended up placing second. Valorie remembers feeling, for the first time in her fourteen years of coaching at UCLA, how great it felt to leave the arena without any "if only" thoughts. For the first time in her coaching career, they had accomplished their goal without regrets and in so doing felt as though they had won the NCAA title. To top it off, "it seemed like every single person in the arena congratulated us for doing a great job with a lot of class." They had performed the most impressive beam set in the history of NCAA gymnastics. "Imagine 6 of the best balance beam performers in the country, all hitting the best routine they are capable of. One impressive routine after another." After the meet the head beam judge told her that judging the UCLA beam team was the highlight of her 25–year career of judging.

In 1997 it was UCLA's turn to take home the trophy. There was a new kid on the block. Georgia, Alabama, and Utah had another contender: Valorie Kondos. For the first time since 1982, a team other than the big three had won the championship trophy.

## ROLE MODELS/MENTORS

*Gregory and Rosie Kondos*—Valorie applauds her parents for giving her the opportunity to be trained in music and ballet.

*Nolan T'Santi*—Although Valorie did not have the natural ability to be a great ballet dancer, Nolan T'Santi acknowledged she could dance and pull off amazing feats on stage. He detected her fluid Mediterranean dance style, and he helped her to understand music, phrasing, and the dynamics of bonding these components.

*George Balanchine*—Valorie met this world-renowned artist at the New York Ballet. He took classical lines and added sensibility to modern movements to assemble what is called the Balanchine look. He was a craftsman of the highest order. He said, "God creates, Woman inspires, and Man assembles." Valorie's philosophy is based on this statement.

Each of these teachers weaves a strong thread into Valorie's philosophical tapestry, which is bound with her mother's compassion and tough-love ethics.

## PHILOSOPHY OF COACHING

Valorie says that everybody appreciates discipline. Athletes also want to be pushed and disciplined. They want to know the rules and consequences for violating rules. Athletes also push to the limit. They also want a leader. Valorie is a proponent of leaders leading, and realizing they will be tested so one cannot just sit back and see how things will work out. Valorie expects each athlete to continue to learn and grow every day of their lives. As long as they can say that they have given their best efforts at the end of every day, she feels they have been successful. She also acknowledges that the road to success is often bumpy. She believes many times there is nothing better for athletes than honesty and tough love. She works to have them see the "big picture" of their lives.

Valorie teaches that life is about making right choices and that making right choices takes strength and helps to develop integrity. It is important to learn from a poor choice and not let it destroy the individual. Valorie believes honesty with others is important and honesty with oneself is paramount, as there is no way one can be honest with someone else unless one is honest with oneself first. She believes if athletes develop this honesty they will progress more smoothly in their college careers, their studying, their classes, their gymnastics, and in their interpersonal relationships. All these things can create stress in a young college student. If they are late for practice, the best explanation for being late is to give an honest reason.

Another major focus for Valorie is to do one's best in all areas of life. This refers to life in the gym, in competition, in the training room, and it refers to the athlete and the coach. Competitors perform in competition as they do in practice. If an enjoyable time occurs in practice "because they are experiencing greatness, it carries into competition." Finally, Valorie feels that one must compete because one loves it.

## CHALLENGES

In her first year as head coach, Valorie tried to become someone she wasn't. She tried to emulate other successful coaches. After her second season as head coach, she knew the majority of her stress was coming from second guessing herself, instead of just following her heart. This realization became a significant turning point.

Even though everyone knew Valorie had not been a competitive gymnast, they knew she was very talented and that in time she would learn the technical aspects of the sport. Judy Holland explained that Valorie was hired because she knew how to handle athletes, and she liked it that, when the team didn't do well, Valorie didn't merely say, "it's ok." Holland also admired Valorie's ability to communicate with her, the doctors, the trainers, and with the team. Indeed, she liked Valorie's attitude of "let's be the best we can be, and let's find a way to get there." The team needed her energy and her attitude. Judy made certain to support her by seeing that she received the needed technical help.

The most frustrating setbacks for Valorie have been injuries to team members. Every year for eleven seasons UCLA has had a season-ending injury; it has usually involved knee reconstructions. Her number one-priority has been to reduce injuries. For the last four years they have ended the season without one injury. Another big challenge has been to find the time to obtain new floor exercise music and choreograph new routines.

## CHANGES IN ATHLETES

UCLA now recruits some of the best athletes in the world. According to Valorie, "This usually means they don't have much tolerance and patience when gymnastics is not going as well they would like it to go." Valorie often thinks, "Part of the problem is that you are too darn talented. If you had to work harder to achieve your goals, you would not get frustrated so easily." Obviously this attitude also brushes off onto their academic performance. These talented athletes are accustomed to immediate results, and they often miss out on the satisfaction that comes from a job well done, regardless of how quickly the results occur. To her, one of life's important lessons is to "enjoy the process."

## LIFE BEYOND ATHLETICS

Valorie is a freelance choreographer with extensive experience in entertainment and gymnastics. Her client list includes Disneyland and a summer figure skating and gymnastics show for Sea World in the summer of 1991. She has also choreographed a summer acrobatic festival held in Lennestadt, Germany.

Valorie was married in the summer of 1998 to Bobby Field, the assistant head football coach. She had known Bobby since arriving at UCLA: "He is the antithesis of what you think a football coach is. He is the ultimate in patience, kindness, and humility. He is a true gentleman."

Valorie likes to read biographies of people like George Balanchine and Johnny Wooden. She likes reading motivational books and stories. She also loves movies and the theater.

## RECOGNITIONS AND ACHIEVEMENTS

### Coaching Recognitions in Division I

- Five PAC Conference Championships: 1993, 1995, 1997, 1998, 1999
- Conference Coach of the Year, 1995
- Regional Coach of the Year: 1993, 1994, 1995, 1996, 1997

- Regional Champions: 1993, 1994, 1995, 1996, 1997, 1999
- National Coach of the Year, 1996, 1997
- National Champions, 1997, 2000
- Twenty-nine Gymnastic Athletes, 46 All-American Honors

Photo courtesy of Florida State
University

# MARYNELL MEADORS
## *Basketball—Charlotte Sting, WNBA*

### INTRODUCTION

Three cousins and an older brother were Marynell's childhood playmates. Little did the foursome know, the lone female was a WNBA coach in the making. Meadors' backyard and its weeping willow tree would provide a training ground for their playmate to achieve coaching eminence. She became a college coach and a premier coach for the Charlotte Sting of the Women's National Basketball Association. And the dream continues.

### PERSONAL DATA

> *Born*: August 27, 1943, Nashville, Tennessee
> *Father*: Herbert L. Meadors
> *Father's Occupation*: Automotive Sales
> *Mother*: Dorothy Dews
> *Mother's Occupation*: Bookkeeper/stenographer
> *Sibling*: Herbert

*Alma Mater*: Middle Tennessee State University—B.S., Physical Education, Health & Recreation, 1965; M.S., Physiology of Exercise, 1966

## FORMATIVE YEARS

The tree-lined streets in picturesque Nashville provided a beautiful childhood environment for Marynell. On the backyard weeping willow tree was mounted a basketball backboard and hoop. In this arena her older brother and his friends gave her an early start with the game. When bored with basketball, they shifted from the willow tree to backyard softball, trampling flower beds in the process. Her mother's flowers had to go; after all, this yard was the neighborhood playground.

Before high school the only sports Marynell participated in were in school physical education classes. It was difficult for this active female to understand why girls didn't have the same opportunities as boys. During her seventh-grade year, she decided coaching would be her profession.

## SPORTS HISTORY

In the tenth grade at Hillsboro High School, Marynell got the opportunity to compete. She played basketball, softball, and tennis. Taking advantage of Nashville's Parks and Recreation League, she became a fine softball player. Thereafter she moved to other sports and changed shoes with the seasons.

By high school graduation she understood the necessity of a college degree prior to a coaching career, so she enrolled at Middle Tennessee State University (MTSU). The school was 30 miles south of Nashville, a nice closeness for a "homebody" like Marynell. At Middle Tennessee, women's teams just being organized needed players. She competed in basketball, softball, volleyball, and even tennis. She described herself as "a tennis home run hitter. "

## DECISION TO COACH

The decision to coach came in the seventh grade; Marynell wanted young girls to have the competitive opportunities she had been denied: "I guess I was on a mission, and I decided we needed to do some competitive things for girls." Her decision to go to college was based on the reality that a college degree was the only road to coaching.

Fortified with her college degree, Marynell was helped by Fran Reil—director of health, physical education, and recreation at MTSU—to land a job at Tennessee Tech as an instructor. During the job interview Marynell asked the department chairman, Dr. Flavious Smith, if she could start some women's sports, he enthusiastically replied "yes." She began with volleyball, two years later she started basketball, and within five years she had begun the tennis program. In each case she was the coach in addition teaching nine classes. Her summer was spent competing on a softball team. In 1972 Title IX passed. Before Title IX, she did not have a budget; after its passage, she was allotted a $100 budget. Comparatively speaking, it was a fair amount of money. When necessary, they supplemented the budget with money earned by clearing rocks from a golf course or by having bake sales. In 1970 basketball was recognized as a varsity sport. The team was nicknamed the "Terrors of Tennessee." They specialized in the fast break and a specialized defense. In sixteen seasons at Tennessee Tech she accrued a 363–138 (.724) basketball record.

After sixteen years at Tennessee Tech, Marynell felt she had accomplished all she could at the small school. An attractive opportunity at Florida State University became available, and she took on the challenge knowing that winning a national tournament would be more likely there. Larger schools were building their programs, whereas smaller schools were not expanding. In rebuilding the Florida basketball program, her team won the Metro Conference. In 1992 Florida State joined the Atlantic Coast Conference, and for three seasons she struggled against such powers as North Carolina, North Carolina State, Duke, Clemson, Virginia, and Maryland. It was an uphill battle all the way. Feeling the futility of the situation, she left after the 1995–1996 season.

Marynell dabbled in broadcasting until the WNBA began to organize and the search was on for head coach positions. The Charlotte Sting management had three criteria for hiring a coach: (1) the coach must build a program from scratch; (2) the coach must have had Division I success; and (3) the coach must have leadership ability. Marynell's credentials placed her at the head of the candidate list, and on March 26, 1997, she was hired as the first head coach and general manager of the Charlotte Sting. The first year with the Sting, she went 15–13. The Comets, the Liberty, and the Mercury were also top contenders. In the second year, Marynell navigated the Sting to another play-off berth, finally losing to the championship team, the Houston Comets. Her regular season record was 18–12. Based on these first two years, she has clearly established herself as a WNBA force.

## MEMORABLE MOMENTS

Winning back-to-back championships in the Ohio Valley Conference at Tennessee Tech in 1982 and 1983 is one of Meadors' favorite recollections. Records attest that her team was a powerhouse—nine out of ten years her teams won 23 games or more.

Her second favorite memory centers on the building process. Taking over the reins at Florida State from a 9–19 team and turning them into a 25–7 team was a success story. Rebuilding and building teams is challenging and one of Marynell's many strengths. Winning the Metro Championship was the capstone experience of a five-year effort. This championship infused her with the texture of success.

Another memorable moment for Meadors was making the WNBA playoffs her first year coaching at a truly elite level. Now her goal is to win a WNBA championship, not just make the playoff. In two years she coached the Sting to a second WNBA playoff and posted an 18–12 win–loss account for a regular season.

## ROLE MODELS/MENTORS

*Bill Smith*—Bill left an impressive mark on Marynell. He coached boys at Waverly Belmont Junior High, and he knew how to develop rapport; consequently, the athletes accomplished amazing things under his leadership.

*Ed Hessey*—Ed was a multi-sport coach back in the sixties. Marynell was impressed with his methods of developing rapport and working with young men. Everyone loved Ed, and Marynell tries to emulate his qualities in her own coaching.

*Emmit Strickland*—Although Emmit was the Waverly Belmont Junior High School principal and not the coach, he was an exemplary leader for young people. He smiled, he was strict, and yet he was able to be a good friend.

These three men took an interest in Marynell and followed her throughout her high school and college careers.

*Jackie Turner*—Jackie was Marynell's tennis and basketball coach and the person who was a powerful influence in her sideline mannerisms. She never showed any kind of emotion, nor does Marynell in coaching situations. Jackie had played basketball and knew the game well. She taught high school chemistry. This intelligent woman had such a talented team she had to be innovative to find playing time for everyone. Marynell admires this patient woman for making a huge contribution to women's sports.

*Eddie Greer, Bill Ingram, and Hale Harris*—Marynell attributes each of these men with being "instrumental in trying to get me as good as I ended up being. "

*Dorothy and Herbert Meadors*—Marynell applauds her parents for providing quality leadership and guidance throughout her lifetime. She is deeply appreciative to them for supporting her in all of her choices.

## PHILOSOPHY OF COACHING

At both the collegiate and professional levels of coaching, Marynell maintains the same philosophical undergirding. Under her system athletes must understand goal setting. In her first team meeting, athletes write what they want to do as a team and then what they want to do as individuals to reach those goals. They do set goals, and she talks to them about the thing she likes from team members, such as hustle, enthusiasm, and wanting to be there. Then she tells athletes she doesn't like tardiness or not giving 100 percent. She expects 100 percent from athletes each time they step on the playing court. She reminds them of their goals and asks them what they want to accomplish each day. She also refuses to allow negativism. Staying positive is a constant reminder, especially when negativism begins to creep into their midst.

According to Marynell, coaches must change with the times. Playing in today's environment is "about achieving goals. You cannot take your eyes off your goals."

## CHALLENGES

The number-one challenge during her early years of coaching was focused on the lack of money. "We spent so much of our own money, but we didn't care because we played for the love of the game." As women's programs have progressed, the new challenge has been recruiting. She believes recruiting will continue to pose a problem because it is a very arduous process.

## CHANGES IN ATHLETES

According to Marynell, athletes are bigger, stronger, and faster. Their dedication is very different than it was in the seventies and early eighties. She feels athletes no longer play for the love of the game as they did in the seventies. In the seventies scholarships were few, but many athletes did not care about a scholarship; they just wanted to play the game. Certainly times have changed, and the woman athlete expects something in return for playing.

In Meador's view, it is presently "cool to be an athlete," whereas earlier it was not so acceptable and athletic females were labeled "tomboys." Now it is prestigious to be a professional player and a collegiate competitor; these athletes are respected.

Overall student athletes have improved every year in Meadors' opinion. She feels that Title IX has helped to initiate school programs, AAU programs, and YWCA programs where the doors are open to all young girls. Camps and clinics have also been created for females to develop budding talents: "Now young women, especially in Tennessee, have a basketball in their hand as soon as they are born."

## COACHING

Currently, Marynell is the only one in this collection coaching a professional team. She explains the difference between professional and college coaching: "The difference between the collegiate level and the professional level is you don't have the personal closeness with the players. You don't have them for five years. You don't have the opportunity to mold them into their lives, and I do miss that about this experience."

Another question posed to Marynell was, "Do professional women relate to teammates in a way different than college women relate to each other?" She responded, "I think the difference is these players may hang out a little bit together, but they are all kind of on their own agendas, but when they walk on the court that agenda has to be team oriented. This is a contrast to college where everybody kind of hangs out together, and they all live together, and they are all right there together most of the time. But in professional sport they pretty much have their own things, like shoe contracts, and their own clinics and things they have to do and appearances they would have to make for their sponsoring companies. "

Marynell sees the enjoyable part of the professional experience as "working with professional athletes who want to win. Their job is to win. They come in, and they work hard. It's the highest level you can coach at, and I have been very fortunate to have started from absolutely nothing and worked into something. I have coached at all the levels and have had tremendous experiences, but the WNBA is really something to see. To go to arenas and see anywhere from 10 to 20 thousand fans is something. It is special because when women first started you had parents in the stands and about forty others and to see something come from that to where we are now has been fantastic!"

In 1997 when the Sting were playing in Houston, one of the reporters saw Marynell laughing and smiling in a very intense game in which the Sting were leading. After the game the reporter asked her, "Why were you smiling?" She replied, "Well, to know where women's sports have come from and where they are right now is just a fantastic feeling." Even so, she still claims to have uneasy feelings going into the season. She wonders if she has the right players and is she using the right system for player success. It has taken a good deal of people to move women's sports to this stage, and Marynell Meadors has contributed to the successful transition.

## FUTURE PLANS

Presently, Marynell is one of the four original coaches in the eight WNBA franchises. She has one more year left on a three-year contract. The fact that four franchises have made changes is of concern for most coaches, including Marynell. She would like to see her contract renewed at least one more time for three or four years. After that she would like to play golf. She says she has been pleased and very happy with what she has accomplished and some of the lives she has touched.

## LIFE BEYOND ATHLETICS

Marynell loves to golf. She would like to retire to a beach-front house with a golf course at the back. She wants to play golf year round and just enjoy the game and people. She describes herself as a "people person." She has traveled to Brazil and Europe, but the trips were mostly work related. When she retires she would like to travel and tour.

Marynell attends the theater when possible. She finds little time for reading, but when she does read, she likes to read and learn. She enjoys Danielle Steele mystery novels. Winning is also another of her hobbies. As a collegiate coach she compiled a 495–game winning record.

Marynell was the first women's coach at a major college to win more than 300 games at one institution. This happened during sixteen years at Tennessee

Tech. She ranks third in most games coached (786), fifth in most seasons coached (26), and seventh in victories (495).

## RECOGNITIONS AND ACHIEVEMENTS

### Coaching Recognitions in Division I

- Two Conference Championships: Metro, 1990, 1991
- Four Conference Championships: Ohio Valley, 1978, 1979, 1981, 1983
- Conference Coach of the Year: Ohio Valley, 1978, 1983
- Conference Coach of the Year: Metro, 1990, 1991
- National Kellogg Coach of the Year, 1977
- Converse Coach of the Year, 1977–1978
- Ranks sixth in most winningest coaches (495)
- First coach to win more than 300 games at one institution
- AIAW Playoffs, 1971–1982
- Coach of the WNBA Charlotte Sting Semifinals, 1997–1998
- Eighteen 20–plus winning seasons

### National Coaching Assignments

- Olympic Festivals 1989 North Team Gold Medal
- Member of Olympics Selection Committee
- Head Coach Jones Cup, 1991
- Assistant Coach Jones Cup, 1992
- Kodak All American Selection Committee
- Member Olympic Festivals Selection Committee

### Other Accomplishments

- Ohio Valley Conference Hall of Fame, 1992
- Tennessee Tech Hall of Fame, 1992
- Ranks third in most games coached in college (786)
- Ranks fifth in most seasons coached (25)

Photo courtesy of Brigham
Young University

# ELAINE MICHAELIS

*Volleyball and Athletic Director—Brigham
Young University*

## INTRODUCTION

Brigham Young Univeristy did not begin keeping records for women's volley-ball until 1969; since that time Elaine Michaelis has coached just over 1,000 matches and has registered 813 victories—the second most in NCAA Division I history. In 38 years of coaching, she has not had a losing season. She has ne-gotiated the long, uphill struggle to provide high-level competitive experi-ences for women athletes in the shadow of tradition and the turmoil of legislation. Her transformation from a child scoring baskets at the hoop in the family feed store to the woman coaching wins on the volleyball court of a ma-jor university was not within a dream's reach for this child of the thirties, born and reared in rural Utah.

## PERSONAL DATA

*Birth*: April 18, 1938, Garland, Utah

*Father*: Arthur Ralph Michaelis

*Father's Occupation*: Feed store owner

*Mother*: Leatha Corbett Michaelis

*Mother's Occupation*: Bookkeeper for feed store

*Siblings*: Max and Lynn

*Alma Mater*: Brigham Young University—B.S., Physical Education, 1960; M.S., Physical Education, 1962

## FORMATIVE YEARS

Elaine, the only daughter of Leatha and Arthur Michaelis, was born in
Tremonton, Utah. Leatha was thrilled to have a daughter. Equally thrilled to
have a girl, Arthur thenceforth referred to her as "ma darlin' daughter." The
Michaelis raised their family in Garland, a beautiful, rural farm community,
nestled in a northern Utah valley. This proved to be a perfect family community. With two brothers and a neighborhood of boys, Elaine was exposed to the
world of sports at an early age. The Michaelis' home, snuggled among cotton-
wood trees, was located adjacent to her grandfather's old flour mill and in
front of the railroad tracks. Leisure hours, aside from those spent at her father's
feed store, were consumed exploring under the stilted mill warehouse and
walking on the railroad tracks; both offered intrigue and challenge.

Wintertime brought the added pleasure of running over banks of drifted
snow in the jaunt to and from school. Her brother, Lynn, was her constant
companion. Together they rode bikes and played the traditional games of
youth. Her mother made certain that her leisure activity was enriched with tap
dance and piano instruction. Elaine, the grade schooler, was especially fond of
music, sports, arithmetic, and the sixth grade teacher.

Daily during these years, she and her buddy, Ralph Cullimore, left school
and headed straight to the family feed store to see her dad. "Dad" Michaelis
supplied them with candy before they busied themselves shooting basketballs
at the store's indoor hoop. Their play was enlivened by the men who came to
purchase cattle feed. It was within the walls of their store young Elaine refined
basketball skills and cultivated a love for sport. Although Leatha Michaelis
longed for Elaine to share interests similar to her own, she understood and
supported her daughter's love for sport and outside activities.

Although Elaine enjoyed house and yard work, she favored cleaning the
store in order to be with her father and the guys who worked there. She loved
listening to the employees and the customers as they bantered about rival
teams and players. In this environment she began to follow major league baseball. From the feed store, her interests were carried to the vacant lots of the
neighborhood. She and her friends formed their own summer leagues in baseball, football, and tennis.

By the time Elaine turned eleven, her father was bishop of a Mormon congregation. Both Elaine's maternal and paternal grandparents were converts to
The Church of Jesus Christ of Latter-day Saints (Mormons). The families' religious fervor seeped into Elaine's soul and shaped the values on which she came
to base all of her decisions. Arthur Michaelis took the matter of being bishop

seriously and centered a good deal of attention upon the youth in his flock. He took the church's girls' softball team under his wing and coached them. No one was more enthusiastic about this than Elaine. She was at his side at practices and games and waited for the day she would be old enough to compete.

The exemplary lives and religious exuberance of Elaine's parents had a profound effect on her. Her father nurtured her love of sport, but it was the way he fulfilled the lofty church responsibilities that inspired her to become a good example for his cause.

Elaine's parents valued and trusted her mature views and opinions. They trusted her ability to make right decisions. This parental respect for her ability to think and act independently at a young age served as a model for her unique leadership style with teams and assistant coaches.

## PLAYING CAREER

Participating in neighborhood sports and on church-organized teams, along with attending college and high school basketball games with her father and brother, provided a sports tradition for young Elaine. High school offered few competitive opportunities for a sports-minded female. She settled for meager opportunities, such as an occasional "Sports Day" at Utah State University and the Bear River High School swim team. A good student, Elaine also joined the school newspaper staff, a capella choir, debate team, bookkeeper team, and the marching team. Church-allied programs consumed Elaine's remaining time. When her circle of friends expanded, she held tenaciously to the commitment to be a good example for her "bishop" father. At church she maintained a perfect attendance record and received all of the awards offered youth. These church-associated activities helped to form many defining values that characterize Michaelis as a coach.

Elaine entered Brigham Young University in the fall of 1956. Although she began with a major in elementary education, she soon switched to a physical education major. Her mother did not share her enthusiasm for the newly acquired major. She worried that teaching physical education might be a career without later life security. Elaine contended otherwise, convincing her that this aspect of teaching would provide a great opportunity to positively influence young people, a concern she felt compelled to pursue.

Intramural sports introduced the joys of competing, and extramural participation provided a heightened competitive experience. Readily earning a place on the extramural rosters of the basketball, softball, and volleyball teams, Michaelis represented BYU at competitions in Colorado, Wyoming, New Mexico, and Idaho. In 1959, at the regional softball tournament in Colorado, Elaine pitched three games in one day—throwing a no hitter and two one hitters.

In her final year, Elaine was named the outstanding senior student. Just before graduation, the Dean of the College offered her a faculty position. She was shocked, honored, and most happy to accept the offer and complete her master's degree along with teaching. Firmly entrenched in a coaching and teaching career, Michaelis moved forward with energy and enthusiasm and geared her future training and study toward improving her expertise as a coach. Aside from the university, her life is consumed by family and church responsibilities.

## COACHING

Elaine's volleyball coaching career at Brigham Young University began in 1962. During her tenure she has established an aggressive volleyball schedule and a remarkable win–loss record. Her early professional years required her to coach several sports, a challenging assignment, but in the process she learned a true love for the life of a coach.

Michaelis' four decades of coaching have reaped countless honors and awards. She was on the board of directors and the executive committee of the original Association of Intercollegiate Athletics for Women. Her unique brand of excellence has touched every sphere of volleyball from playing court to committee room. In so doing, she has carved a unique niche among her peers with her devotion to fair play. Her unfettered nudge for fair play prompted former BYU Women's Athletic Administrator Phyllis C. Jacobson to declare, "Elaine has implemented an ethical and moral standard that does not vary, a nonjudgmental attitude and way of being with athletes. She exhibits good faith and continual belief in athletes. Even when they disappoint her, her faith and belief continues unshaken." On another occasion Jacobson quipped, "I have always said if anyone were to judge me, I would want it to be Elaine Michaelis, as she is the most fair person I know." Throughout her career, Michaelis' athletes have been noted for making "Honor Calls," an action not required by rules or officials.

Since records first began to be maintained in 1969, Elaine has amassed an incredible 813–204–5 record. Proving she remains at the top of her profession, Elaine's BYU team reached the NCAA Regional finals for the third straight year while posting a 31–4 record in 1998. Her team has reached the NCAA Elite Eight five times in the last seven years, including a trip to the Final Four in 1993.

## PHILOSOPHY OF COACHING

According to the Michaelis philosophy of coaching, motivation is overplayed. She feels that self-motivation is the best motivation and further feels if a player plays for excellence, then the player will be motivated while playing. Nonmotivated players usually do not feel challenged, so the solution must be found in goal setting and providing tough competition. Furthermore, Michaelis feels some athletes need to be calmed down, others need to be encouraged to have fun, and others keep motivated by themselves. While this is true of athletes, Coach Michaelis is motivated by the challenge, the focus, and the strategy of the game. She is fascinated by strategic plays and figuring out opponents' offensive patterns.

Mingled in with Elaine's philosophy of coaching is a different belief about losing. Contrary to the belief subscribed to by most coaches, namely, that values gained by losing can be learned by winning, Michaelis believes just the opposite. She concludes that often times a loss will teach more than a victory because players are more attuned to learning and will work harder to improve. Coaches, too, are energized in the process and find better ways to achieve success. Contrary to these views, she knows too many losses can be demoralizing, and, although she has never had a losing season, she claims to have experienced enough losses to keep humble.

## CHANGES IN ATHLETES

Elaine notes that athletes have changed somewhat over the years. Before scholarships were granted to women to participate in sports at the collegiate level, athletes played because of a pure love of the sport. Today, with the rewards of participating including scholarships, not every athlete competes solely for the love of the sport. However, she also notes that today's athletes start playing at a much younger age and are more committed to conditioning and preparing to compete at a Division I collegiate level.

## MEMORABLE MOMENTS

Elaine recalls that one of the greatest thrills was to accomplish the goal of winning the title in the toughest region, the West, and earning a berth on the NCAA Final Four roster. This happened in 1993. In conjunction with this goal, she has always delighted in following the family lives and accomplishments of former team members.

## ROLE MODELS

*John Wooden*—John Wooden, the well-known UCLA coach, impacted Elaine's philosophy because he was more than a coach; he was an educator. He saw athletics as an integral part of the total university. His formula for success was geared toward helping young people to achieve in any life venture.

*Leona Holbrook*—Leona Holbrook was a distinguished professor of physical education at Brigham Young University. Well known as an international leader in physical education, Holbrook inspired Elaine to understand the profession of physical education. Michaelis learned about university life, how to be a professional, and what it means to have excellence as a standard while observing this great leader.

## LIFE BEYOND ATHLETICS

Elaine enjoys reading, playing the piano, listening to music, and gardening.

## FAVORITE BOOKS

Elaine's favorite subjects for reading include philosophy, biographies, self-help, and church.

## FAVORITE MOVIES

Elaine enjoys film biographies.

## FUTURE PLANS

During Elaine's career, she has gone from coaching four different women's sports, to specializing in volleyball, to overseeing one of the top women's athletic programs in the country.

Presently, Elaine claims she is too involved to think about much more than making life better for the athletes she serves as Brigham Young University Women's Athletic Director and Volleyball Coach.

Elaine has been a steady force of inspiration and example to those with whom she has associated. Never without her critics, she has emblazoned a style and a consistency that make her predictable and productive in fulfilling her own deep-seated sense of "mission" for Brigham Young University and the Mormon church.

## RECOGNITIONS AND ACHIEVEMENTS

### Accomplishments as a Player

- Player awards were not given when Elaine was a player.

### Coaching Recognitions in Division I

- Thirty-seven years of coaching
- Regional Championships, 6 AIAW titles: 1969, 1970, 1972, 1974, 1975, 1976
- Conference Championships (22 in 30 years):
    Six ICCWPE: 1969, 1970, 1971, 1972, 1973, 1974
    Five Intermountain Athletic Conference: 1975, 1976, 1977, 1978, 1981
    Five High Country Athletic Conference: 1982, 1983, 1986, 1987, 1990
    Six Western Athletic Conference: 1992, 1993, 1994, 1996, 1997, 1998
- National Finishes Ranking
    AIAW 2, 4, 5, (2 times), 6, 7 (2 times), 8, 9, 13
    NCAA 3, 5 (7 times), 9 (4 times), 17 (5 times)
- Conference Coach of the Year
    IAC, 1981
    HCAC, 1982, 1983, 1986
    WAC, 1993, 1994, 1996, 1997

- Regional Coach of the Year
    District VII, 1996
    AVCA Tachikara Region I, 1987
- Finalist National Tachikara Coach of the Year Award, 1987
- Sixteen All Americans, 43 honors, and 5 Academic All Americans
- Second all-time winningest coach
- Nine international tours: 1978, 1979, 1983, 1987, 1988, 1989, 1991, 1995, 1999
- Tachikara Victory Club: 500 wins 1987, 600 wins 1991, 700 wins 1994, 800 wins 1998
- AVCA 700 Career Wins Award, 1995
- AVCA 800 Career Wins Award, 1998

## National Coaching Assignments

- Board of Directors and Executive Committee for AIAW
- Selection Committee, 1986–1987

## Other Recognitions

- Utah Summer Games Hall of Fame, 1987
- Hall of Fame of the Utah Network for Girls and Women in Sports, 1990
- Volleyball Festival Distinguished Service Award to USA Volleyball, 1993
- Honoree of Salt Lake City Old Time Coaches Association, 1993
- BYU Cougar Club Dale Rex Memorial Award, 1994
- AVCA Founders Award, 1996
- Twenty-five offices and positions in athletic and volleyball organizations

Photo courtesy of University
of Virginia

# JANE MILLER

*Lacrosse—University of Virginia*

## INTRODUCTION

Jane Miller's neighborhood game-playing pals set the stage for her to acquire athletic skills and nurture an interest in sport. Basketball dominated the hoop-filled community and pulsated with children at play. This early exposure to sports channeled Jane toward a career in athletics.

## PERSONAL DATA

*Born*:  October 21, 1950, Brockton, Massachusetts

*Father*:  John Miller

*Father's Occupation*:  Accountant

*Mother*:  Phyllis Seaver

*Mother's Occupation*:  Secretary

*Siblings*:  Pamela, John, and Gail

*Alma Maters:*  Northeastern University—B.S., Education, 1973; University of North Carolina, Greensboro—M.S., 1979

## FORMATIVE YEARS

A few years after Jane's birth her parents moved to a family-oriented place in Easton, Massachusetts. This neighborhood was a wonderful place for children. Youngsters of all ages could be found playing basketball, softball, and football. Several of the neighborhood boys played on the boys' high school basketball team while Jane played on the girls' basketball team. John, her brother, was her constant companion and their time together helped advance her athleticism.

## SPORTS HISTORY

The transition to high school sports was easy for Jane. She started with field hockey, basketball, and softball and played all three sports over the next four years. Her excellent coaches, Sue Rivard and Gloria Ferrandino, guided her teams in the Hockomock League to a championship or a second place in each sport every year.

While in the eleventh grade Jane knew she would probably spend the rest of her life involved in sport. With the help of her high school counselor, Ms. Sylvia, Jane was admitted to Northeastern University in Boston. Northeastern did not have a softball program, so Jane played field hockey, basketball, and lacrosse. She had learned lacrosse in a high school physical education class.

At Northeastern she majored in physical education, which was a five-year program. The program provided ample experiences in teaching elementary school, junior high, and high school physical education. After graduation she was offered two different teaching opportunities. One was at a public school and the other was at Milton Academy, a private prep school. She chose Milton Academy because of the opportunity to pursue lacrosse. She taught there for four years before leaving to pursue a master's degree at the University of North Carolina at Greensboro. After completing a master's degree Jane took a job at Longwood College. The school, in Farmville, Virginia, enrolls 2,500 students—small enough to allow a healthy interchange between students and faculty. She taught classes for physical education majors and was the assistant basketball coach and the head lacrosse coach. Here athletes were focused and goal-oriented and the small student body accorded the faculty opportunities to guide major students in career choices. Jane coached at Longwood College until 1983, when Linda Southworth, lacrosse and field hockey coach at the University of Virginia, endorsed her nomination to replace her as coach.

The move from a small college to a large university was a challenge. Virginia's Linda Southworth had developed an enviable program and expectations were high for the new coach. Jane knew it would be demanding just to maintain the program level. She also knew it would be an arduous task to move to another level of excellence. Reflecting on the move, Jane said it was "scary" but "the best move I ever made." A limited teaching schedule made it possible to focus on coaching two sports. At Longwood she had learned that she was better as an assistant than as a head basketball coach, but she also learned that she was a very good lacrosse coach.

For ten years Miller was a two-sport coach. In the early years over 50 percent of the athletes crossed over from field hockey to lacrosse. In time the number of dual-sport athletes declined. Today Virginia has just five athletes who play both sports. Although coaching the same players in both sports made coaching easier, it helped to have Julie Dayton for an assistant as well as an efficient support staff. Without both, Miller felt coaching two sports would have been impossible. Julie Dayton assisted during eight seasons making significant contributions. By 1990 Miller and Dayton had spearheaded a very successful program.

Miller's 1991 team practiced harder than they played. They had a tremendous work ethic, and team members bonded to each other. Certain individuals reaped the fruits of their aspirations—currently Julie Meyers is the head coach at the University of Virginia, Bonnie Rosen is the head coach at the University of Connecticut, and Jenny Slingluff is the head coach at North Carolina.

Jane Miller was an assistant coach of the World Cup Lacrosse team in 1986 with Josie Harper, head coach, and **Sue Delaney Scheetz**, assistant coach.

## ROLE MODELS/MENTORS

*John and Phyllis Miller*—Jane's parents have been exemplary in loving, encouraging and supporting their children.

*Sue Rivard*—Jane's physical education teacher was an excellent teacher who supported students and the community.

*Gloria Ferrandino*—Jane's physical education teacher, Ms. Ferrandino, took the time to take Jane to her Lacrosse Club Association on two occasions, introducing Jane to the game of lacrosse.

*Jeanne Rowlands*—College basketball coach Rowlands was the kind of person people respond to in a positive way. Athletes gave all they had in trying to achieve her expectations. She was a role model, she stood for all the right things, she supported and encouraged, and was very good at what she did. Rowlands was one of the first women coaches to read men's basketball books and utilize their offensive and defensive schemes, a cutting-edge leader in her era of women's basketball.

Jane describes this special woman: "Besides members of my family Jeanne was the most influential person in my life. The lessons I learned from her as a player, as an assistant coach, and in the classroom have served me well in my own career. She taught me that the experience of sport included more than winning and losing. She created a family atmosphere. She taught us to compete hard, to strive for excellence, to enjoy the experience, to value team, and to never sell ourselves short. Jeanne was an innovative teacher and coach who led the way by example."

When Jane went to Virginia, Linda Southworth had the same family approach. Virginia was a good fit for what Jane feels is the most important aspect of her coaching style.

*Marilyn Cairns*—Lacrosse coach Cairns encouraged Jane to play club lacrosse, and that eventually led to her four-year United States lacrosse squad experience.

*Priscilla Bailey and Dorothy Sullivan*—These two women mentored Jane as she began teaching at Milton Academy.

## MEMORABLE MOMENTS

Miller cites playing in the first AIAW National Championship for women's basketball as one of her most memorable moments in sport. The championship was held at West Chester State University, and she played on one of the first-ever teams selected for the tournament.

A second highlight came when her lacrosse teams won the NCAA championship in 1991 and 1993. The experiences of the teams had changed the career paths of several members of the teams as some became coaches who had not intended to do so prior to their team experiences. Three of these people are already head coaches: Jennie Slingluff, University of North Carolina, Julie Meyers at Virginia, and Bonnie Rosen at the University of Connecticut. The members of the 1991 and 1993 teams remain extremely close. Perhaps the most dynamic player on those teams was Cherie Greer. As a freshman in 1991, Greer added tremendous speed and athletic ability to an already talented team. Since that time she has been voted the 1997 MVP in the World Cup competition and is known as the world's greatest player. Reminiscing brings a smile to Jane's face: "I actually changed my coaching philosophy in 1991. I told the players to just play fast and take risks. They took it, and ran with it, and we reaped the benefits of two National Championships."

During the year in between the national championships, Virginia lost a final four thriller to the University of Maryland, and the year after the 1993 championship they lost a final four thriller to Princeton University. From these experiences, Jane takes not only fond memories, but lifelong friendships with cherished people and the knowledge that they share something very special. For Jane, it has been building a family outside of her birth family and then bringing these two families together and sharing what she loves with a wide circle of wonderful people.

## PHILOSOPHY OF COACHING

Hard work is the fundamental component for success in a Jane Miller–coached team. Hard work is emphasized in practice and in competition, but she also knows how to create an atmosphere to bond team members. A family atmosphere is extremely important to Jane in coaching and in life away from coaching. She views the family dimension as the vitality of her successful coaching career.

Being a conservative person, she developed a conservative and structured coaching style. Staff members convinced Miller in 1991 to loosen the reigns and allow the team "to play loose and fast." The structure remained, but they were given the freedom to do what no other Virginia team had ever had the freedom to do. This new dictum allowed them to win two national championships in three years and place in the final four the third year.

Eventually Jane made a paradigm shift from coaching to become the senior women's administrator. Presently she is the associate athletic director at the University of Virginia. Jane works directly with student-athletes and coaches. She is doing exactly what she wants to do. Since becoming an administrator, she has served on 13 university committees along with 17 different committees in the athletic department.

## CHALLENGES

Although Jane coached basketball for a short period, and wanted to do well because Jeanne Rowland had been such a positive influence, she also knew that her strengths and talents as a coach were better suited to lacrosse.

## FAVORITE BOOK

*The Memoirs of the Ya-Ya Sisterhood.*

## LIFE BEYOND ATHLETICS

Jane spends a good deal of time reading all sorts of fiction and nonfiction books. Other spare moments are spent in all sorts of sport activities, especially running and golf.

## FAVORITE MOVIE

*Steel Magnolias* is Jane's favorite movie.

## RECOGNITIONS AND ACHIEVEMENTS

### Accomplishment as a Player

- United States Lacrosse Team Reserve and Squad, 1972–1976

### Coaching Recognitions in Division I

- Regional Coach of the Year, 1991
- National Coach of the Year, 1991
- Two National Championships, 1991, 1993

## National Coaching Assignments

- World Cup Assistant Coach, 1986
- U.S. Lacrosse Squad Coach, 1985–1991

## Other Accomplishments

- Athletic Hall of Fame, Northeastern University, 1983
- Virginia Lacrosse Hall of Fame, 1996

Photo courtesy of University
of California, Los Angeles

# BILLIE MOORE

*Basketball—University of California, Los Angeles*

## INTRODUCTION

The rolling hills of eastern Kansas, dotted with windmills and wheat fields, were homeland to the first woman coach of an American Olympic basketball team. Billie Moore was the woman. Surely this singular honor pleased her father, also Billie, who nurtured and coached his young daughter in sports from third grade through college.

## PERSONAL DATA

> *Born*: May 5, 1943, Humansville, Missouri
>
> *Father*: Billie Moore
>
> *Father's Occupation*: Teacher, principal, and coach
>
> *Mother*: Glestner Robinson
>
> *Mother's Occupation*: Homemaker
>
> *Siblings*: John (stepbrother), Shirley (stepsister), Nancy, and Terri
>
> *Alma Maters*: Washburn University—B.S., Physical Education, 1966; Southern Illinois—M.S., Physical Education, 1968; Washburn University—Honorary Doctorate, 1999

## FORMATIVE YEARS

From Missouri, the place of Billie's birth, the family moved to Kansas where they lived in several different small Kansas communities. Finally the family established themselves in Westmoreland, a small town close to Manhattan, Kansas. They lived in this northeastern Kansas town from the time Billie was three until she left to get her master's degree. The Moores were a blended family. After the death of Mr. Moore's first wife, he was left with two children. He eventually married Glestner Robinson, and Billie was one of their three children.

Westmoreland had a population of about 500. There were 40 students in the high school, and 18 in Billie's class. The family was closely knit; they had little money, but neither did those who lived close to them. At home they played lots of card and board games. In such a small community, families created their own social life. Card playing was popular among groups of couples, and they held their weekly card games in each other's homes. Holidays were spent with the family, and the extended family was within a two-hour drive of their home, making visits to grandparents a frequent event. Family vacations were usually spent in the Ozarks area by lakes.

## SPORTS HISTORY

Westmoreland provided the right locale for youngsters to flourish. Girls' and boys' sports played a vital role in the school and in the community. Billie began her sports career in third grade, and in each sport she played, her father was the coach. The two of them filled their leisure hours with football, baseball, softball, and basketball. Looking back reminds Billie that had she been raised in a big city, athletics as a pastime or a career may not have been possible.

To be entirely accurate, it must be said that Billie began varsity basketball in the fifth grade. Several men in the community, noting her skill, approached her parents, and attempted to convince them to let her play on the boys' team. Her mother put her foot down and refused. At that time in the mid-west (1955), distinctions were not made between girls' teams and boys' teams. Billie was fortunate to get such a broad background in sports, and she virtually fell in love with athletics. Throughout her public school days, she competed in sports, and, starting at age 12, she played softball in the American Softball Association's summer league. Her father was the coach on those teams, too. When Billie finished grade school, her father became principal of the high school and so he continued to coach the teams Billie played on. The teams were composed of school kids, but the school did not sponsor any athletic teams.

As a sophomore in high school Billie played for a team in Manhattan, Kansas. Ohse Meats sponsored the team—an employee from the company had seen her play and recruited her to play for the team. The company also convinced her father to accept a position as company personnel director, thus relinquishing his principalship. When he changed jobs, he began to assist Billie's new team, and the family moved to Topeka, Kansas. In the winters she played AAU basketball for Oshe Meats, and her dad coached that team, too.

All too soon it was college time. Wayland Baptist College in Plainview, Texas, had the best AAU basketball team in the country, so naturally Billie had an interest in going there. With the help of her high school physical education teacher, she attempted to get admitted, and in the process she learned that Wayland was not, at the time, an accredited institution. That dream ended abruptly, and instead she attended Washburn University in Topeka. After her second calculus class, she switched from a math major to physical education and minored in math and history. Her long-term goal was to get a degree in law.

## DECISION TO COACH

The change in major redirected Billie. She graduated mid-year after four and a half years and started looking for a job. The physical education teacher at Boswell Junior High School was pregnant, so they hired Billie to finish the year. She stayed on another year. It was a "tremendous experience." The junior high was typical with between 600 and 700 students. She was the only physical education teacher for the girls, and she coached all the teams. Play days offered the main opportunities to compete; there were very few leagues. During the second year at Boswell, some people from Washburn University submitted Billie's name to the National Institute for Basketball. Two coaches were invited from each state for the hands-on clinic. The coaches were divided up into teams, and they were put through all kinds of drills and plays. Billie wound up on the same team as Charlotte West, who was at Southern Illinois. Impressed with Billie, Charlotte recruited Billie to go to work on a master's degree. At the University of Southern Illinois, located at Carbondale, Charlotte named Billie as her assistant coach. Billie's father finally retired from coaching, and Billie started to play softball for the Raybestos Brakettes, probably one of, if not the most formidable women's softball team in the U.S. at the time. One of her teammates was **Sharron Backus**. Another teammate was Lou Albrecht, who was then the women's athletic director and the basketball coach at Cal State University at Fullerton. Lou had a chance to go into private business and was giving up the collegiate scene. Lou suggested Billie give a call and submit an application. She interviewed and was hired to be the basketball coach and the women's athletic director.

Billie's primary attraction was not to coaching, but to teaching in the professional preparation of physical education teachers. She wanted to teach upper division classes. That was her major motivation for going to Cal State, Fullerton, so Billie went to Cal State and coached for eight years. Billie was hired prior to the 1969–1970 season as the third coach in school history. She started a dynasty that led to an immediate national championship in 1970. In the first four seasons her teams only had one regular season loss. They won seven WAIAW Region 8 championships and took three seconds and one fifth to go with the national championship.

Billie became a national figure in women's basketball. By 1975 Billie was the coach of the national team. In 1976 she coached the first-ever U.S. Women's Basketball Olympic Team in Montreal. In 1976 Cal State became a founding member of the Western Collegiate Athletic Association Conference. **Linda K. Sharp**, also featured in this book, was one of Billie's players. Billie led Cal State after the 1976–1977 season. By this time, six years after Title IX, larger institutions were starting to make some serious commitments to women's sport, especially basketball. Billie had several offers from name schools but had little interest in leaving California. Once the schools that dominated men's athletics decided to embrace women's sports, the inclination and ambition to make their women's teams dominant became a goal as well. That led to a discussion with Judy Holland, the athletic director for women's sports at UCLA. Billie was hired by UCLA and started another dynasty which lasted sixteen years until 1993 when she retired.

In her first year at UCLA, 1977–1978, Billie's team went 27–3, won the conference, the region, and the national championship. In her career Billie won 9 conference championships and took her team to eight top-ten finishes. She went to post-season play 16 times.

In 1993 Billie retired from full-time coaching at UCLA. Billie's father passed away in 1989 and that had been a difficult time for Billie. She really had thought about retiring after the 1990–1991 season. Her enthusiasm waned. Her battery was dry. Just empty. Just burned out. She had never wanted to just coach. Now it was just getting to be a job. Since retiring she has been offered many opportunities to coach in the ABL, the WNBA, and on the college scene. She feels she no longer has the emotional energy to perform at that level. She clearly came to this realization in 1992 when UCLA beat Texas to go to the sweet 16. Cathy Oliver, her assistant, said to her "you don't seem to be very excited or something." Billie replied, "I would just as soon be playing golf or something." It just wasn't fun any more. The flame for that kind of competition had burned out.

Now Billie spends her time doing basketball camps, consulting, and working with the WBCA and several Division I programs. Billie and Pat Summit do the basketball academy, now in its fourth year, and have over 300 high school and Division I coaches participating.

## RECOGNITIONS AND ACHIEVEMENTS

### Coaching Recognitions in Division I

- Nine Golden West Conference Championships: 1969–1976
- Seven WAIAW Region 8 Championships: 1970, 1971, 1972, 1974, 1975, 1976, 1977
- Two PAC 10 Championships: 1977–1978, 1978–1979

- College Basketball Coach of the Year, 1978
- Two AIAW National Championships: 1969–1970, 1977–1978
- Two ACAA Regional Championships: 1978, 1979

## National Coaching Assignments

- Head Coach World University Games, 1973, 1975
- Head Coach Pan Am Games, 1985
- First-ever women's basketball Olympic coach, 1976—won silver medal

## Other Accomplishments

- U.S. Selection Committee since 1976
- Kodak All-American Selection Committee
- Kansas Athletic Hall of Fame, 1997
- Women's Basketball Hall of Fame, 1999

Photo courtesy of University
of Alabama

# SARAH PATTERSON

*Gymnastics—University of Alabama*

## INTRODUCTION

Sarah Patterson has created a unique gymnastics dynasty at the University of Alabama. The unique part is that her husband, David, is the assistant coach, and together they have chartered a program based on their mutual love for gymnastics.

## PERSONAL DATA

 *Born*:  December 31, 1955, Endwell, New York

 *Father*:  Marshall Singer

 *Father's Occupation*:  Manager for IBM

 *Mother*:  Ruth Stiles

 *Mother's Occupation*:  Worked for IBM

 *Siblings*:  Susan and Shelly

 *Husband*:  David Patterson

 *Children*:  Daughters Jessie and Jordan

 *Alma Mater*:  Slippery Rock State College—B.S., 1977

## FORMATIVE YEARS

Born in upstate New York, Sarah resided there until her father was transferred to Huntsville, Alabama. In this predominately white neighborhood, the children found daily excitement in hide 'n seek and kick ball from the close of school until dark. In the summer Sarah and her sisters, Susan and Shelly, arose early to attend their 7:30 A.M. swimming lesson. After the lesson their mother took them home for breakfast and then back to the pool where they spent the rest of the day.

Holidays were especially pleasant because their mother had a love for parties and activities for their family and others. A sport family, her mother and the girls watched football with their father. Physical education was also Sarah's favorite elementary school subject. In the seventh grade her interests shifted to gymnastics, jazz band, marching band, and the dance team.

## SPORTS HISTORY

Sarah's parents moved to Binghamton, New York, during her ninth-grade year. This year she got her "first real coach." The coach, Jo Childs, inspired Sarah to choose a physical education teaching and coaching career. Even though Sarah wanted to be a physical education teacher, she had only participated in gymnastics, swimming, and dancing. So Jo Childs, a fine athlete and teacher, took the time to teach Sarah in basic sport skills.

Even though Sarah's parents had not attended college, it was assumed that Sarah would attend college. Looking into various schools of higher education, she knew she wanted to go where she could participate in gymnastics. After looking at Slippery Rock State College, Kent State, and Pennsylvania State, she decided Slippery Rock offered the program she wanted. The school was small, a six-hour drive from home, and it had an excellent reputation for preparing teachers and coaches.

Although Slippery Rock was a fine school, Sarah had to adjust to a new gymnastics coach every year she was there. Even though this was unfortunate, she still developed the skills to attend the AIAW Nationals in Colorado Springs. The competition pushed her to learn new skills and become a more all-around competitor.

## DECISION TO COACH

After graduation, at 22 years of age, Sarah was hired to coach gymnastics at the University of Alabama. The Alabama program was dying. Sarah became the fifth coach in five years. After four losing seasons Sarah was the only one that expected success.

Shortly after accepting the job (1978) Sarah called David Patterson, with whom she had worked one summer at a gym in Huntsville, Alabama, to offer him the assistant's job. David was a diver on the Alabama Swim Team and, even though he had just completed a successful freshman year on the team, he decided coaching gymnastics was more in line with his interests. He received a tuition scholarship and started his sophomore year at Alabama as an assistant to Sarah. Over time, Sarah and David's relationship became personal as well as professional. They were married in 1982. Tongue in cheek, David still claims they married for job security.

Now, after twenty years of working together, they have developed an excellent coaching style where one compliments the other. Sarah credits David as the better technical coach whereas she flourishes in the artistic realm. He's laid back and she's the typical type A personality. Sarah knows the administrators, and David is best friends with the maintenance people. Together they have produced a winning alliance.

Sarah credits her boundless energy, enthusiasm, and naïveté with pushing the Alabama program further than one might within reason expect. She knew what she wanted to do and went about doing it. The work paid off immediately for the team that had never enjoyed a winning season. The Sarah-and-David team produced a 23–11 record in their first two years. By 1982 they had recruited a class of predominately juniors, and they finished the season 11th nationally. This was the first year the NCAA had sponsored women's nationals, and only the top ten squads qualified. By the end of 1983, the team, now mostly seniors, not only qualified for nationals but started a six-season trend. Fourteen times they placed in the top five, three were national championships, four third-place finishes, and three fourth-place finishes. For 14 seasons they have qualified for the Super Six. The Alabama athletes have won 11 individual national championships, and Alabama has produced 26 All Americans who have collectively won nearly 100 All-American honors. Alabama was the 1998 season attendance leader, averaging 10,301 persons per meet.

## MEMORABLE MOMENTS

One of Sarah's best memories occurred in 1996 when the Crimson Tide team won the national championship in Tuscaloosa on their home court. The previous three years they finished nationals in second place. In 1996 they were picked to be number one. As they proceeded into their last rotation on the vault, Sarah began to wonder if they could pull it off. Then she saw 50 alumni seated together in the center section with husbands and children. When she looked up from the end of the vault runway and saw all of them standing and cheering for Alabama, it was a breathtaking scene. She remembers thinking, "It doesn't matter whether we win or finish fourth, look at these women and look at what David and I have done to contribute to their lives." It was then she felt like a winner, and the actual winning or losing faded into the background. That moment epitomizes the reason the Pattersons continue to coach. Their contribution extends beyond the winning and the losing; it is centered in the lives they hope to touch. Alabama won, but Sarah never forgets the emotion that washed over her when she looked up to an alumni once again united.

Recently Sarah said, "Winning championships, at one point in time, was the ultimate for us. That has changed. We still enjoy winning and that's why we do this, to win meets and championships, but the relationships with the kids are why we stay in it. I mean, in terms of watching them mature as young women, watching them go off and get married, seeing them as professionals, and seeing their careers flourish. The biggest rewards now are seeing these young women come through our program and really blossom. That's how we measure success."

A second major memory happened when the Tide sold out Coleman Coliseum to 15,043 fans. Sarah knew they had been building up to a sell out because they were attracting crowds of 12,000 and 13,000. She knew they were gradually inching towards being sold out. The day was February 1, 1997, when the media relations person came to report, "We have sold out, in fact we have turned 400 people away." Outside people were scalping tickets. The event was Alabama vs. Georgia. It was a sobering moment when the lights dimmed and the team marched in, greeted by a deafening crescendo of fans. A big introduction followed; when the lights came on there was not an empty seat in the arena. Sarah realized, "I've been working 18 years for this moment." She so enjoyed the moment she didn't want the competition to start; she just wanted to savor the sound, the crowd, the team, and the feelings. She wanted the moment to last forever.

## ROLE MODELS/MENTORS

*Jo Childs*—Jo taught Sarah basic sports skills. She also helped to engender in her a disciplined work ethic.

*Cheryl Levick*—Cheryl Levick, now the associate athletic director at Stanford University, was Sarah's fourth Slippery Rock gymnastics coach. Prior to her coming, Sarah almost quit gymnastics. Cheryl motivated Sarah to stay, and wisely assigned her to assist in coaching and choreographing routines.

## PHILOSOPHY OF COACHING

Sarah and David's basic coaching philosophy has changed little over the years. Developing the whole person remains paramount along with recruiting, coaching, and promoting the sport. Although the job has not changed, the breadth of responsibilities has changed significantly.

Athletes are carefully recruited to fit the environment and the program. Newcomers know the coaches will do anything within the rules to help them succeed. Their first coaching priority is to care for them as young women and then as gymnasts. They only recruit individuals who want coaches to be highly involved in their lives. Their athletes know they will monitor their classes; they also know they will be assisted by tutors and academic advisors. They know Sarah will talk to their parents, and they know they are going to be part of a team family. Each athlete comes to realize she will be loved and cared about. The

Pattersons feel that taking care of each person will contribute to the happiness of the athlete and enable each to accomplish her athletic potential.

The first two to three weeks of the school year are spent in conversations with athletes and helping new team members make a successful transition. Sarah claims they deliver on promises, and athletes know that their promises will become reality.

## CHALLENGES

Legendary Alabama Football Coach Bear Bryant hired Sarah. Bryant loved winners, male or female. Every time the gymnastics team did well, they got more money in the budget and more support. The team usually went over the allotted budget, but Bryant liked the fact they were winning and making money too.

The biggest challenge the Pattersons faced was changing the mindset of the spectators and teaching them they could love traditional sports and also love gymnastics. They wanted to make gymnastics a family entertainment alongside the more traditional sports.

Trying to get newspaper coverage was another big challenge, but when fans started filling the seats, the media had to pay attention. Today they get media coverage not because the media understands the sport, but because the public demands coverage.

Near the beginning of the program they lacked equipment, they shared a gym with the volleyball team, and they passed out flyers in parking lots to advertise their meets. Today one sees a full house of spectators and a successful program as a result of the untiring work of Sarah and David Patterson.

## CHANGES IN ATHLETES

The female gymnast has evolved from a slightly built, petite woman to a female with a strong body that is powerful and explosive. Fifteen years has changed the physical attributes of the athlete being recruited today. One of the biggest challenges the present-day gymnastic coach has is making the sport fun—this is necessary because today's gymnasts have been enrolled in gymnastics programs for so many years they have almost lost the ability to have fun. Sarah also feels the emphasis has to be changed from the "me" mentality to a "we" mentality. Obviously this must be done so the team concept will prevail. Being responsible to teammates is a motivating factor most gymnasts have not had. Sarah brings in former athletes to explain to the team how things were in the early days. They discuss how they traveled to meets in vans and stayed in the least expensive hotels and ate at fast food places. Sarah tries to teach the teams of today that what they now enjoy comes from the legacy earned by earlier teams. Knowing the history is very important in maintaining a thankful attitude rather than the entitlement attitude that is rampant in some areas. Ninety-nine percent of the Alabama athletes prefer the team concept.

Any big organization runs the risks of diminishing individuals, and so Sarah believes it is important for the fans to know the team and the coaches in a personal way. The Pattersons make a conscientious effort to facilitate this kind of relationship and atmosphere with their fans.

## LIFE BEYOND ATHLETICS

Noting the difficulty in maintaining balance in her personal life, Sarah credits David with being the better one at balancing. David sets the parameters. He reminds Sarah how many nights it has been since they were at home; he admonishes her if it is time for a family night. "Family night" is when they and their two daughters spend quality time together all in one room. Such nights are planned. Also Wednesday night is the family's church night.

David likes playing golf and fly fishing, but he doesn't get much time to do either. Most of their away-from-gymnastics time is spent with their children. To just stay at home and enjoy the family is considered a luxury. Their daughter Jessie once remarked to a friend, "Gymnastics season is never over at Pattersons."

When David Patterson became ill, priorities at the Pattersons' house changed. After suffering an injury moving equipment, David had an x-ray thinking he may have done some serious damage. During a lunch break the team physician beeped David on his pager and asked if they would come to his office. They knew something was wrong. The doctor reported David had a two-inch cancerous tumor. Sarah came unglued and fell to the floor sobbing. David was calm. Sarah was so physically sick she couldn't get past the word CANCER. Finally David said, "If you can get up off the floor, I think he has something good to tell us." But Sarah thought, "Oh no, I have two children and I'm going to be by myself. How am I going to do this? How will I provide? "

Well, they pulled a team of surgeons together and ten days later David had surgery. Sarah said, "Those were the longest ten days of my life." David tried to go to the gym those days, but it was very hard on him. Now that is behind them, and, as a result, Sarah does twice as much work for charities, etc., because she feels it is a way to give back because David was given a second chance. She feels, "The good Lord is not yet ready for David Patterson. He still has a lot of work to do and a lot of lives to change." Sarah and David firmly believe they have a mission to perform and part of that mission is to contribute to their athletes and to society in some unique ways.

During these difficult days it was hard for the team, especially the upper class women; they struggled all year to get on their feet. At the same time, Sarah was amazed at the alumni and community who called to offer to help with the children, the program, or whatever else they might have needed. Sarah still calls the support "unbelievable. "

David and Sarah continue their journey of a team serving a team. They are an exemplary couple who personify hard work, enthusiasm, and love for those with whom they work.

## RECOGNITIONS AND ACHIEVEMENTS

### Coaching Recognition in Division I

- Three Conference Championships, SEC: 1988, 1990, 1995
- Fifteen Regional Championships: 1983, 1984, 1985, 1987, 1988, 1989, 1990, 1991, 1992, 1993, 1994, 1995, 1996, 1998, 1999
- Conference Coach of the Year, SEC: 1985, 1995
- National Coach of the Year: 1986, 1988, 1991
- Three National Championships: 1988, 1991, 1996
- Thirty All Americans, 104 honors
- Super Six Qualifier 12 out of 15 times

### National Coaching Assignment

- World Games, 1983, 1997 Silver Medal

# CATHY RUSH

## *Basketball—Immaculata College*

### INTRODUCTION

Boating, fishing, and clamming granted untold hours of intrigue and fun for a bright-eyed youth named Cathy. Her father fished when not at work, and he and an uncle built a boat-launching dock. By the time Cathy was ten, she and her sister and two cousins each owned a small motor boat. Pampered by family-focused parents, Cathy professes to have had "the best of childhoods. "

### PERSONAL DATA

*Born*: April 7, 1947, Atlantic City, New Jersey

*Father*: John Cowan

*Father's Occupation*: Atlantic City electric supervisor

*Mother*: Alice

*Mother's Occupation*: Convention speaker recorder and transcriber

*Sibling*: Alice

*Husband*: Ed Rush

*Children*: Eddie and Michael

*Alma Mater*: West Chester State—B.S., Physical Education and
Health, 1968; M.S., Physical Education and Health, 1972

## FORMATIVE YEARS

Her small hometown supported an old two-room elementary school. One
teacher was assigned to each room. There were fourteen children in one classroom including Cathy, her sister Alice, and their two cousins; kindergarten,
first, and second grade were all housed in the same room. The other classroom
was for the sixteen students in the third, fourth, and fifth grades, making the
school's enrollment total thirty students. The school was small, but it had a
wonderful atmosphere for learning. Cathy still treasures the memory of those
youthful years.

The small neighborhood throbbed with imaginative youth who created
many of their own games. They played street games, basketball games with a
hoop on a telephone pole or a garage, and other seasonal sports were introduced in the vacant lot.

## SPORTS HISTORY

When Cathy reached the eighth grade, she played 6–on–6 basketball, and
her team made it to the county tournament. She averaged 30 points per game
and was such a force the newspapers labeled her "Big Gun." The middle
school did not offer other sports. In high school she was the county high
point-scoring champion. During her sophomore year, returning high school
students were told the school had dropped girls' interscholastic sports. The
announcement was accepted without complaint. However, when a new
teacher (who had been on an exhibition gymnastics team at the University of
Maryland) came, things changed. He started a gymnastics team, and Cathy
joined and was soon appointed the team captain. For three years Cathy toured
with the team, putting on half-time shows and demonstrations in elementary
schools. She loved the trampoline enough to make it her exhibition specialty.

Oakcrest High School was brand new Cathy's freshman year. There was a
multitude of vibrant young teachers along with a few older, more experienced
teachers. Cathy thought it was the best of schools and the teachers were excellent. Cathy graduated second in a class of 300. For the most part, young
women of her age aspired to be either teachers or nurses. She chose to be a
teacher.

Wanting an experience away from home, she applied to West Chester State
and was accepted. Cathy majored in physical education and played basketball
for two years before losing interest after Lucille Kyvallos, the basketball coach,
left. She switched to gymnastics and competed there for the remainder of her
time at West Chester.

## DECISION TO COACH

Obtaining a coaching job was easy. First she taught at Springfield High School in Springfield, Delaware County. She taught health, physical education, and coached field hockey, lacrosse, and basketball. The teacher whose place she had taken returned after a sabbatical leave, and Cathy went to General Wayne Junior High to teach. There she taught seventh and eighth grade physical education and health. Near the end of her two-year stay at General Wayne, the basketball coaching job at Immaculata opened; the gym had burned down making a challenging situation for a new coach.

Prior to accepting the position, she knew about the gym. Even though a new one was under construction, it did eliminate home games during her first year. It was challenging, but she found a 4 P.M. to 6 P.M. practice spot at the Catholic convent across the street.

After she began coaching, she told her husband Ed, who was an NBA referee, that she had some really good players. Ed said, "Yeah, sure you do." So practice started and they were a pretty good team. Almost all the players commuted to the school. They had won eight games in a row. When they showed up for the ninth game, two of the girls were late—they had been in a car accident. Theresa, now **Theresa Shrank Grentz**, suffered a broken collar bone and missed the last four games of the season. The Immaculata team finished the first season 10–2.

By Cathy's second year at Immaculata, the Association of Intercollegiate Athletics for Women (AIAW) had set up a regional and a national tournament schedule. The regional tournament entry was earned. There were 16 teams. All teams played four games in three days to save the expense of a night's lodging. Their uniforms were box pleated tunics and blouses, bloomers, and gym shoes with high socks. They won Thursday, Friday morning, and they knew if they won the game on Friday night they would head to the national tournament. They won in the regional finals; they played West Chester State and lost 70–38.

The national tournament was held at Illinois State University. They didn't have any money, so the nuns in charge of the school said they would get everybody to help out. It was determined that $3,000 would be necessary. After meeting in the school's rotunda where groups such as the Mother's Guild, the Parents Association, and students had gathered, it was determined $2,700 had been raised—just short of the $3,000 needed. Cathy was disappointed she had to leave three players at home. An airline program was found affording students between the ages of 12 and 21 a standby flying opportunity for half price. They left without any support personnel, flew to Chicago, rented cars, and drove to Illinois State. Cathy didn't know anyone there. First they played Indiana, then Cal State, Fullerton, coached by **Billie Moore**, then the Mississippi University for Women. After every game Cathy called Ed to say "we won." His response was, "Who do you play next?" When Cathy would tell him, he would say, "Don't be disappointed if you lose." They made the finals, only to play Cathy's alma mater, West Chester State, the same team who drubbed them 70–38 in the regional final. This time the outcome was different: Immaculata slipped by notching a 56–52 win to became the 1972 National Champions. The following year Renie Portland and Theresa Grentz returned. This was previous to press guides and school-furnished warm-up—in fact, each player had a different color warm-up suit. That season they played at West Chester State before a crowd of 5,000. That was the beginning of increased publicity and newspaper articles promoting women's basketball. They rented high school gyms, charged admission, and thousands poured in to watch. Immaculata won the AIAW national championship three years in a row: 1972, 1973, and 1974. In 1975 and 1976 they came in second and in 1977 they took fourth. In 1977 Cathy resigned and became a full-time mother.

As a result of Cathy's success at Immaculata, she was invited to become involved with the Women's National Team. In 1975 she took the team to the Pan American games and later to the world championships. She also served on the Olympic committee.

## MEMORABLE MOMENTS

"My most memorable moment by far occurred in 1973 when we played the nationals at Queens, New York." A local radio station came to broadcast their games. Most important to Cathy, the players' families were there. Their friends and all of the Immaculata nuns were there too. In the semifinal game the team was down 12 points with three minutes left. With 26 seconds left, they were tied. **Marianne Stanley** shoots with three seconds left. The ball comes off the rim. Theresa Grentz goes up and tips the ball in. The next day they played Queens for the national championship.

## ROLE MODELS/MENTORS

*Ralph Platt*—A basketball coach and English teacher who was blessed with a tremendous sense of humor, Ralph Platt used it make the teaching and coaching an enlivening experience.

*Lucille Kyvallos*—Lucille coached basketball at West Chester State. She was advanced for her time in understanding basketball preparation and game strategy. Cathy acclaims Kyvallos as having an "amazing insight and mind for the game."

## PHILOSOPHY OF COACHING

A good deal of time was spent on defense and in teaching players their roles. An athlete's willingness to fulfill a particular role was prerequisite to playing on Cathy's teams. She fashioned teams in a way she could get the most out of each based on what they did best. Her players understood what they needed to do in comparison to other teams of the era. It was important to have an intellectual understanding of what should be done and why. They were taught to be very patient and very disciplined. Smart, disciplined players like Theresa Grentz and Marianne Stanley helped her to implement the core of her philosophy.

## CHALLENGES

In this era few female programs were blessed with money. At times fundraising was used to alleviate the problem. One such project involved selling toothbrushes to generate some money. As the team became better, it became necessary to travel, escalating the need for money. The development and admissions offices both recognized the impact of good publicity on alumni contributions. Being in the New York–Baltimore–Washington, D.C., area helped the publicity. The publicity came fast and furious enough to cause Cathy to wonder, "Now that we have it, what do we do with it? "

## CHANGES IN ATHLETES

Cathy feels that the upside of the changes are physical. They are bigger and stronger and taller. There are 6'1" athletes now playing guard positions who are also good inside players. Formerly, a shorter athlete played the guard position. Now, 10, 11, and 12–year-old children are as good as high school players of the seventies. On the downside, attitudes have changed. Young women used to like feedback, they loved to be taught, they loved to be coached. Currently they don't want to hear any criticism. Cathy feels like they are saying "been there, done that, I know all that stuff." To that attitude Cathy's reaction is, "If you know it all, why is it you don't do it so well?" Cathy believes that although many athletes are turned off, they still need the organization that the coach can bring to help them maximize their talents. She sees a need for athletes to learn how to negotiate, how to make decisions, and how to work within a team.

## LIFE BEYOND ATHLETICS

Cathy met Ed Rush when she was a freshman at West Chester State. Their first date was to a basketball game. Two years later they began dating again and were married. In 1972, while at Immaculata, she had her first son, Eddie. Practice had started, and so he became a regular at her daily practices. During the next season, September of 1973, she was pregnant with Michael. He was born after the national championships in 1974. Cathy resigned to become a full-time mother for the next three years.

Her husband Ed was an NBA referee. Eddie is a captain in the Marines and a jet pilot. Michael is employed with the NBA.

Cathy started doing basketball camps in the early seventies. She did one camp with 45 kids. Her colleagues were impressed with the idea, and the next year she had 90 and soon reached 600. Presently Cathy runs camps at eight different campuses. She has a strong network of people. Collectively they sponsor camps for all ages and in many different sports and activities. In 1999 there were 9,000 participants.

In addition to running camps, Cathy likes to snow ski, water ski, and body surf. The family plays golf together. She enjoys reading and is especially attracted to books on history, historical novels, and mysteries. Theater is also a favorite activity.

## RECOGNITIONS AND ACHIEVEMENTS

### Coaching Recognitions in Division I

- Five Eastern AIAW Championships: 1971–1976
- Three AIAW National Championships: 1972, 1973, 1974
- Produced 4 All Americans

### National Coaching Assignments

- Pan Am Games, 1975, Gold Medal
- Coach of the Year, 1973

### Other Accomplishments

- Pennsylvania Hall of Fame, 1987
- Philadelphia Big Five Hall of Fame, 1996
- Member of the U.S. Olympic Committee for Basketball, 1975, 1976
- Delaware County Athletics Hall of Fame, 1992
- Color Commentator for NBC, CBS, ESPN, PRISM, and the Sports Channel
- First woman coach to be named Coach of the Year, 1973

Photo courtesy of University
of Florida

# MIMI RYAN

## *Golf—University of Florida*

### INTRODUCTION

Mimi Ryan's competitive past was limited to Play Days and Sports Days—competitions which usually featured softball, basketball, swimming, and volleyball. They were organized around the notion that females required a different competitive experience than their male counterparts. In this respect, Ryan exemplifies the female athlete of a day long past. Most of today's coaches know little of the Sports Day tradition that reigned over women's sport during the fifties.

### PERSONAL DATA

*Born*: April 1, 1936, Troy, New York

*Father*: John Ryan

*Father's Occupation*: Electrician

*Mother*: Mildred Pratt

*Mother's Occupation*: Telephone operator in the New York governor's office from the time of Franklin D. Roosevelt to that of Nelson Rockefeller

*Alma Maters*: Tufts University—B.S., Physical Education, 1958; Bouvé-Boston School, 1958—Physical Education Degree; University of North Carolina, Greensboro—M.Ed., 1964

## FORMATIVE YEARS

Mimi grewup in Latham, a suburb of Albany, New York. This rural New York town was dotted with farms and children, mostly boys, engaged in the activities that occur around farm life. Horseback riding and playing the traditional games of baseball, basketball, and football created lively activity for Mimi during her early years.

## SPORTS HISTORY

As a young teenager, Mimi became interested in golf. "Chasing a little white pill around a golf course" was her father's impression of the game. He simply could not understand why anyone would want to play golf. Neither he nor his wife played the game, that is until they gave Mimi lessons—then they took up the game in "self-defense." At sixteen, Mimi was playing golf at Normanside Country Club, playing in club events, but she gave it up when she went to Bouvé.

Organized sports for girls in Mimi's high school followed the "Play Day" model. That is, schools selected the number of girls needed for a team and sent them to the host school. The host school then created new teams comprised of girls from several schools. The new teams chose a name and competed together in a round-robin tournament. Competitions were usually held all day on a Saturday. A social generally followed the competition where the winners were announced and awards were given.

Bouvé-Boston School, part of Tufts University, was a special school with a national reputation for preparing physical education teachers and physical therapists. That is why Mimi attended Tufts. The school ran a very structured program for its students. After a long rigorous day in the classroom, intramurals were contested in the evening; everyone participated, and Mimi played every sport offered. Mimi graduated from Tufts with a B.S. in education and a physical education degree from Bouvé. Her first position was teaching junior and senior high health and physical education in Livingston, New Jersey. She dearly loved this time of teaching, and she liked living near New York so she could attend the theater. Golf was put on the back burner because she could not find time to teach and play golf. After teaching five years, Mimi wanted to get her master's degree. She applied and was accepted at the University of North Carolina–Greensboro. After completing her master's degree in Educational Administration in 1964, she was hired to teach physical education at Pennsylvania State University. The sports programs at Penn State were considered varsity sports, and during her five years at Penn State she coached the golf team and the bowling team—having written her master's thesis on golf augmented her coaching credentials. Mimi remained at Penn State from 1964 to 1969 co-directing the DGWS Women's National Collegiate Golf Tournament in 1969. Nine years later she directed the 1978 AIAW National Collegiate Golf Tournament.

Penn State was advanced in their approach to women and sport. Prior to the AIAW and NCAA involvement in women's sport, Penn State ran a national collegiate golf tournament in 1969 sponsored by DGWS. This provided Mimi with many contacts in the golf world. Also, taking players to a tournament in Florida in 1965 afforded another opportunity for her to meet all of the right people. When the Florida job opened up she called and asked about the job. On that call she was asked, "Do you want the job?" Her answer was a resounding yes, and the job was hers. No interview on campus, just a telephone call, an offer, and a yes answer sealed the coaching position.

Golf at Florida, unlike golf at Penn State, was a club program, with a golf budget of only $200 that first year. When the team traveled to play other schools, each team member had to pay her own expenses. Finally, a number of physical education teachers from all over Florida met in Orlando with the "pure purpose" of starting varsity sports. Mimi returned and asked the chairperson of the women's physical education department to arrange a meeting with the dean of the physical education college so as to inform all concerned of the plans of the women to start a varsity sports program. Although they had the go-ahead for the program, the money was there and then the money was not there. Finally, student athletes went to the president of the university to get the muscle for the athletic department to give them the money to attend the National Collegiate Tournament. In the mid-seventies, with the aid of Title IX, the scholarships and budgets were increased. No reasonable budget was denied. Climate conditions in Florida were excellent for recruiting, and the academic programs were equal to the climate. Student athletes who attended Florida were happy and successful. Mimi Ryan's athletes chalked up one of the best graduation rates in the country, and those with degrees are now making inroads into the profession.

## MEMORABLE MOMENTS

Winning the first national championship was certainly an event to remember. But as exciting as the first one was, the second national championship was especially exciting. The second championship was more special because her five players were named All Americans before the tournament started. According to Ryan, this had never happened before and has not happened since. That year Mimi was also named coach of the year and was one of the original inductees into the Women's Coaches Hall of Fame. During the tournament, although they were ranked number one, they were three strokes behind after the first day and the team came from behind to win the tournament by eight. Their motivation was to win the tournament for the team, for her, for themselves, and for the school. Mimi did not have to apply any motivational techniques—they generated their own. Ryan's team was one of the first in the country to use a sports psychologist. They started using Psychologist Pete Taylor in 1985, and won the next two national championships.

The University of Florida was a wonderful place to coach and Mimi felt fortunate to have spent her coaching career there. She didn't have money struggles after Title IX, she didn't have to struggle to get a golf course, and the athletic association was very supportive. Looking back, she did not feel that she had any great obstacles to impede her success. Mimi Ryan retired from coaching in 1994; she had always told her players "do what is fun, when it is no longer fun . . . get out!"

## ROLE MODEL/MENTOR

*Ellen Griffin*—Ellen was one of Mimi's graduate school professors and one of several women who helped found the LPGA. Ellen's infectious enthusiasm caused students to love her classes and Mimi was impressed with her deep love for teaching. Ellen Griffin taught Mimi that athletes should learn something from each competitive experience and have a good time in the process.

## PHILOSOPHY OF COACHING

As described earlier, the Ellen Griffin philosophy had a profound impact on Mimi Ryan's philosophy. Mimi believes in self-motivation, hard work, academic achievement, and good team atmosphere. Basically, her philosophy translated into "one day, one hole, and one shot at a time."

Ryan claims that today's athletes have been pushed by parents toward the dollar sign at the end of the tunnel. They have to be told when to practice, and they are not as willing to devote the necessary time and effort to achieve excellence in their skills. Many believe that just because they come to a good golf school the skills will come with little or no effort. Many athletes get scholarships and feel that it does not matter if they play well. Even athletes claim they have been pushed by their parents and rewarded for mediocrity. There is an attitude of "if I play well, what will you give me?" Ryan feels that athletes must play for the sheer joy of playing.

## LIFE BEYOND ATHLETICS

Mimi is finally getting to play golf. Strange as it may seem, even though she was a golf coach, the opportunity to play seldom arose. Gardening is a favorite pastime, and she is especially interested in growing roses and working in the rose garden. She loves to read. She enjoys the challenge of jig-saw puzzles and crossword puzzles. She also treasures time spent visiting the friends she made during her coaching years.

To those seeking a satisfying career Mimi advises, "do it if you love it." To her, money is not a good reason for a career choice: "it usually will not bring happiness or prosperity. "

## RECOGNITIONS AND ACHIEVEMENTS

### Coaching Recognitions in Division I

- Six SEC Conference Championships: 1981, 1982, 1984, 1986, 1987, 1991
- Conference Coach of the Year, SEC: 1984, 1985, 1986
- National Coach of the Year, 1986
- Two National Championships: 1985, 1986
- Sixteen Top 5 NCAA Finishes
- Entire team named All Americans in 1986
- Produced 25 All Americans
- Forty-six team titles
- Two players on World Cup Team
- Two Broderick Cup Winners: 1985, 1986
- Four players on Curtis Cup teams

### National Coaching Assignment

- NCAA Team vs. Japan, 1985

### Other Accomplishments

- Gladys Palmer Award, 1990
- National Golf Coaches Association Hall of Fame Inductee, 1986
- University of Florida Athletic Hall of Fame Inductee, 1996
- *Golf World*'s panel to select top twenty rankings

Photo courtesy of Princeton
University

# CHRIS SAILER
## *Lacrosse—Princeton University*

## INTRODUCTION

The ability to work effectively within a system is a notable trademark of Chris Sailer. When Chris took over the Princeton program, she demonstrated the ability to create a winning tradition without scholarships, designating an innovative leadership style.

## PERSONAL DATA

*Born*: October 29, 1959, Abington, Pennsylvania

*Father*: Lambert Sailer

*Father's Occupation*: Teacher, Haverford High School, Pennsylvania

*Mother*: Barbara Dalrymple

*Mother's Occupation*: Homemaker

*Siblings*: Kathleen, Maureen, and Jennifer

*Alma Maters*: Harvard—A.B., 1981; University of Massachusetts—M.S., 1985

## FORMATIVE YEARS

During the first nine years of Chris' life, she resided in northeast Philadelphia. Through the third grade, she attended Olney Elementary School in Philadelphia. This area was without playing fields. Most games were played on concrete roads and pavements. At Manoa Elementary School, a new world of opportunity opened when she started playing fifth grade field hockey. Philadelphia was a hotbed of competition for field hockey and lacrosse. Although Chris' sisters were not sports-minded, she found playmates who sharpened her sporting energies. The Sailer family did not have a lot of money, and they did not have many vacations. They lived ten minutes from relatives, and their mother's sisters' children were like their own siblings. Their parents took them on day trips to New York City and Washington, D.C. Their station wagon managed two parents and nine kids, affording beach trips to the Jersey shore and various sightseeing excursions.

## SPORTS HISTORY

The elementary school physical education teacher, Mr. Blessing, encouraged children to participate in a variety of sports in his classes. In sixth grade Chris played softball and field hockey. The school system was set up so that seventh graders went to the junior high school. One of her female teachers was the coach, Phyllis Corl Pillard. She still teaches and coaches at Harriton High School. Phyllis was the first to coach Chris in field hockey and lacrosse. She was also her seventh-grade physical education teacher, and she took a lot of interest in the kids on the team and in her classes. Chris mingled with many fun-loving, talented athletes during the upper grade-school years. Athletes were taken to local colleges to observe college games beginning in the seventh grade, thus exposing them to role models and opportunities. As the coaches gave their time and energy to these young athletes, strong bonds were also developing.

Chris was the family's athlete; she competed in basketball, field hockey, and lacrosse all through junior and senior high school. Julie Soriero coached Chris in high school basketball and counseled her as she applied for college. Harvard was one of the six schools of higher education to which she applied. Harvard was on the list because Val Walchack, lacrosse coach, had played lacrosse at West Chester State with the Harvard lacrosse coach, **Carole Kleinfelder**. Kleinfelder recruited Chris based on Walchack's recommendation. Chris became interested in Harvard and was pleasantly surprised when she was admitted.

Plans to major in physical education were changed—Harvard did not offer that major; so figuring four years of varsity field hockey and lacrosse would provide the needed coaching background, she majored in psychology. Early exposure to many outstanding role models made coaching an easy choice. Graduating from Harvard and entering the coaching field raised a few eyebrows; most who questioned this move thought she should be doing something else. She still jokes about how she brought the Harvard graduate salary average down when she became a coach. Her parents were very supportive of her career choice; they favored her doing something that would make her happy. She claims her father got over wanting her to become a lawyer or a doctor fairly quickly. Although she felt her parents knew she had always wanted to teach or coach, she believed they thought that going to Harvard meant she would choose another career. Now they are spectators at many of her games and extend reinforcement and approval. After graduation, Sailer played for a number of district teams. She played on the New England Lacrosse team for eight years and the national squad for one year in 1983.

After graduating in 1981, Chris took a job at Choate-Rosemary Hall prep school in Connecticut. She taught classes in behavior, ethics, psychology, and human development and coached field hockey and lacrosse. She remained at Choate for three years. During this time she developed a great love for the school, but prep school teaching was very demanding—one had to be in the dorm with the kids, on duty in the evenings, and frequently on weekends. Thinking of her future, she challenged herself by enrolling in the sport management program at the University of Massachusetts. While there, she was assistant to **Pam Hixon**, the lacrosse coach. She served her internship at the University of Pennsylvania, where she worked in the athletic department as an administrative assistant to Ann Sage, the field hockey and lacrosse coach. After completing the internship, she remained there for the balance of the year. During her job search that spring, she uncovered the lacrosse head coaching position at Princeton University.

Taking over as head coach of the Princeton lacrosse team became her next challenge. When she took the helm, it was necessary to assemble components for a winning team. The team was too familiar with losing—some athletes were satisfied with a win or a loss. Changing this mindset was gradually accomplished by boosting self-confidence, setting high goals, and activating the desire to win. Recruiting strong athletes also advanced the process. In her third year at Princeton, they made it to the final four. This was an important achievement for the seniors; reaching higher goals had happened far more rapidly than Chris had anticipated. Winning 3–9 in 1987, 7–7 in 1988, by 1989 the attitude change was complete; the record was 14–3. In 1989 Chris lost three seniors, and six more in 1990, necessitating another season of rebuilding. By 1992 they were strong again. Four out of the last six years they have won the Ivy League title; twice in ten years they have established an undefeated record in conference play. They have been ranked in the top ten all ten years. They have also been six times in the final four; finalists in 1993 and 1995; and in 1994 they were NCAA national champions. Chris envisions coaching as long as it is enjoyable and as long as she feels like an effective coach. She is not looking beyond coaching.

## MEMORABLE MOMENTS

Early victories were success milestones for Chris and the team. The first time they beat Penn State was in 1989. Over the years they have developed great rivalries, but their first time defeating Penn State left a lasting memory.

Another memorable moment happened the first time Princeton beat Harvard during Sailer's tenure—in 1993, the last year they won the league title. It was just like having a monkey on their back. It was the one team they could not beat. Even though they had a good team, when pushed against Carole Kleinfelder's Harvard team they were ineffective in weaving the critical components into a winning pattern. Once they won, it was like they had overcome a major a mental block and it was special; in fact, it was key to future playingfield successes.

Obviously, winning a national championship provided another great memory. In the preseason, the senior captains pulled out T-shirts with the front printed "1992 final four, 1993 finals, 1994——." On the back of the shirt it said, "The time has come." So the team was focused and committed to reaching goals. When Princeton came up against Maryland and Coach **Cindy Timchal**, her boosters claimed Maryland was not only the best team in the country, they were the best team that had ever been assembled. They were touted as being unbeatable, having not lost a game. Princeton thought they could have the best team ever for them and not win just because Maryland was good. Chris' team defeated Maryland, and watching the poise with which Princeton played was another great moment for Chris. At 34 she hoped she had not reached her professional peak.

## CHALLENGES

Probably the biggest challenge was beginning the two-year process of building a program that had faltered, as was earlier discussed. Chris knows Princeton is a wonderful place to coach, and a place where equity reigns. She has an exceptional relationship with men's lacrosse—they share facilities fairly. She gets administrative support and has not experienced the horror stories that have converged on other campuses. Like other coaches, she would like more press coverage, but for now she is largely satisfied.

## ROLE MODELS/MENTORS

*Phyllis Corl Pillard*—Chris feels fortunate to have had Phyllis during her high school years. Phyllis sparked Chris' love for sports. Having somebody take that kind of interest in her really made her appreciate what it meant to be active and involved.

*Averil Haines*—Haines was a teacher and coach of Chris' in the eighth grade. Julie Soriero and Val Walchak coached her in high school. Having these three women in her life at that particular time was critical in guiding Chris to focus her life.

*Julie Soriero*—Soriero had just graduated from college when she began teaching at Haverford. She was Chris's tenth grade teacher and a constant support for her in high school. Julie was somebody Chris could always talk to and could learn from in terms of how it was to play in college.

*Carole Kleinfelder*—Carole showed Chris how to build a collegiate program. She showed how it could be done by upgrading your schedule and by demanding a lot. She modeled assertiveness in dealing with the athletic department and would always be wanting to improve the program, the program's reputation, and the benefits for the women in the program. She had the team's interest in mind all the time.

There were few great role models in women's athletics during Chris' early years. Observing these quality women helped Chris to feel it was okay to be a female athlete.

## PHILOSOPHY OF COACHING

When asked about her coaching philosophy, Chris explained that, apart from lacrosse, she expects athletes to demand excellence from themselves. To go all out all the time, to work as hard as possible. The Princeton team motto is "hard work beats talent when talent doesn't work hard." She teaches athletes to aim high and take risks. Setting sights on goals and working hard day in and day out places goals within reach. The road to success is a long road, assuring one that little things culminate into positive results.

## CHANGES IN ATHLETES

Sailer feels that there has definitely been a change in athletes over the last 12 to 15 years. The level of fitness and training is much higher. The demands and the expectations coaches place on athletes require a year-round dedication to specializing in a sport. Today's athletes train harder, lift weights, and see themselves as athletes. They are not happy just having opportunities to play on a team; they want more and they have high expectations.

## LIFE BEYOND ATHLETICS

Chris likes to use her vacation time well. She has a place at the beach and loves the time she spends there. She has a boat and that is what she likes to do in the summer when she is not recruiting or running camps. She likes socializing with her friends—that really is relaxing for her. She likes to travel and read mysteries and books on the *New York Times* bestseller lists. The family, parents, and sisters live within a half hour of each other in Pennsylvania, so they see each other often. They come to the games with their kids.

## RECOGNITIONS AND ACHIEVEMENTS

### Accomplishments as a Player

- All-Conference Ivy League, 1980, 1981
- National Lacrosse Team Member, 1983
- New England Lacrosse Team for 8 years

### Coaching Recognitions in Division I

- Conference Championships: 1990, 1993, 1994, 1996, 1997
- National Coach of the Year, 1993, 1994
- National Championships, 1994
- Runners up, 1993, 1995
- Final Four, 1989, 1992, 1996
- Elite Eight, 1998, 1999
- Produced 23 All Americans

### Other Accomplishments

- New England Lacrosse Hall of Fame, 1996
- Harvard University Club Hall of Fame, 1997
- Haverford High School Sports Hall of Fame, 1998
- President of the Intercollegiate Women's Lacrosse Coaches Association

Photo courtesy of Penn State
University

# SUSAN DELANEY SCHEETZ
*Lacrosse/Assistant Athletic Director—Pennsylvania State University*

## INTRODUCTION

Eva Denlinger encouraged Susan Delaney Scheetz to pursue a teaching career rather than a secretarial profession. Denlinger was Susan's teacher, coach, and guidance counselor at Brandywine High School. Vonnie Gros at West Chester State further challenged Sue to try competing in lacrosse. Spurred by their counsel, she began teaching and coaching in junior and senior high and subsequently moved to a high profile position in the world of college sports.

## PERSONAL DATA

*Born*: March 6, 1947, Wilmington, Delaware

*Father*: John Delaney

*Father's Occupation*: Foreman for Dupont

*Mother*: Madeline Windett

*Mother's Occupation*: Homemaker

*Sibling*: John, Jr.

*Alma Mater*: West Chester State College—B.S., Health and Physical Education, 1969; M.Ed., 1975

## FORMATIVE YEARS

Susan's early education was in Catholic schools in Delaware. First at Saint Helena's and then at Saint Mary Magdelene, and, of course, she was taught by Catholic sisters. Susan puns "they got me into the right habit!" It is evident by this comment that Susan developed a sense of humor early in life.

## SPORTS HISTORY

The Catholic Youth Organization (CYO) leagues provided Susan the first opportunity to play organized sport. She was eleven when she started playing basketball and softball. The leagues in which she participated were under the auspices of the CYO and the city of Wilmington. Sports were a serious venture in these leagues and Ray Pankowski, the girls' basketball coach, even held play and strategy sessions in his home. After attending her ninth-grade year at Springer Junior High School, she attended Brandywine High School where she continued to compete in basketball and softball and got started in field hockey. At Brandywine, the girls competed on varsity teams, played in a conference, and shared facilities equally with the boys' teams. This was an unusual situation for girls in the 1960s. In 1965 Susan received the "B" Award as the outstanding female athlete.

Eva Denlinger, Susan's basketball coach, was instrumental in facilitating Susan's admittance to West Chester State College and directing her to a career in education. Again Susan played softball, basketball, and field hockey. When she met Vonnie Gros, the lacrosse coach, Gros made a point of teasing her about playing the wrong sport. While on the softball field, Susan found herself watching the lacrosse players and admired the fluid nature of the game. Watching kindled a desire to be part of the team, so in her sophomore year she quit softball and took up lacrosse. The next three years at West Chester were filled with basketball, field hockey, and lacrosse. She was also fully immersed in preparing to become a certified teacher of health and physical education.

## DECISION TO COACH

In 1969, while completing a teaching practicum experience in Media, Pennsylvania, a teaching position became available at Indian Lane Junior High in the same district. Susan was asked to take the position. Besides teaching 30 classes per week, she coached field hockey, basketball, and lacrosse. When Penncrest High School needed a lacrosse coach in 1975, Susan moved to Penncrest to coach lacrosse and later, in 1980, to run the women's physical education department. During her scholastic coaching career, she coached lacrosse and field hockey for thirteen seasons and basketball for ten. In eight seasons coaching lacrosse at Penncrest, she amassed a 90–20–3 record and a 1979 state championship.

Following a time of personal loss and conflict that included the death of her father and separation from her husband, Susan took a sabbatical leave from

Penncrest to become an assistant coach at Pennsylvania State University. Her intentions were to return to Penncrest after a year, but this never materialized because she accepted the opportunity to stay at Penn State. She served for three years as the assistant field hockey coach and the assistant lacrosse coach. In 1985 she became the head women's lacrosse coach, replacing Gillian Rattray. She served as head coach until 1989 when she gave up coaching to become the assistant athletic director. Still fulfilling this assignment, she is the administrator for thirteen women's sports.

Her elite experiences included coaching the U.S. Women's Lacrosse Squad from 1982–1989, coaching for the British Tour in 1987, coaching for the World Cup Team in 1986, and coaching the U.S. versus Canada in 1984.

## MEMORABLE MOMENTS

"When I would see student athletes move on and have success at the college or the U.S. level, that to me was rewarding." This highlight is only superseded by winning the high school district/state championship. Sifting through other secondary school memories also brings satisfying thoughts of players who may not have been the most outstanding athletes, but who were exemplary in implanting team spirit, improved their skills and their confidence, and left school with greater self-assurance.

The year 1987 was a thrilling year: it was the year they won their first national championship. They were not expected to win, and that was fine with Susan because she prefers being the underdog going into a National Championship. This win was especially "sweet" as Penn State had a goalie who not only was playing goalie for the first time, but it was also her first year to compete in lacrosse. To win its first NCAA title, Penn State had to reverse a regular season loss at the hand of top-seeded Temple University 7–6 in the championship after losing earlier to them 10–7. Penn State led 4–1 at the half, then built a 7–3 margin before Temple narrowed it to a goal with six minutes to play. Penn State protected its lead with pinpoint passing and a determined defense. It was a thriller, and it was capped off with Susan being named Coach of the Year.

Winning the second National championship was more difficult and involved more pressure on the coach and the team because the fans expected another win. Pollsters made it sound as if all Penn State needed to do was walk onto the field and they had an automatic win. Rated number one preseason, seeded number one, and ranked number one post-season, the Lady Lions were favored to win their second national title in three years. Penn State survived a late charge by the previously unbeaten Harvard team to win the championship game 7–6. Half-way through the season Susan figured this might be her last year to coach as it appeared a new opportunity was on the horizon. Assistant Athletic Director Della Durant had announced her retirement and Penn State officials had suggested Susan to fill the position. Susan's long-range goals included athletic administration, and even though she was looking to coach a few more years, she could not afford to pass up the opportunity to remain at Penn State. In four years of heading the lacrosse program she had produced a 67–9 record, two national championships, and two runners-up.

Associate Athletic Director Ellen Perry said of Susan when she was named assistant athletic director, "Moving Sue from the sidelines to the administrative offices is something of a mixed blessing. While we gain the value of her skills as an administrator, we lose an exceptionally successful coach. The same attributes that made her successful as a coach, the detailed preparation, the ability to motivate individuals to work as a team, the sense of anticipation and the competitive spirit, can successfully be transferred from her old responsibilities to her new ones."

## ROLE MODELS/MENTORS

*Eva Denlinger*—Eva Denlinger was Susan's high school teacher, coach, and guidance counselor. Eva encouraged Susan to make plans to become a teacher and coach.

*Vonnie Gros and Carol Eckman*—Susan was coached by both of these women at West Chester State College. Vonnie was the field hockey coach and Carol coached basketball. Susan claims both of these women were excellent mentors for her, and she feels she owes much of her coaching success to them. Under Eckman's leadership Susan was a teammate to **Marion Washington** and Linda Hill McDonald. This team won the First National Invitational Championship for Women's Basketball in 1969.

## PHILOSOPHY OF COACHING

Respect for the uniqueness of the individual athlete is the central focus of Susan's coaching philosophy. Branching out from the individual, she believes a coach must create an environment where team members unite in the pursuit of excellence. Her personal goal was to make certain athletes became better than they were when they entered the program. Creative drills are planned and practiced in a demanding atmosphere. Skill mastery is one of her paramount goals. Analogies, quips, and puns are used extensively to help players remember important items relating to game play. It is her belief that one must be a good teacher to be a good coach, and success is keyed to quality preparation.

Mentoring coaches without meddling is a challenge in her administrative role. Long term she is focused on becoming the best in the business. Reigning over thirteen different women's sports keeps her in constant contact with students and gives her a continuing opportunity to mentor the new coach.

## CHALLENGES

Susan considers herself lucky to have had some of her early athletic experiences at a time when many other females had little or no opportunity to compete. Being part of the growth of women's athletics has been very rewarding.

Facilitating the needs of a broad-based sports program is an enormous task. Fundraising is key as institutions try to meet gender equity obligations without cutting men's sport opportunities.

## CHANGES IN ATHLETES

Athletes bring a good deal of experience into present day college and university programs. They far exceed the athletes of the eighties in their backgrounds of experience and travel. They question more and their parents are more involved in the program and in questioning coaches.

Susan is concerned that some of the athletes feel they are more important than the overall program.

## LIFE BEYOND ATHLETICS

Susan is a self-proclaimed "frustrated golfer" who also likes to ski. Easy-reading books are her favorites because she can put them down and come back to them easily. High on the reading list are books by James Patterson and Barbara Taylor Bradford.

*Fatal Attraction*, *Raiders of the Lost Ark*, and *An Affair to Remember* are her favorite movies. Her favorite television series is *The Practice*.

## RECOGNITIONS AND ACHIEVEMENTS

### Coaching Recognitions in Division I

- National Lacrosse Championships, 1987, 1989
- Runners-up, 1987, 1989
- National Coach of the Year, 1987, 1989
- Produced 14 All Americans
- Three National Team Players

### National Coaching Assignments

- World Cup Coach, 1986
- National Lacrosse Squad Coach, 1982–1998
- USA Coach vs. Canada, 1984
- All American selection committee, 1985–1987
- Coach for U.S. tour to England, Wales, and Scotland, 1987

### Other Accomplishments

- Pennsylvania Lacrosse Hall of Fame, 1988
- West Chester State University Hall of Fame, 1990
- Delaware County Hall of Fame, 1998

Photo courtesy of Southwest Texas
State University

# LINDA K. SHARP

*Basketball—Los Angeles Sparks; Southwest
Texas State University*

## INTRODUCTION

It was a big step to become head coach of the Los Angeles Sparks. Prior to doing so, Linda Sharp had been a grammar, middle school, and high school
teacher, a university teacher and coach. Earlier, Linda coached basketball at
Southern California and at Southwest Texas University. While at Southwest,
she was asked to return for a coaching position at the University of Southern
California. On that same day, just two hours earlier, she verbally agreed to accept the Sparks head coach position. Even though the agreement was verbal
she did not turn back when USC made a second proposal substantially increas-
ing the monetary value of their earlier bid.

## PERSONAL DATA

    *Born*: Okmulgee, Oklahoma, March 14, 1950

    *Father*: G.W. Sharp

    *Father's Occupation*: United States Army

    *Stepfather*: Frank Thompson

    *Stepfather's Occupation*: Driller on an oil rig

*Mother*: Juanita Gleason

*Mother's Occupation*: Homemaker

*Siblings*: Gary, Toni, and Frank Jr.

*Alma Maters*: Fullerton Community College—Associate Degree, 1970; California State College, Fullerton—B.S., Physical Education/English/Biological Science, 1973

## FORMATIVE YEARS

By the time Linda was three, her parents were divorced and her mother had married Frank Thompson. Shortly thereafter the family moved to California where they made frequent moves until Frank found employment on an oil rig. They eventually settled in Cypress, California.

A fourth grade teacher, Mrs. Snider, a fifth grade teacher, Mr. Smith, and Linda's grandmother, Grace Gleason, all contributed to Linda's sports participation. Mr. Smith even went to the playground with Linda and taught her to shoot baskets and spin a basketball on her fingers.

## SPORTS HISTORY

Linda was launched into sports when her mother discovered that her young daughter did not have any serious interests. Her concern prompted a newspaper search for an activity that might interest Linda. The probe yielded an advertisement for Bobby Sox Softball, so she asked Linda if she would like to play on a softball team. Linda said "yes" and was introduced to a wonderful competitive experience.

Sports for junior high kids were mostly confined to sports days with very few competitions against other schools. Linda participated in every sport the school offered, but she preferred softball, track, and basketball. Changing schools disrupted her social and sporting ties and was generally disconcerting because the changes occurred too often. At John F. Kennedy High School it was different because she was there three years. She was active in student body affairs as well as sports and drew friends from both activities. In addition, she played badminton, field hockey, volleyball, basketball, softball, and track. She tried out for the swim team but was less successful. At John F. Kennedy High School, Linda became the first female to be awarded the title "best overall athlete." She starred as a point guard. Her athletic accomplishments were supported by two of the most influential people in her life: her mother and her grandmother, Grace Gleason. They both loved sport, especially her mother. The men in the family preferred to read books or watch movies.

Linda competed for the Anaheim Stars softball team, a counterpart team to the Orange Lionettes. At that time, the Orange Lionettes were one of the best softball teams in the country. Recruited by the Lionettes, she was unable to accept their invitation because the family was without a phone and the transportation necessary for her to attend practices and games.

High school graduation forced Linda to decide between marriage and college. Cognizant of the difficulty of combining the two, she decided to follow earlier educational plans for college—much to the disappointment of her boyfriend and parents. (Three months later her boyfriend married.)

The selection of Fullerton Junior College was a good choice for Linda. Her friends were there, and they had winning athletic teams—both important factors. A special attraction was their basketball program—they had the best basketball team and an excellent coach compared to other schools. At Fullerton Linda majored in physical education and prepared to coach; she had dreamed of teaching and coaching since she was twelve. Linda played on the school's basketball and softball teams, and on the B squad for volleyball. From Fullerton JC she moved on to California State in Fullerton. Her basketball team, Fullerton State, won the state tournament every year she played for the school. The first year, they won a berth in the national championship at Illinois State. The tournament featured 16 teams. Sometimes the teams played two games in a day—the 1970s were famous for this kind of competition; it was tiring but not unusual for the era. Her senior year, 1971–1972, the team won state and went to North Carolina for the national championships. They took third in the tournament after losing a game to West Chester State. **Marianne Stanley**, Basketball Coach at the University of California, Berkeley; **Theresa Grentz**, Basketball Coach at the University of Illinois; and **Marian Washington**, Basketball Coach at the University of Kansas also played on other teams in the tournament.

Graduation for most usually means a job with new challenges, but not in Linda's case. The job market was flooded with teachers seeking employment. She managed a part-time job at St. Mary's and was also a substitute teacher. It didn't take long for Linda to quit substitute teaching because it seemed like "glorified baby sitting." Finally, Mater Dei High School in Santa Ana, California, hired Linda—they had tired of her constant telephone calls seeking employment at the school.

Two classes in American literature made up her first-year teaching schedule along with teaching physical education and coaching. The second year she became school athletic director and also coached basketball, volleyball, softball, and started programs in tennis and track. She did this for three years while leading the basketball team to a 63–7 record. Good news travels and before long the University of Southern California sought Linda to be their assistant basketball coach. She was hesitant because she loved teaching high school and knew it would pose a new set of challenges. She said yes but kept her high school position and managed to fulfill both by starting at 6 A.M. with the high school team, then teaching all day, then driving to Los Angeles to assist with the varsity squad and coach the JV team. She was back home by 9 or 10 P.M. each evening. When the year concluded, USC offered her the position of head coach. This was 1976; women were just beginning to receive full-time salaries for coaching. USC had only managed to win five games before she arrived, and in 1977–1978 they went 11–13, in 1978–1979, 21–10. To Linda it seemed like an overwhelming uphill battle. By 1979–1980 USC was clearly on the basketball map for women. In 1980–1981 USC made it to the NCAA final four with a 23–4 record. The McGee sisters and Cheryl Miller put them in the basketball history books. USC won back-to-back national championships in 1983 and 1984. In 1982 and 1987, Linda served as head coach for the U.S. team in the USA Jones Cup, and in 1987 she was named head coach in the World University Games.

In 1989, after posting 271 wins, Linda left the University of Southern California for Southwest Texas State University. In 1994 she became the 26th most active women's basketball coach in Division I history winning 350 games. The Los Angeles Sparks, of the newly formed Women's National Basketball Association (WNBA), hired Linda away from Southwest Texas. After a mere few weeks, and a 4–7 record, Sparks General Manager Rhonda Windham announced Linda had been relieved of her duties as head coach. The Sparks had hired three coaches in two years and compared to the other WNBA teams, delivered a poor record.

## MEMORABLE MOMENTS

Keeping in touch with former athletes provides flashes of an indelible past. To Linda, contacts with prior athletes are as cherished as the memory of winning her first national championship. That championship was especially unforgettable as it was the first nationally televised women's basketball championship and it left her "nervous and shocked." USC was playing Louisiana Tech; at half-time they were down 11 points. The USC kids were so upset that Linda just stood in the back and tried to figure out what she was going to do. Walking to the front to address the team she turned and smiled at them. Linda said the players looked at her as if they thought she was crazy; apparently it gave them the confidence needed to align their energies and focus to win by 2 points. Hard work had played in their favor. After the win they were invited to the state capitol to meet the governor and receive his congratulations; they were also invited to the White House to meet President Ronald Reagan; this was a new experience for women in sport. But they were unable to go to the White House because the university did not provide the funds.

The following year USC came right back and won the championship again. Winning the championship the second year was much more difficult. This time the final match was against one of the most outstanding coaches in women's basketball, Pat Head Summit, and her University of Tennessee Club. USC hosted the championship in LA which added more pressure. The same players were on this year's team, and they were down two points at half. She did the smile routine again, it worked and, much like the previous year, they won again. This time they were granted the honor of meeting with President of the United States Ronald Reagan.

Another prominent reflection from Linda's memory bank focuses on her experiences while coaching the national team against Team-China in Zagreb, Yugoslavia in 1987. China had a 6'8" 340-pound post player, Zheng Hzaxia, currently playing for the LA Sparks. Linda claims it took half the U.S. team just to guard this phenomenal woman. "We were down by 18 points at half time, but came back to win in the closing seconds." Without a doubt, Sharp claims, that was the greatest comeback she ever witnessed in her coaching career.

## PHILOSOPHY OF COACHING

Fashioning one's coaching philosophy takes time and experience. With Linda, the process started by observing those who coached her. When she heard or observed their nuggets for success, she put her spin on the ideas and created her own unique scheme. Consequently, the Sharp philosophy vibrates with components gleaned from past coaches. Also, her ever-supportive mother and grandmother played a significant role in formulating a coaching concept.

Working with youth provides a rich source for grass-roots learning. Young people are honest and offer a reliable fountain of feedback to coaches wise enough to listen and learn. Linda has been wise enough to incorporate their suggestions in improving all areas of her coaching technique.

Another cornerstone to Linda's coaching philosophy and success was formulated around teaching fundamental skills, teaching discipline, developing a standard for helping team members to understand each other, and showing athletes how to have fun while learning. The theme: "Whatever you do, you need to enjoy it"; otherwise what is not enjoyable and fun becomes drudgery. It is her belief that to enjoy the program, athletes and coaches must be able to communicate. Another thing she stresses is "never give up, fight to the bitter end." Being willing to adapt her coaching style to each team's strengths has helped her teams win big games. She has no reservations about changing strategies or schemes in the middle of a game. Coaches must be able to adapt a game plan around each team's abilities. Because each player brings something different to a team, the coach must capitalize on individual talents.

To play tenacious defense is another must for Linda's coaching plan. Her teams have always been at the top of the conference in scoring defense, opponent's scoring percentage, and rebounding. One press guide described her this way: "Flexibility may be her best asset as a coach, but honesty and hard work make her an even better person." Integrity is also very important to Linda; she will not mislead someone to attain goals. Keeping her word, even when it is a tremendous sacrifice to herself, is without a doubt one of her paramount virtues.

## ROLE MODELS/MENTORS

*Juanita G. Thompson*—Linda's mother loves sports and has always been a model of constant support for her daughter.

*Grace Gleason*—Linda's grandmother also loved sports and encouraged Linda throughout her sporting career.

*Betty Lancaster*—Coaching Linda in high school in softball and basketball, Ms. Lancaster was stern, but she gave athletes freedom. She encouraged, supported, and respected Linda and her leadership abilities.

*Ms. Marilyn Matson, Mrs. Scott, Ms. Shirley McBride, and Ms. Jean Agee*—Each of these women coached Linda, and she feels that they each made a contribution to her as a coach and athlete.

## CHALLENGES

One of the main challenges Linda had to deal with was not having a facility. While coaching at USC, the team had to practice off campus. They played at Orange Coast Junior College or Riverside Community College. Because it was difficult to get the sports arena that was owned by the city, they played in the old North Gym. People can't believe that they played and practiced there. It made it very difficult and frustrating to schedule quality opponents. There were many positive things happening that year (1986) in other top programs, and they should have happened at USC to keep the program on top. By 1989 the frustration was too much, so Linda decided to move on.

## CHANGES IN ATHLETES

One of the biggest changes Linda sees in present-day athletes is that young people now play ball for scholarships rather than for the love of the game. For example, they play basketball because it is paying for their education, and they wait for the coach to motivate them because they most often do not have that intrinsic quality. Whereas when she played, "we busted our butts playing and loved the game; we didn't need somebody to motivate us. Now one only sees this internal motivation in the great players."

## FUTURE PLANS

Change has been Linda Sharp's constant. Raised in a family that moved often during her early years, she learned to manage change. Although an educator at heart, Linda's coaching career is marked by focus, energy, and resiliency. Currently, Linda is looking at future coaching opportunities; her talents will not be overlooked for long.

## FAVORITE AUTHORS

John Grisham, Danielle Steele, and Pat Riley are among Linda's favorite authors.

## FAVORITE BOOKS

Linda finds books about sports most enjoyable.

## LIFE BEYOND ATHLETICS

In her spare time, Linda enjoys sewing, golfing, traveling and reading.

## RECOGNITIONS AND ACHIEVEMENTS

### Coaching Recognitions in Division I

- Five Pac 10 Conference Championships: 1981, 1982, 1983, 1984, 1986
- Six Regional Championships: 1980, 1981, 1982, 1983, 1984, 1986
- Conference Coach of the Year: 1983, 1984
- National Championships: 1983, 1984
- Runner-up, 1986
- Five All Americans
- Women in Sports Programs Coach of the Year, 1983

### National Coaching Assignments

- Junior Olympics Silver Medal, 1979
- Olympic Festival, 1979
- World University Games, 1987
- Three Olympics
- Eight National Team Players
- Jones Cup Silver Medal, 1981

### Other Accomplishments

- Converse Hall of Fame, 1990
- U.S. Olympic Team Selection Committee, 1984–1988

Photo courtesy of Texas Tech
University

# MARSHA SHARP
*Basketball—Texas Tech University*

## INTRODUCTION

Daughter of a bank president, Marsha Sharp spent her early life in Tulia, Texas. Much of the family's early activities were centered around their Southern Baptist church.

## PERSONAL DATA

> *Born*: August 31, 1952, Oak Harbor, Washington
>
> *Father*: Charles Sharp
>
> *Father's Occupation*: Bank president
>
> *Mother*: Mary Dell McCloud
>
> *Mother's Occupation*: Physician's insurance clerk
>
> *Siblings*: Pam and David
>
> *Alma Maters*: Wayland Baptist—B.S., Physical Education, 1974; West Texas State—M.S., Education, 1976

## FORMATIVE YEARS

Charles and Mary Dell Sharp were high school sweethearts. They both graduated from Tulia High School. Charles went into the U.S. Navy for several years, and their first daughter, Marsha, was born in Oak Harbor, Washington, where he was stationed. Returning to civilian life, Marsha's father pursued more schooling and moved into the banking business. He became president of several banks in Texas and Carlsbad, New Mexico. When Marsha was in the seventh grade, her family returned to their Tulia, Texas, roots where she spent her junior and senior high school years. The Sharps were a religious family, so naturally they focused life around their Southern Baptist religion and the church programs. Marsha's parents wanted their children to experience America, so they loaded the family in their yellow station wagon and combined camping with their travel. In time, they visited the original 48 states. During her eleventh year, her grandfather died, leaving her father to manage the farm located on the outskirts of Tulia. The whole family became involved in the enterprise. Hauling hay, feeding hogs, and all the tasks of farm labor seasoned Marsha to understand hard work and physical labor. Farming left a lifelong impression that hard work is prerequisite to becoming good at something.

## SPORTS HISTORY

Sports were not available where Marsha attended elementary school. Charles Sharp was a sports fanatic, and he was a good athlete. He coached a little league baseball team in Lubbock, Texas, when Marsha was just eight years old. She accompanied him to practices and, when there were too few players, she got to play. On game days she stood behind the back stop and watched because she was a girl. She was not allowed to play even though she was as skilled as many of the boys.

All of this changed when the Sharps moved to Tulia where sports for girls were offered. Marsha joined the basketball team, and she competed on school basketball teams from eighth grade through high school. She also played tennis and ran track and competed in the long jump and the triple jump. The assumption was that Marsha would go to college, but she never entertained the possibility of becoming a coach as most high school coaches were men.

Being a homebody, Marsha was interested in a college close to home. She settled on Wayland Baptist University, where the Flying Queen basketball team was well known and considered the best in the country from 1940 into the early 1980s. Neil Record, a former pastor of Marsha's, was in charge of recruitment for the small school. He encouraged her to indicate she wanted to participate in the basketball program. Actually, she was going to Wayland for two reasons: she was a Baptist and she had an academic scholarship.

Although basketball was not her main interest, she played basketball for four years at Wayland Baptist. Harley Redin, a basketball pioneer and innovator, was the coach. During her final year she was coached by Dean Weese. The basketball team was called the Flying Queen because the sponsor, Claude Hutcherson, traveled in small planes and this was almost unheard of in those days. The team was flown from the east coast to the west coast to compete in states with teams that were mostly AAU affiliated. Some games were played with junior college teams and, in a few cases, regular colleges. Most of the big schools did not even have women's teams at the time. It is amazing that Marsha actually played basketball for two pioneering schools, Tulia High School and then Wayland Baptist. Wayland Baptist featured one of the strongest basketball teams to ever play in those early days of women's competition. Marsha was part of these early programs just because her home was geographically located in the right spot. She was never more than twenty-five miles from home during this time period.

Political science was Marsha's original major; she wanted to become an attorney—that is, before she caught the coaching "bug." Competing and associating with school peers who talked about their coaching dreams attracted her to the same dream. The new plan called for another major, so she changed to physical education and English. Equipped with an undergraduate degree in physical education, she moved directly into a master's program at West Texas State University where she received a master of science degree in education with a health specialization.

## DECISION TO COACH

Having made the decision to coach early in her college career, Marsha was afforded the opportunity to coach Wayland's freshman team during her junior and senior years. In the 1974–1975 season, she served as a graduate assistant coach. Upon receiving her master's degree, she took a job at Lockney High School as basketball coach and head track coach. Coach Weese played a significant role in helping her obtain the job. Not many schools will hire a 22 year old with no coaching experience. Weese told the school that he felt that the coaching experience she had at Wayland with the freshman team and as his assistant qualified Marsha for the position. Coaching for six years at Lockney, Marsha put together a 126–63 record with district titles in 1976, 1977, and 1979.

After six years at the high school, Jeanine McHaney, who started all of the women's programs at Texas Tech, recruited her as the assistant coach there. The head coach came from the University of Nevada, Las Vegas. The two coaches each taught part time in the physical education department that first year. At the end of the first year, the head coach resigned. Again Marsha was in the right place at the right time. Now 29 years old (in 1982), Marsha Sharp was named head coach of the women's basketball team at Texas Tech. Currently she is in her seventeenth year at the helm. In 1983 Sharp's Lady Raiders made their first NCAA tournament bid. Between 1991 and 1996, Marsha recorded five back-to-back conference championships, five sweet-sixteen appearances, and a national championship in 1992–1993. She also coached the Olympic festival teams in 1987 and 1990. In 1994 she was the head coach of the West Team that advanced to the Gold Medal Game.

## MEMORABLE MOMENTS

For Marsha, winning is winning regardless of the grade level. She believes it is about expending time and energy with a group you care about, so the feeling is the same. When she won district titles at Lockney, her feelings then were almost identical to her feelings of winning the conference championship. Watching kids become successful, sitting down with them to learn what their dreams are, and trying to help them achieve their dreams is also part of the good feeling. The relationship she has with athletes is what drives her to excel. She loves to win, but the most important part is that she likes to watch the process of success take place. She believes it is wonderful to be able to provide growth opportunities through scholarships, travel, and competition as these occasions produce maturity.

Filling the coliseum in 1992 and winning that conference championship in front of 8,300 fans was a definite career highlight for Marsha, especially when she remembered starting with 200 fans ten years earlier—this was a great accomplishment. Also, in 1992 the Lady Raiders won the national championship. That year she says they had the best chemistry of any team she's ever coached. They were absolutely unselfish; they had a focus and a competitive edge different from any team she had coached to that point. An athlete by the name of Sheryl Swoopes joined the team and moved them to a new level of excellence. Winning the national championship was a life-changing experience for Marsha. It resulted in such a flood of publicity and recognition that at times it was overwhelming. The community of over 225,000 people turned on its ear when Tech won. When the team arrived home to the football stadium, they were greeted by 40,000 fans. The athletes showed their academic colors, too; every single one of them graduated. The average crowd in 1997–1998 was 7,900, placing Texas Tech's attendance record as number four in the country.

## ROLE MODELS/MENTORS

*Harley Redin*—Without doubt, says Marsha, Harley Redin is one of her prime role models. Redin had a way of making those around him feel like champions. He surrounds himself with great people and great players and then employs a hard work ethic coupled with certain standards. Under his leadership athletes attended classes and did things correctly because "we're going to uphold the Flying Queen tradition." He often told the team, "We've got a lot to uphold, we better go to work!"

*Dean Weese*—Marsha worked for Dean her final year at Wayland. She credits this man with being the best of her teachers and the one that influenced her most. She was fascinated with his ability to develop players and take them to different levels by demanding their best.

## PHILOSOPHY OF COACHING

Marsha describes her coaching style as not based on emotion. She claims, "I do not stand on my head and do cheers in the dressing room." She believes motivation of teams comes through relationships built over long periods of time. She wants to look at faces and know hard work has brought them to where they are. When they won the national championship, the athletes motivated themselves, and she believes this is the way it works most of the time—great teams don't need coaches to spend quality time motivating them.

Nearly 100 percent of her players have graduated. That success is likely due to the fact that she stresses to her players the importance of making the most of their opportunity to get a top-flight education while playing basketball in a first-class program. The product of a strict work ethic, Marsha believes in a basic approach to life. She sees no conflict with the idea that there is no substitute for hard work. Honesty and integrity and success are important parts of one's life. With academics as the focal point, it leads to success on and off the court. Upholding the Texas Tech tradition is also high on her philosophical list of critical elements. Her own beliefs and methods have been combined with what she has learned from Harley Redin and Dean Weese.

## CHALLENGES

Clearly, any woman coach who coached a college team in the early eighties faced the same kinds of challenges. Success was a necessity, especially where people didn't want women's athletics to succeed. Most programs were separate, and for the men to share facilities and recognition was viewed as a hurdle to their own success, and they fought against it. Women at Tech had to overcome that and become accepted and respected. One of the toughest things was to draw spectators at women's events. Playing in front of from 150 to 200 people in those early years discouraged coaches and athletes. Presently Tech draws an average of 8,800 spectators per game. Getting acceptance and media attention helped and changed over time.

One of Marsha's big challenges was assembling a team to compete against the University of Texas. They had to be ready to play or be ready to be embarrassed. They finally made it. The anticipation inspired hard work and focus. Getting to the "sweet sixteen" five years in a row makes playing in the "sweet sixteen" almost a tradition.

Marsha is well-known in Lubbock; she claims to know about 6,000 of her fans. Having stayed close to home has created a situation that may be unparalleled. Most of her family lives close by. She says she knows every back road and small town in west Texas. She says she knows every eating place in every small town and every Dairy Queen in west Texas. Lockney alumni are some of her biggest fans and have season tickets to all the games. What Texas Tech has done financially to build a package that incurs fan support has given a terrific boost to the program. She believes loyalty is what makes it all work. And she believes in loyalty.

## LIFE BEYOND ATHLETICS

Marsha is an associate athletic director with a bit of slack being given on the administrative end so she can maintain her basketball program at a high level. She likes to golf. Her father has been ill lately, and she has helped out when needed. She likes to travel, and she has hosted cruises for a student association every summer for the past five years. Her community service entails speaking to various groups and serving on a number of boards and committees.

Marsha likes to read historical novels, biographies, and current-event publications. She likes theater and movies. She gets videos of the movies she misses during the basketball season.

## RECOGNITIONS AND ACHIEVEMENTS

### Coaching Recognitions in Division I

- Six Conference Championships, SWC: 1993, 1994, 1995, 1996; Big 12: 1998, 1999
- Conference Coach of the Year, Big 12: 1998, 1999
- Regional Coach of the Year, 1996
- Coach of the Year—Women's Basketball News Service, 1993
- WBCA Coach of the Year, 1994
- National Championship, 1993
- Six All Americans, 24 Awards
- One Olympian

### National Coaching Assignment

- Olympic Festivals

Photo courtesy of University of
North Carolina

# KAREN SHELTON

*Field Hockey—University of North Carolina*

## INTRODUCTION

As a West Chester State athlete, Karen not only lettered in field hockey, she led her team to three AIAW Championships. While at West Chester she also lettered three times on the lacrosse team. Twice an Olympian on the United States Field Hockey team, she claimed the 1984 Los Angeles Olympic experience "was my most proud moment because I represented my country on my home turf." It was at the 1984 games that the United States Field Hockey Team brought home a bronze medal.

## PERSONAL DATA

> *Born*: November 14, 1957, Honolulu, Hawaii
>
> *Father*: James Shelton
>
> *Father's Occupation*: Career Officer, Pilot, U.S. Army
>
> *Mother*: Gertruey Dansberg (Judy)
>
> *Mother's Occupation*: Housekeeper
>
> *Siblings*: Michael, Greg, Robert, Mark, Kimberly, and Virginia
>
> *Husband*: Willie Scroggs

*Husband's Occupation*:  Associate Athletic Director, former UNC
   Lacrosse Coach

*Child*:  William

*Alma Mater*:  West Chester State—B.S., 1979

## FORMATIVE YEARS

The Shelton children were spread over a 20-year span. Karen had three
brothers. Playgrounds, brothers, and living on military bases populated with
children helped develop her athleticism. Prior to entering high school, Karen
had attended four different elementary schools. The frequent moves strength-
ened family ties. When she enrolled at Paxson Hollow Junior High School in
Marple Newtown, Pennsylvania (a Philadelphia suburb), she began to develop
ties with students and teachers.

The first organized team sport for Karen was field hockey. Karen
Kostenbander coached the team, and she also taught physical education and
health. Karen also enrolled in Kostenbander's eight-week summer program in
field hockey and basketball. The itinerary included both sports daily in a
three-hour block. Karen loved the activities and never missed a day. The venture advanced her skills in both sports. Her self-proclaimed "tomboy" interests made her a valuable part of the athletic events where she competed with
her three brothers. At one time, her athletic skills were so much better than
that of other girls of the same age that it caused her embarrassment.

Such an early start in athletics proved fortunate as it presented opportunities to go on bus trips and compete against other schools while in junior high.
Many of Karen's professional colleagues didn't begin sports competition until
high school; Karen had already played basketball and run track while in junior
high. At Marple Newtown Senior High School, Karen continued basketball
and track and began playing lacrosse. The college students who instructed in
the summer camps encouraged Karen to get a college education, so as a high
school senior she made plans to enroll in college at West Chester State.

West Chester State sponsored four field hockey teams. Athletes began on
the freshman team and worked up to the varsity team. Karen made it to the
third team her freshman year, the varsity team her sophomore year, and during
her junior year she made the national team. Vonnie Gros coached West Chester's varsity team, and she also coached the national team.

During Karen's West Chester State career, she led the field hockey team to
three AIAW championships (1976, 1977, and 1978), and she was awarded the
Broderick Award, a prestigious recognition of the nation's top collegiate
player. Lettering in field hockey, she also lettered in lacrosse three times, and in
her senior year she was named West Chester's Outstanding Female Athlete.
Karen played on the Olympic teams in 1980 and 1984. After the 1984 games
she retired from the national team—she had been a member of the U.S. National Team from 1978–1984.

## DECISION TO COACH

Karen's dream to become a teacher was fulfilled at West Chester State. While student teaching she was astute enough be an assistant coach at Franklin and Marshall College, a Division III school. In the fall following her graduation (1979), she became a high school assistant coach, trained for the national team, and worked for the Michelin & Ness sporting goods company. The job took Karen to high schools in Pennsylvania, New Jersey, and Delaware where she marketed field hockey sticks. After playing on the Olympic team in the spring of 1981, the University of North Carolina head field hockey coach, Dolly Hunter, called her to interview for her position. Dolly was retiring and felt an obligation to help the school find a replacement. UNC's team was ready to develop into a national power. Dolly wanted to see a good coach with aspirations fill the position, so she sought strong candidates.

Karen went to the interview in a half-hearted, disinterested way. She was still on the national team and time constraints made an assistant coaching position a more attractive job, as she planned to compete in the 1984 Olympics. UNC offered a $7,700 salary and expected the coach to live in Chapel Hill. Karen told Dolly she wasn't interested, but Dolly persisted and convinced her to go to the campus, look at the facilities, and meet the team. So Karen drove to Chapel Hill just to look things over. The experience changed her life. Just looking helped her to see the university, the community, and it revealed a vision of what might be developed at the school. The athletic department didn't have a problem with her competing while coaching because the position was part-time. Karen took the job.

The first thing Karen looked for was good assistants to lead when she was with the national team. Next she upgraded the program with clear goals and objectives. Having a recognizable name in field hockey circles and being on the Olympic team made it possible to attract some top athletes. The strong academic reputation of UNC was another attraction. So her name, the school's fine academic reputation, and the lure of a beautiful campus gave the new coach a platform from which to hone a field hockey club worthy of a national reputation.

The dream and the plan became reality: UNC has received considerable national recognition since Karen stepped up to head the program. Now some of the best recruits come to UNC, and playing schedules have expanded regional boundaries to include regular competitions with many top teams.

Karen didn't ask for money to improve the program, but the coaches drove vans to competitions, stayed in inexpensive hotels, assigned four athletes per room, and ate in fast-food restaurants. They followed this plan for two years without asking for additional money, and then UNC started to expand the scholarship money. At that time, the NCAA allowed just nine scholarships; Karen was slated with three. The next year they added the fourth, and over several years they boosted the team to the NCAA maximum. Scholarships are still split but "blue chip" athletes receive full scholarship. In a recruiting year two of the best athletes in the country are identified, and UNC goes after them with an offer of a full scholarship. Subsequently, she seeks the "diamond in the rough" athletes who can run and develop; these people are offered partial scholarships, rewarding them as they continue to develop.

Former UNC Athletic Director John Swofford says of Karen, "Karen is one of the premier coaches in college athletics. Her team represents us in a first class fashion in every respect, on and off the field. That is a credit to Karen's leadership and her coaching expertise as well as her values."

## MEMORABLE MOMENTS

During her sophomore year, Karen played on the West Chester team that won the AIAW championship. The experience remains memorable as it was her first championship. Next came participating in the 1984 Olympic ceremonies in Los Angeles as part of the national team. Even though she was retiring and getting married in November, the Olympic experience was "absolutely my proudest moment" because "I represented my country on my home turf and, of course, we won the Bronze Medal."

Among her great coaching wins, the most significant and memorable was the defeat of Old Dominion for the first time. Old Dominion had long excelled and bested UNC for years, until UNC finally got the edge to drub the outstanding team. Since then, Coach Anders' Old Dominion team and Karen's UNC team have developed "a healthy rivalry based on mutual respect." Karen believes **Beth Anders** is the greatest collegiate coach in the United States. She admires Beth's "brilliant coaching mind," and the fact that she is able to develop teams that play the same way year after year. Karen marvels at Anders' ability to accomplish this continual feat of excellence.

The University of North Carolina has won four NCAA Championships: 1989, 1995, 1996, and 1997. They were devastated by losing in the finals in 1993 and 1994. The losses resulted from sudden-death penalty strokes. Going into the 1995 championship they were strong, young, and blessed with a lone powerful senior. This young woman had shown her formidable abilities by leading the team to a 24–0 season. The recent memory of losing in two previous championships added a good deal of pressure to the 1995 contest. UNC had been referred to as a "choker." In fact, one of the James Madison athletes announced, "ACC stands for Another Carolina Choke!" Sure enough they had to play James Madison in the semifinal; this was the same team that had defeated them the previous year. They also had to play Maryland, the team that defeated them in the 1993 finals. UNC, in spite of previous losses, was a wonderful team; they worked hard without complaining, and they were again with one lone senior who was also a significant leader. Much to their relief, UNC ran away with the game. The score was 2–1 at the half, and they finished strong with a 5–1 score. The following year they had four outstanding seniors. The team did not go undefeated (23–1), but they repeated their winning, giving

UNC its third national championship in seven years. Karen was named National Coach of the Year in 1995 and 1996; her conference championships totaled 14.

## ROLE MODELS/MENTORS

*Karen Kostenbander*—Karen admires the strong personality and inspirational methods that set Kostenbander apart from other teachers. It was nice for Karen to have someone outside the family who could give her extra attention. Karen Kostenbander was the person she turned to when she needed to talk.

*Cheryl Madigan*—Cheryl coached at Marple Newtown Senior High and was instrumental in influencing Karen to become a teacher-coach.

*Vonnie Gros*—Vonnie was another outstanding mentor. She helped Karen's career both at West Chester and on the national team. She groomed her to become an Olympian. Karen applauds Gros as "a wonderful human being with a brilliant field hockey mind who provides leadership to help athletes appreciate the difference between right and wrong."

## PHILOSOPHY OF COACHING

Karen's coaching success formula is based on finding at least two great blue-chip athletes who can lead. She teaches the team to be humble and to never think they are better than anyone else. She also teaches "the best team does not always win . . . the winner of a contest may be the one who performs the best at the moment or has luck." Having her players avoid injury is also high on her list for success—it is one of the critical components of the winning mix.

Players' respect is a crucial part of team success. Referring to her three championship teams, she notes they had great respect for each other. Molding twenty young women into a team means overcoming personality conflicts. Binding themselves into a championship team requires respect and understanding. In the process, athletes must learn to appreciate the hard work each person contributes to the common goal. Respect for teammates must flow into respect for opponents. A team can get a "flukey goal and out shoot the opponent 36–5 and still be defeated." This is why Karen teaches we "don't go into a game assuming anything."

Karen emphasizes hard work. She feels it is important to understand that worthwhile things never come easy and that success is rooted in hard work. It is also important to enjoy the little victories along the way rather than only looking to the end result: "To appreciate the journey and the means, so when everyone works hard and stops, the entire team feels good about the work accomplished, and they can feel pride in little things."

Attitude is next on the agenda. Karen likes athletes who nurture attitudes that soar over challenges and solve problems. She teaches athletes to identify the problems and at the same time to identify the actions necessary to overcome the problems. The "bring-it-on mentality" readies one for everything including the weather, the umpires, the specific opponents, or a specific player on an opposing team. Athletes must be able to handle their best shot and prove that they can overcome obstacles and self-imposed problems. Whining and complaining does not fly with Karen.

## CHALLENGES

Early on, sharing a practice facility with the football team posed problems. From 1981 until 1987, the field hockey team not only had to wait for the football team to practice, but they also had to wait until the marching band finished rehearsing. The field hockey team practiced at 7:30 P.M. for many years because the astroturf was so essential in developing a nationally powerful team—all of the nation's top teams played on astroturf. After Title IX and gender equity studies, the football team was told they must share prime practice time with the field hockey team. Now they practice from 1 to 3:30 P.M.

Although Karen understands the necessity for strong football and basketball programs, she feels it is a hindrance to operate under the attitude that football is more important than field hockey or that football players are more important than field hockey players; all athletes are student-athletes.

The respect she receives comes from having developed a successful program. Before she won three national championship titles, she did not receive the same measure of respect. But, for whatever reason, her name is now mentioned along with names such as Anson Dorrance, **Sylvia Hatchell**, and Dean Smith. This is a well-deserved change.

## CHANGES IN ATHLETES

In Karen's opinion, present-day athletes are pampered. They have more expectations of "what can you do for me?" They all want to get material things from team membership, instead of just playing for the passion of the game. Karen says she has a passion for the sport. She knows coaches such as Beth Anders also have a passion for the game. But today not as many students share that same passion. Many wonderful athletes have passed through her program; in 1997, she had six senior leaders who were outstanding young women. That was the most enjoyable year for her because they felt a passion for the game. Such athletes are few and far between, and earlier athletes had a healthier work ethic than present competitors.

## FUTURE PLANS

Karen wants to coach for four or five more years. UNC is building a new facility; they are going to build a locker room and meeting space where they can view tapes. She claims she does not want to be an old coach. Moving into the administration side of the game is appealing, as is conducting summer camps, or co-coaching. Karen expects to finish her coaching career by the time she reaches 50.

## LIFE BEYOND ATHLETICS

When Karen came to UNC, her office was next to the men's lacrosse coach, Willie Scroggs, who had feathered his cap with three national championships. Willie Scroggs and Karen were married in November of 1984 after the Olympics. Their son William was born in 1990. Young William likes the athletic atmosphere, and he enjoys the attention her team showers on him—who wouldn't? He is a soccer player and is starting to play basketball. Her husband currently serves as the associate athletic director.

Karen is also an avid golfer. Willie courted Karen on the golf course. He was the one who taught her the game, and they still enjoy golfing together. She likes to read historical novels and *The Winds of War* by Herman Wouk is her favorite. When she can muster the time, she also enjoys gardening.

## RECOGNITIONS AND ACHIEVEMENTS

### Accomplishments as a Player

- Three-time Broderick Award Winner: 1977, 1978, 1979
- National Collegiate Player of the Year, USFHA, 1983
- National Team, 1978–1984
- Two-time Olympian: 1980, 1988, Bronze Medal
- World Cup Team: 1979, 1983
- Played on three AIAW National Championship Teams

### Coaching Recognitions in Division I

- Fourteen ACC Conference Championships: 1983–1991, 1993–1997
- ACC Conference Coach of the Year: 1986, 1987, 1988, 1989, 1994
- Regional Coach of the Year, 1994, 1995
- National Coach of the Year, NCAA, 1994, 1995, USFHA, 1996
- Four National Championships: 1989, 1995, 1996, 1997
- Twenty-one All Americans, 29 Awards
- Three Olympians, 2 Alternates

### National Coaching Assignment

- Olympic Festivals Coach of West, 1987

### Other Accomplishment

- United States Field Hockey Hall of Fame

Photo courtesy of Temple
University

# TINA SLOAN GREEN

*Field Hockey and Lacrosse—Temple University*

## INTRODUCTION

"I'm thankful to God, to Temple University, and to all the people that supported me in my career. I have a burning desire to give back. The next decade of my life will be spent giving back to the world and the African American Community. Hopefully I will repay some of the debts I owe because without sport, I would not have been able to provide my family with many of the advantages they have enjoyed." This promise was voiced by Tina Sloan Green after completing a highly successful coaching career.

Tina rose to athletic and academic excellence through the nurturing and encouragement of parents who valued education.

## PERSONAL DATA

>*Born*: April 27, 1944, Philadelphia, Pennsylvania
>
>*Father*: Norwood Sloan (deceased)
>
>*Father's Occupation*: Electrician, Philadelphia Naval Ship Yard
>
>*Mother*: Sally
>
>*Mother's Occupation*: Homemaker

*Siblings*: Norwood, Gene, Cordelia, Leonette, Beatrice, and Teresa

*Husband*: Frank Green

*Children*: Traci and Frankie

*Alma Maters*: West Chester State University—B.S., 1966; Temple University—M.Ed., 1970

## FORMATIVE YEARS

Nurtured in a two-parent home along with six brothers and sisters, Tina's parents encouraged each child to receive a high school education. Neither of them had earned a high school diploma, but they valued education. Tina attended grade one through grade eight in a small school in Eastwick, Philadelphia. The school's graduating class was thirteen students, and Tina was not just a leader, she was a fine student.

Before entering the ninth grade, she was designated as gifted and selected as one of twenty African American young women to attend Girls' High School for the academically gifted students of Philadelphia. At this elite school, Tina, though educationally disadvantaged, determined she was truly advantaged because it had been her privilege to be born to exemplary parents. Tina's parents, Norwood and Sally Sloan, were deeply religious people. They endowed their seven children with high-minded values. These values accorded Tina essential guideposts for all her personal and professional endeavors.

## SPORTS HISTORY

Girls' High School offered a new sphere of opportunity, and it did not take Coach Jane Weitzenhoffer long to discover Tina and recruit her to play field hockey, basketball, and volleyball. A talented athlete, Tina made varsity in each sport within six weeks. Excelling in athletics granted Green the platform to distinguish herself among an accomplished student body of primarily white, upper-middle-class youth. Prior to attending Girls' High School, her sporting experiences were confined to kick ball and stick ball on the streets of Eastwick, Philadelphia. Girls' High School was a subtle change for a girl schooled in a black, lower-socioeconomic community. Weitzenhoffer's invitation opened a refreshing window of possibility.

Green's first real athletic experience arose at West Chester State College with Coach Vonnie Gros. Gros coached field hockey, and she was a member of the United States Field Hockey Team and the United States Lacrosse Team. This expert teacher and coach realized Tina's athletic potential and helped to hone her athletic skills. Today, Green lauds Gros and Weitzenhoffer as the most memorable of her mentors.

## DECISION TO COACH

The positive influences and advice of female coaches, coupled with Tina's love for sport, aroused her desire for further education. She graduated from West Chester State with a degree in physical education and began teaching at Unionville High School in the Philadelphia suburbs. Green made history being the first African American to teach at the school. There she organized and coached the school's first lacrosse team and was an assistant basketball coach and a physical education teacher. This hefty schedule of coaching experience furthered her desire to give back to the black community.

Green also wanted a social life, so she obtained a teaching position at William Penn High School. This urban, economically disadvantaged black school in Philadelphia was fortunate to hire Green, and she felt fortunate, too; it was like being at home. Here she was assistant basketball coach and coach of her worst sport, swimming. The assignment turned into a wonderful learning experience. She found that kids excel regardless of background or color when given a good mix of opportunity and exposure and that with these ingredients kids performed as well as those with ample resources.

## COACHING

From William Penn High School she moved to Lincoln University. Lincoln's black male student body was being transformed into a coeducational school. She was appointed basketball coach, cheerleader squad coach, and physical education teacher—she even found time to start a lacrosse team. Lincoln afforded Green a broad latitude for experimentation. The young women came with few athletic skills, so Tina began with the basics. Building on basics, the basketball team improved enough to beat Cheney State College, the team coached by the well-respected basketball coach **Vivian Stringer**. This would be the one and only time she defeated Stringer's team. Tina was especially happy at Lincoln because at an all-black institution racism was not a glaring issue. After four years at Lincoln, Green became restless for an opportunity to coach elite athletes. Her own competitive level had won her membership on the United States Lacrosse Team that had competed in Australia and Great Britain. She was ready and eager to work with highly skilled athletes.

In 1974, Tina Green was hired at Temple University as a teacher and the coach of the field hockey, lacrosse, and badminton teams. Her salary was $11,000 per year. Temple University teams had club team status and as such they received little competitive respect. When Tina attended lacrosse and field hockey meetings, coaches dismissed the thought of considering Temple as a legitimate contender; they actually scoffed at the idea. However, Tina knew before long the tide would shift to favor Temple. After five strenuous years, Green's recruiting produced athletic females with positive attitudes and the will to win. Newly instituted athletic scholarships helped draw skilled athletes, and Green's venture bore fruit. By the late seventies, Temple University's lacrosse team was winning. In the eighties, lacrosse at Temple University was known and respected in athletic circles across the country. In 1982 the team took their first national championship. They did it again in 1984 and repeated the performance again in 1988. The 1988 season was fabulous: they defeated every team they played, plus they won the national championship. The eighties belonged to women's lacrosse at Temple University.

Like others of her generation, Green credits her many opportunities for achieving coaching excellence to being in the right place at the right time. Although in the right place at the right time, Tina knows that Affirmative Action gave her prospects that otherwise would have been closed to a black female. Indeed, students at Temple University amplified the call for African Americans to be given opportunity at their institution and this, no doubt, helped assure Sloan Green a slot to gain a professorship while distinguishing herself as a coach. Nonetheless, Tina was somewhat unique, too. As a ten-year-old she regularly organized and coached other youngsters in sporting events. A child who grows up running this kind of an operation will naturally dream bigger and dare to envision herself as a career coach.

For every individual who receives the world's accolades, there is usually one who stands in the shadow as a buttress to the visible one. Frank, Tina's husband, is her buttress. Frank encourages her in every major professional decision. He encouraged her to move to Temple University, he encouraged her to accept and seek professional assignments, and in her absence he manages meals, children, and home. When she is discouraged, he sustains her hopes and dreams, and they become his too.

## CHALLENGES

As for challenges, Tina's perspective is that successful people look on obstacles as temporary conditions in need of solutions. Citing the example that although she won the national championship in 1984, she did not receive the coach-of-the-year award knowing full well that had she been from a different racial background she would have received the award without question. To spend too much time lamenting this unreasonable oversight saps one's energy; therefore she refuses to worry about the trivial because it is not worth the energy.

## PHILOSOPHY OF COACHING

Tina attributes her coaching strengths to rich experiences she has had as an athlete, an underdog, a parent, and a teacher. Drawing from this well, she is able to identify with parents and athletes. She feels that because she has been there, her talent for motivating athletes is one of her greatest assets. She teaches athletes that obstacles are part of life, and a successful person looks at an obstacle as a temporary condition. In her own life she de-emphasizes the trivial to avoid sapping energy. This philosophy keeps her from spending undue time wondering why it took ten years to be named coach of the year. This honor came only after she had recorded a perfect season and garnered the national championship the same year. Yet other coaches received coach of the year by winning the national championship and without a perfect season. It would appear that race played a major part in her incredible coaching accomplishments being overlooked.

Tina teaches athletes to know what they want out of life, to define goals, and then to concentrate on the positive. Coaching circumstances have not been graced with blue-chip athletes, the best equipment or facilities, but she feels that she had something more important—heart. To her, heart is the willingness to win and to achieve in spite of the odds. From coaching she has learned that when people believe, they are miraculous. For Green, the most rewarding part of coaching is to work with athletes who are written-off by other coaches as not quality athletes or people who become outstanding lacrosse players and outstanding students. She also finds it rewarding to hear from them years later and know what they have accomplished. The culmination of her twenty years of coaching is to watch kids grow up. The most exciting moments in Tina's coaching career came each time she won a national championship. Each title was an exhilarating experience; nothing could recapture the excitement of these three moments in coaching. Tina's coaching philosophy is simple: "be the best that you can be, and that is all I will ask."

## ROLE MODELS/MENTORS

*Norwood and Sally Sloan*—Tina's parents were the most impressive of her role models.

*Eloise Cuker*—Just one year older than Tina, Eloise was an outstanding African American student athlete at Girls' High School.

*Jane Weitzenhoffer*—Jane Weitzenhoffer was the high school coach who recruited Tina to play field hockey, basketball, and volleyball. Weitzenhoffer saw Tina's potential and made certain she participated in athletics.

*Vonnie Gros*—Vonnie Gros was Tina's coach at West Chester State. Gros recognized Tina's great athletic ability and helped her to become better in all of her skills.

Obviously when athletes achieve their best, great ones emerge and the team can reach untold possibilities. Perhaps Tina's Temple University lacrosse team was the most diverse team in the country. This reality spurred Tina to deal with economic, social, and ethnic diversity in a very individual way.

## FUTURE PLANS

Tina Sloan Green retired from coaching after 17 years. She retired "when lacrosse was feeling good about me, and I was feeling good about lacrosse." She had coached three teams to national championships, two to second place standings, and four to third place finishes. When she left coaching, the lacrosse team was ranked in the top ten.

Tina and Frank's daughter is a junior in college at the University of Florida. She played on the 1998 University of Florida NCAA championship tennis team. Their son Frankie is a nationally ranked tennis player for boys 14 and under (Junior Tennis). Naturally she would like to enjoy some of their competitive events. Tina also wants to watch their careers and give her husband a break. Now the academic world claims her time.

In addition to writing about her experiences, she has authored chapters in several books and co-created the Black Women in Sports Foundation. The goal of the Black Women in Sports Foundation is to guarantee black women an opportunity to participate in sport at all levels, not just as athletes. Green is a model spokeswoman for blacks and carries the banner that will continue to open windows of opportunity for those who have faced limited opportunity in a world filled with possibilities. She wants to expose African American girls to all sports because she knows they can excel in any sport. Her attitude is filled with zest and a promise to foster change in incremental steps and touch the lives of individuals one at a time. In the same personalized way she energized athletic teams, Tina's level of "giving back" benefits not only the community and the nation, but also the world.

Tina has been described by fellow professionals as quiet, modest, strong-willed, uncanny in self-confidence, a noncomplainer, and a truly fabulous person. She was further painted as one who is loved by athletes, and colleagues say she is firm, tough, and decisive.

## RECOGNITIONS AND ACHIEVEMENTS

### Accomplishments as a Player

- All-American Field Hockey, 1965, 1966
- National Field Hockey Squad, 1966
- National Lacrosse Team, 1969–1971

### Coaching Recognitions in Division I

- National Coach of the Year, Lacrosse, 1988
- Seven Final-Four appearances: 1979, 1983, 1985, 1986, 1987, 1989, 1990
- National Champion, AIAW, 1982
- National Champion, NCAA, 1984, 1988
- Produced 23 All Americans
- Produced 8 National Team Players

### Other Accomplishments

- First African American head coach in the history of women's intercollegiate lacrosse

- Athletic Hall of Fame, Temple University, 1994
- Athletic Hall of Fame, West Chester State University, 1988
- National Lacrosse Hall of Fame, 1997
- Co-founder of Black Women in Sports Foundation

Photo courtesy of University
of Delaware

# JANET A. SMITH
*Lacrosse—University of Delaware*

## INTRODUCTION

Janet Smith claims the University of Delaware is the only lacrosse team to have won a national championship on a football parking lot. Obviously, Janet is not only a fine coach, but she is also a superb athlete—she played four years on the United States Lacrosse Team and was inducted into the Lacrosse Hall of Fame and the University of Delaware Athletic Hall of Fame, both singular honors.

## PERSONAL DATA

*Born*:  August 1, 1944, Philadelphia, Pennsylvania

*Father*:  Charles E. Smith

*Father's Occupation*:  Boeing Aircraft

*Mother*:  Esther Weiss

*Mother's Occupation*:  Homemaker, then sales associate at Lord and Taylor

*Sibling*: Pamela

*Alma Maters:* Ursinus College—B.S., Physical Education, 1966; West Chester State University—M.Ed., 1973; University of Delaware—Ed.D., 1995

## FORMATIVE YEARS

Born into a family who lived in the Philadelphia suburbs, Janet enjoyed early years enlivened by the ever-present activities of same-aged neighborhood children. Life was easy then—creating new games or playing hide-n-seek, kick ball, dodge ball, or football. At Enfield Elementary School, gym classes were her favorite as was summertime play in a softball league.

## SPORTS HISTORY

Janet started playing softball in a league while in fourth grade. The junior high she attended did not offer softball, but they did have basketball and field hockey. She played basketball in the seventh grade and then went out for field hockey in the eighth grade. It was fortunate for her that she lived in this area because they had very good athletic programs at Temple University and Ursinus College. The schools she attended either had physical education teachers who had attended these schools and were well prepared, excellent instructors or student teachers from one or the other of the schools who were also well qualified. Two of her teachers had been All-American field hockey players. Jean Edenbarn Stiles, who was one of her field hockey coaches, was one of the All-American field hockey players. During these impressionable years, Janet wanted to become either a math teacher or a physical education teacher.

Janet attended Springfield Township High School in Montgomery County, Pennsylvania. She played field hockey, basketball, and lacrosse for three years. Mary Anne Harris, an All-American field hockey player, coached the basketball team and was assistant field hockey coach. Her physical education teacher, Jane Vaché, was also the head hockey and lacrosse coach. The combination of these three outstanding coaches not only provided excellent coaching, but they caused Janet to think about coaching as a future profession. When thoughts of higher education emerged, Janet naturally thought of Temple University, Ursinus College, and West Chester State. She was also impressed by a high school history teacher's wife, Marge Watson, who coached lacrosse at Ursinus—the school had developed many All Americans in both field hockey and lacrosse. Many graduates of Ursinus had also competed for the national teams. After applying to all three schools, and being accepted by the same, she chose Ursinus. Scholarships were not available at the time.

Janet majored in physical education and played field hockey and lacrosse all four years. She was on several all-college teams in both sports. Her most noteworthy recognitions came after college when she was named to the U.S. developmental squad in 1967–1968 and went on to make the Philadelphia lacrosse team and the U.S. reserve lacrosse team. From 1970 to 1974 she played on the United States Lacrosse Team and took three international tours.

## DECISION TO COACH

Janet's first teaching position was Pottstown High School. She taught physical education and health and was assigned as head coach of field hockey, lacrosse, and the junior varsity basketball team. Five years at Pottstown opened new interests, and when a friend told her of an available opportunity to teach at the prestigious Tatnall School, a private school in Wilmington, Delaware, she investigated the job. The school wanted an elementary physical education teacher who could coach lacrosse and field hockey. The job was especially attractive because the incoming lacrosse players had played since the fourth grade as opposed to the ninth grade. She accepted the job and also became assistant varsity basketball coach and head seventh and eighth grade basketball coach. Concurrently while teaching and coaching at Tatnall, Janet earned a master of education degree (1973) from West Chester State University. Sanford School, a private school in Hockessin, Delaware, learned of her talents and secured her to start a physical education program and reorganize their athletic program. For two years she carried out assignments much like she had at Tatnall and was also the girls' athletic director.

While sitting in a hockey camp (1979) surrounded with hockey coaches, Janet heard talk that the University of Delaware was looking for a head lacrosse coach and an assistant field hockey coach. The next day, after thinking about the possibility, she applied for the position, received an interview, and was offered the position. The assignment was to coach and teach lifetime activities and skills to physical education majors. It took just two years for Janet to launch the Delaware Blue Hens to a nationally competitive level. The team won the Division II AIAW National Championship in 1981 and 1982. By 1983 they took the NCAA Division I National Championship title. Throughout the eighties she served in numerous national and regional administrative capacities and produced nine All Americans, seven of whom made it on to the national squad. In 1997 she was inducted into the Lacrosse Foundation Hall of Fame and the University of Delaware Athletic Hall of Fame. In 1989, Janet resigned from coaching to become a full-time teacher of physical education in the physical education teacher preparation program. She is an associate professor at the University of Delaware in the Department of Health and Exercise Sciences. She was inducted into the Delaware State Sports Hall of Fame (May 1998) and inducted into Ursinus College Hall of Fame for Athletes (October 1997).

## MEMORABLE MOMENTS

Teachers often instruct more than one youngster from the same family; so it was with Janet at Pottstown. She had coached a young woman who came from a family of seven. At the University of Delaware, she again taught two sisters from this family. It was exciting for her to teach these young women in a college setting.

Remembering championship athletes and teams stirs deep emotions for Janet. Reflecting on a Division I championship brings nice memories of by-gone days where five freshmen who became starters in 1981 actually competed on the team for four years. At this time, the team was under AIAW Division II; they won the AIAW Division II championship two years in a row. In 1983 the NCAA assumed governance of Women's Athletics, resulting in the program moving to Division I. The 1985 team won the national championship.

## ROLE MODELS/MENTORS

*Jane Vaché*—Jane Vaché was Janet's high school physical education teacher and coach. Vaché was prominent in lacrosse and had coached the U.S. touring teams. This mentor aroused Janet's interest in becoming a physical education teacher.

*John Wooden*—John Wooden is the much-celebrated former UCLA basketball coach. Janet has used bits and pieces of Wooden's "Pyramid of Success" and has also used inspirational quotes and ideas and passed these on to players.

## PHILOSOPHY OF COACHING

During her first year of collegiate coaching at the University of Delaware, Janet remembers the first day of try-outs early in the spring of 1979, thinking, "This is like a candy store, so many good players." All the kids could catch and throw. So it was a matter of teaching them what her philosophy was and getting them to buy into it. She strongly believes it is important for athletes to understand where the coach is coming from so the team can be a unit. As Janet had been coached by All Americans and had been on the national squad, she readily recognized the necessity for a group of players to work together to succeed.

To her, conditioning is a basic necessity, but she does not believe in running for the sake of running. If athletes push themselves through drills, they need not go to great extremes in conditioning programs like many other athletes do. Her athletes didn't have scholarships; they were there because they wanted to be, so they had to enjoy what they were doing. She stressed, until her last day of coaching, the idea that athletes must enjoy what they are doing because this is the only way they benefit the most from the experience. At the same time, she encouraged athletes to play the best they could; if they lost, it was all right because they lost fair and square.

Lacrosse was a team game, a passing game, and interceptions were a must. She stressed the catch-cradle-pass game and emphasized, "You've got to catch it and immediately get rid of it. If we move the ball around, nobody can stop us as they won't have time to set up a zone."

When Janet came to Delaware, she started reading about mental imagery. She tried to get players to think about their positions specifically and then play the best mental game they had ever played: seeing the interception, shooting the ball past the goal keeper, making the catch and so forth. They could see themselves doing it, and they started believing it. Often at half time she would finish what she had to say, and the team would quietly work on mental imagery. It must have worked—the team won three national championships back to back.

## CHALLENGES

One incident, and the only one that really stands out in Smith's memory, occurred when the men's lacrosse team had a field of their own, and the women's lacrosse team did not. It is her claim that Delaware is the only lacrosse team to have won a national championship on a parking lot. The women's field was a grass area that was used for a football parking lot. On rainy days one of the male coaches would bring the team over to practice on her field—understanding that when men play lacrosse they literally tear up the field. "So they would come and play on our field, and we both played crossways on the field. One day it was just too much and I said, 'If you are going to practice on my field, I am going to practice on your field.' So she started to take her team over to the men's game field, and he said, 'No, he would leave.' That was the last time that ever happened."

Funding usually poses an obstacle in most athletic programs. "At that time, the university did not have scholarships for women's lacrosse. Parents would come to visit with their daughters and ask, 'What will you give me for my daughter?' It was a like a meat-market mentality. The money spent on recruiting an athlete these days is ridiculous."

## CHANGES IN ATHLETES

When the NCAA assumed governance and the AIAW became defunct, a big change occurred in how recruiting took place. Women were forced into recruiting the same way the men recruited. Under AIAW rules, schools were allowed to hold auditions. Athletes were actually invited to a school to audition, thus allowing coaches to watch athletes perform without extensive travel and money expenditure. In this system, recruits could be placed in game situations to assess their skills. That is no longer possible under NCAA rules.

## LIFE BEYOND ATHLETICS

Having completed her doctorate, Janet is currently an associate professor teaching full time in the teacher-preparation program at the University of Delaware. However, she still likes to attend and support the teams in their athletic events. She likes to garden and loves her flowers, her two dogs and three cats, and her country home. She enjoys reading nonfiction and especially likes reading about and observing wildlife.

## RECOGNITIONS AND ACHIEVEMENTS

### Accomplishments as a Player

- National Team Reserve, 1968–1969
- National Team Member, 1970–1974
- U.S. Tour to Australia, 1969
- U.S. Tours to Great Britain, 1970, 1975

### Coaching Recognitions in Division I

- Four ECAC Conference Championships: 1983, 1984, 1986, 1987
- Conference Coach of the Year, 1984, 1989
- Regional Coach of the Year, AIAW, 1981, 1982
- Three National Championships, AIAW Division II, 1981, 1982; NCAA Division I, 1983
- Nine All Americans
- Two National Team players, seven squad members

### National Coaching Assignments

- U.S. Squad Assistant Coach, 1982–1986
- USWLA Selection Committee, 1980–1985

### Other Accomplishments

- Lacrosse Foundation Hall of Fame, 1997
- University of Delaware Athletic Hall of Fame, 1997

Photo courtesy of University of
California, Berkeley

# MARIANNE STANLEY
*Basketball—University of California, Berkeley*

## INTRODUCTION

It was on the playground across the street from her home where Marianne's Uncle Jack, her father's twin brother, took her for her first basketball lesson. He took her after she "hounded him to death to take her and show her how to shoot the two-handed underhand shot." That constituted her first basketball lesson and started the chain of events leading to a career in coaching the game.

## PERSONAL DATA

*Born*: April 29, 1954, Yeadon, Pennsylvania

*Father*: James Crawford

*Father's Occupation*: Superintendent, Yellow Cab Company/ Salesman, Lance Co.

*Mother*: Marjorie Halt

*Mother's Occupation*: Homemaker, reading teacher

*Siblings*: Suzanne, Jim, Marjorie, Richard, Paul, and David

*Daughter*: Michelle

*Alma Mater*: Immaculata College—B.S., Sociology, 1976

## FORMATIVE YEARS

Life for Marianne started in Upper Darby, a Philadelphia suburb situated just outside the border of West Philadelphia. The houses were row houses, and the neighborhood was fairly densely populated. The Crawfords lived on an end street directly across from a playground. She had plenty of neighborhood kids with whom to play, and she took advantage of every waking moment outside of school work or chores to go to the playground and practice shooting basketball hoops and playing all sports.

Marianne attended Saint Lawrence Elementary School, a first through eighth grade Catholic school. The school was fairly strict and did not offer gym classes, but it did support Catholic Youth Organization (CYO) programs.

## SPORTS HISTORY

Marianne the sixth grader participated in extracurricular school activities and in a well developed sports program sponsored by the Catholic Youth Organization. In the early 1960s many of the public schools did not have organized sports programs, but the kids in Philadelphia and the Philadelphia suburban areas were afforded tremendous opportunities to participate in well developed and well established CYO programs. Organized basketball became 12-year-old Marianne's dream come true.

Another Catholic school, Archbishop Prendergast High School, was where she received her secondary education. The school had more than 2,500 female students and her graduating class was more than 600 strong. Marianne continued to compete in the Philadelphia Catholic League basketball program where they had formed a sixteen-high-school competitive schedule. Marianne also found the time to compete in the softball program.

In addition, Marianne competed at every level in grammar school and high school and in AAU teams as well. She reports to have had some very influential coaches. In grammar school Kathleen Morgan coached basketball, and in high school Barbara Mooney was her coach for all four years. Her softball coach was Ann Condon. These coaches combined their skills to lay a sturdy foundation for Marianne's athletic career. Her AAU coach was Marti Byron, a Philadelphia legend.

None of Marianne's family had attended college, but when she was in the ninth grade she began to take all the college-prep classes necessary to be on the right track for college. By the time she was a sophomore, she was really serious about going to college.

When college enrollment time arrived, she registered at West Chester State University. It was considered one of the finest teacher colleges in the mid-Atlantic area and was especially well recognized in Pennsylvania. It was also just a 45–minute drive from the Crawford home. Marianne was happy to attend West Chester as she was familiar with the school and knew they had a fine basketball team coached by Carol Eckman. Marianne enrolled in physical education teacher education and remembers after the first three days wondering, "What am I doing here? The basketball team is good, and I don't know what else to major in, so teaching physical education sounds good."

At that point she thought the school was a little too big for her in some ways, and she really didn't want to teach physical education. The choice was based on her love for sports and kids. Knowing she did not want such a physical education career, she left West Chester and enrolled at Immaculata College declaring a sociology major.

## DECISION TO COACH

After six years of dating Rich Stanley, Marianne married him in May after her junior year in college. In that same year (1975), Immaculata went to the final four where she saw signs about Title IX and the opportunities for women in athletic careers. She could see herself as a coach and knew she could combine her love for sport and work with young women. Marianne's daughter, Michelle, was born in October of her senior year. After graduating, **Cathy Rush** asked Marianne to be her part-time assistant basketball coach at Immaculata College. Marianne accepted and took Michelle with her to practices and to home games. Cathy's two little boys and Marianne's little girl looked like siblings getting an early courtside start.

While at Immaculata her teams played in four national championship games, and she became visible in basketball circles. Looking for a full-time position, she applied at several places and interviewed for a "dream job" at West Point. She was a finalist but lost out to ten-year veteran coach Joe Ciampi. Next, Old Dominion's Athletic Director Jim Jarrett, traveled to Philadelphia for an interview with her and after the discussion it seemed like a good fit, so she accepted the job.

In her first year at Old Dominion, the team won thirty games. One of the players Marianne inherited was Nancy Lieberman; another was Inge Nissin. Those two led the Old Dominion team to three national championships, one NWIT, and two AIAW national championships. Nancy Lieberman moved on to have a stellar international career and currently coaches the Detroit Shock in the Women's National Basketball Association.

When Marianne started as a head coach, at the age of 23, she was only a year older than Nancy and Inge. Marianne recognizes such opportunities do not occur these days. She claims it took her about five years to feel fully competent, confident, and comfortable in honing the skills to do the job the way she thought it should be done. Having come from Immaculata, she knew her standard of excellence had to be the caliber of a national championship team.

After Old Dominion won the NCAA National Championship in 1985, Marrianne began another job search feeling she needed to make a move. Old Dominion had been great in supporting her, and she felt the athletic department's leadership was outstanding. They were clearly ahead of their time in supporting women's sports. She was invited to apply at several prestigious schools. Michelle, her daughter, was 12 $\frac{1}{2}$ years old, and she felt that Michelle really needed to be closer to her family. So she took a job at the University of Pennsylvania. UPenn had a non-scholarship program, and it had been a losing program. The school had rigid academic standards, and it was a greater challenge than she had supposed. The mentality which accompanied losing was difficult for her to accept because it was the antithesis of everything she believes sports should stand for. She also knew she could not transform a group of 18–21 year old youngsters into overnight winners. They, too, had set ideas, but she took the challenge to try and resuscitate the foundering program at UPenn.

While at the University of Pennsylvania, Marianne made good use of time by attending the Wharton School of Business continuing studies program. It took two years before she felt the need to examine other prospects that were emerging. The lack of athletic scholarships made it difficult to recruit top-caliber players to UPenn. The head-coaching job opened at the University of Southern California in 1989, and she was hired for the position. The USC team went 8–19 her first year, and in the three subsequent seasons USC made post-season appearances in the NCAA tournament and finished in the Elite Eight in the 1991–1992 season. The hiring mandate given to Marianne was "get us back to where we were in the championship years of the mid-eighties." The key to success was to attract talented competitors, and luckily Marianne signed an outstanding player, Lisa Leslie. Lisa Leslie and a superb class of recruits empowered USC with the talent to move from an 8–19 team to a 23–8 team and finish in the Elite Eight.

In the summer of 1993, after another successful season (22–7), Marianne approached the USC administration for gender equity salary. "To make a very long story short, I was fired over equal pay!" Even though Marianne was unsuccessful in her bid for equity, several other institutions around the country have acknowledged the contributions of women coaches and compensate them accordingly.

In 1994 Stanford coach Tara Van Derveer was preparing to take a leave in order to coach the Olympic women's basketball team for a year and arranged for Marianne to work for her at Stanford as a marketing assistant on a part-time basis. She started in January of 1994 and remained there for ten months before taking a leave to prepare for the equity trial. Again, in March of 1995, Marianne was seeking a job. Tara invited her to co-coach at Stanford with Amy Tucker, Tara's long-time assistant. The two coaches struck a 29–3 record and made an NCAA final-four appearance.

At the end of the season Marianne applied for the head coach's job at the University of California, Berkeley. She negotiated a four-year contract. Presently she is in a rebuilding mode.

In addition to Marianne's collegiate career, she had considerable international experience having coached or assisted ten different U.S. teams, including gold medal wins in the 1983 World Championships, 1986 Goodwill Games, and 1986 World Championships.

## MEMORABLE MOMENTS

The first championship Marianne coached was in North Carolina. It was special because her former coach from Immaculata, Cathy Rush, was courtside doing network television commentary. For her it seemed like a continuance of the legacy they had shared; now the mentor was watching her student coach a national championship team in the second year of her career. The team went 35–1 that year.

The second big highlight was in 1979 at the championships held at Central Michigan. The year for Old Dominion's team had been excellent, and when they got to the final they had to play against a great Louisiana Tech team coached by Leon Barmore. The height of Old Dominion athletes really helped as they had a 6'5" player and a 6'8" player. This was a great asset as they were able to win the championship against Tennessee, and what a significant win for Marianne's Old Dominion team.

The third highlight occurred while hosting the Russian Olympic team in 1979. The Russian team had a player, Julianna Semiova, who was 7'3" and weighed 280 pounds. For years the Russian women had dominated basketball at the international level and at the Olympics. Julianna had been the main factor in that domination. The Russians had not lost a game in 21 years. This was their first trip to the United States. Julianna was a very skilled player, but she had trouble moving around well because of her size. The Norfolk facility had never been sold out until the Russians came . The cold war was still on. There was a hysterical atmosphere, and at half-time the score was tied, and Marianne actually ran to the locker room with excitement. It was the first crowd of over 10,000 for women's basketball. Old Dominion kept up with the Russians until four minutes to go, and the Russians pulled ahead and won by 10 points. It was the closest score spread of the tour, and they had put a scare into them—that did not often happen.

Finally, the memory of playing in four national championship games as a college athlete: "It was a high almost too good to be true."

## ROLE MODELS/MENTORS

Marianne had the unique experience of being coached by women at every level from grammar school to college and to the AAU teams. These coaches were "capable, caring and ambitious role models, every single one of them was female."

*Kathleen Morgan*—Marianne's first coach was nurturing in a very personal way. Marianne felt "she walked on water."

*Barbara Mooney*—Barbara Mooney understood kids. Marianne was a very headstrong youngster, and Mooney helped to instill discipline in her. She sat beside her on the bench when she lost her temper and composure. This woman not only understood kids, but she also understood the game, and she helped Marianne to grow both in the game and off the court. Barbara was a very successful coach and one of the best in the Philadelphia Catholic League.

*Marti Byron*—Marti coached the Philadelphia Teamsterettes AAU team. Marti was an icon in AAU circles in Philadelphia. She made a significant contribution to the game and to Marianne at a time when very few people really invested their resources and time in young women and their athletic pursuits.

*Cathy Rush*—A good deal of the vision Marianne has about coaching philosophy and basketball is attributed to Cathy Rush. "I can't even begin to tell you how indebted I feel to her." Cathy was a good coach who started the team off with a bang. The team orientation was very convincing: they learned they had to be unselfish. Cathy knew how to blend player talents into a cohesive unit. "She had a great defensive philosophy and was tough on fundamentals. She was a tremendous teacher and had the ability to pull the best out of each and every player on the team."

## PHILOSOPHY OF COACHING

Marianne is intense and passionate about what she does. Once players see that is a good thing, they understand her better. She tries to emulate the strengths of past mentors. After her players get past their initial apprehensions, they find out that Marianne is an approachable person and coach.

She believes in getting together with players off the court so they know she is interested in other aspects of their lives. She wants the athletes to know they are important outside of basketball, too.

Marianne teaches doing well at what one chooses to do. To her, basketball is a perfect microcosm of life. It provides a safe environment to develop skills and learn through experience. Basketball teaches one that getting knocked down is not the end of the world as it is possible to get back up and move forward.

Teaching fundamentals, paying attention to details on the court, and personalizing skills are all critical components of coaching. She does not believe in "trying to squeeze athletes into a cookie cutter mold. You tailor skills and spend a great deal of time trying to draw out the best from each player in terms of their special talents."

## CHALLENGES

Being a single mother was a challenge while Michelle was growing up. Michelle has now graduated from college and teaches elementary school disabled kids in Phoenix, Arizona.

Getting the support of the administration at the University of Pennsylvania was difficult and was really a contrast after having been at Old Dominion, which was on the cutting edge in terms of support for women's athletics.

The gender equity suit was a real strain, and yet it opened the way for other women around the country to get equal pay for same-role coaching. The suit made it difficult for a long while in terms of finding another job, but Marianne practices what she teaches. Get up and go again. Having supportive friends as she does has been very much appreciated. Marianne has a tremendous ability as a coach who knows how to teach and inspire and motivate youngsters to perform.

## CHANGES IN ATHLETES

The good changes are inherent in the opportunity women have to pursue sports. Today it is "cool to be an athlete." When Marianne was in college, she paid her own educational expenses for the first three years. In her senior year she was awarded a "$500.00 talent scholarship," not an athletic scholarship. Two "talent scholarships" were awarded that year, one to a female in music and the other to Marianne. Obviously such a mentality operated in the mid-seventies. Now, due to Title IX, there are all kinds of "athletic" scholarships available for women.

The other side of change suggests fewer and fewer females come to sport for the sheer love of the game. It is Marianne's belief that many first love sport because they love the physical activity. "Along the way the pure love of the sport can become jaded." Marianne and most of her generation paid for their own education and bought their own shoes, warmups, etc. She, like other coaches, believes it doesn't matter how much athletes receive, most still want more. The coach and the school can never do enough to satisfy the demands of many athletes. Noting this to be a sad commentary on what has happened in sport, she tries to instill the idea that one must develop an appreciation for everything provided in the athletic arena.

## LIFE BEYOND ATHETICS

Marianne likes the notion of continuing her education. She is an avid book collector and is especially endeared to women and minority authors. She loves movies and is partial to epic films like *Lawrence of Arabia* and *Doctor Zhivago*.

## RECOGNITIONS AND ACHIEVEMENTS

### Accomplishments as a Player

- Olympic Team Finalist, 1976
- All American: 1974–1975, 1975–1976
- Played in Four AIAW National Championship Games, 1973–1976

### Coaching Recognitions in Division I

- Regional Championships: 1979, 1980, 1981, 1982, 1983, 1984, 1985

- NWIT, 1978
- Three National Championships: AIAW, 1979, 1980; NCAA, 1985
- Six Final-Four Appearances: 1979, 1980, 1981, 1983, 1985, 1996
- PAC Ten Conference Co-Coach of the Year, 1996
- Nineteen All Americans, 10 Kodak All Americans

### National Coaching Assignments

- Olympic Festivals, 1981
- World Championships, 1983, 1986, 1993 Gold Medal
- Goodwill Games, 1986, Gold Medal
- Pan Am Games, 1991

Photo courtesy of Rutgers
University

# VIVIAN STRINGER

*Basketball—Rutgers University*

## INTRODUCTION

"A basketball player is artistry in rhythm and motion—when she finally gets it." This is Vivian Stringer's appraisal of an athlete's polished performance. To view an athlete as "artistry in motion" makes sense as many of Vivian's own talents were germinated and cultivated by a father who used the organ as his artistic medium. In the humble company-owned home, Vivian's parents taught her she could do anything she wanted to do, but they also warned that some situations would require her to use her ingenuity to find a way to accomplish her desires.

## PERSONAL DATA

*Born*: March 16, 1948, Edenborn, Pennsylvania

*Father*: Charles H. Stoner

*Father's Occupation*: Mine Worker and Musician

*Mother*: Thelma

*Mother's Occupation*: Homemaker

*Siblings*: Verna, Charles, Timothy, Madelin, Richelle, and Jack

*Husband*: William Stringer (deceased)

*Children*: David, Janine, and Justin

*Alma Mater*: Slippery Rock University—B.S., 1971; M.S., 1972

## FORMATIVE YEARS

Edenborn, Pennsylvania, was a small coal-mining town populated by between three and four hundred people. Vivian had her beginnings here. The family lived in a company-owned home on the city's main street. All of the houses were essentially alike. Stop signs and stop lights were unheard of, but there were several taverns and three or four churches. When one gave directions, Main Street was the reference point. A neighbor was as likely to reprimand a child as the child's own parent. Children belonged to the community, and the community helped to raise the children.

Many children came from the surrounding area to attend school. The elementary school educated students from grades one through eight. The teachers most often had been there long enough to lay claim to having taught their students' mothers, fathers, aunts, and uncles. Vivian's Latin teacher, Mrs. Yanger, still stands out in Vivian's mind as a strict disciplinarian who held high expectations for her students, especially if she had worked with other family members. This woman was quick to inform students if they had not done their best and what her expectations were for them.

Vivian's father was a coal miner. He mined five days a week, but on the weekends he exchanged mining tools for an organ. A jazz organist, he also played the organ for the local church. Music was a constant in the Stoner home. Sometimes the family spent hours playing various instruments; often their music sessions would go until 3 o'clock in the morning. Mr. Stoner played the organ, and Vivian was on the piano (she started piano in second grade). There was a saxophone, a trombone, a singer, and a rhythm section of kids playing pots and pans. On Saturday musicians often came to jam at the Stoner house. The front doors were opened and townspeople gathered on the porch to enjoy the music. Vivian and her sister eventually tried out for the well known Ted Mac Amateur Hour televison show.

An intelligent, energetic man, Vivian's father made certain the family visited the zoo, the museum, and similar educational sites. Little money was available for vacations, so the family took their trips to the mountains. Because Vivian's father had started a family at a very young age, he lacked a formal education; therefore he pushed his children, as did their mother, to work hard and complete their homework each night. All six of the Stoner children went to college; Vivian, Tim, and Verna earned college diplomas.

## SPORTS HISTORY

The small coal-mining community did not provide girls' sports. In high school Vivian became a cheerleader, which put her close to sports even if it was on the sideline. However, at other times during the week and on the weekends, she played basketball with boys on the varsity teams. This helped satisfy her interest in competition.

Vivian's piano teacher was very encouraging, and as a result Vivian felt that to be a musician like her father would be ideal. By the time she reached high school, she realized she wanted to get out of the community. Vivian recalls, "I was a person who had regular dreams and visions." Watching television promoted her dreams, especially when she saw people all dressed up. She would think, "I want to do that." She wanted to do something that would be important and have a positive effect on the lives of many of people. With such a dream she planned to attend college.

One of her teachers suggested Slippery Rock State College, because of its excellent reputation. Based on this suggestion, and the fact that it was a three-hour commute from her home, she chose Slippery Rock. During her freshman year, Vivian met her future husband, William D. Stringer. At the time, William was a senior and a member of the gymnastics team as well as the track team. He came from a farming family of nine children, and all but one of the nine had graduated from college. Bill was serious, honest, genuine, and very giving of himself. He graduated from college and went on to medical school for two years. Eventually he turned to exercise physiology after dropping medical school because it was too difficult for him to be in New York away from Vivian.

Originally Vivian wanted to teach in a high school, but she changed her mind when she recognized that she would have to teach students who did not want to be in school. This motivated her to complete a master's degree to broaden her professional choices. In July 1971, William and Vivian visited Cheyney State College in Cheyney, Pennsylvania. She was fortunate because Cheney State President Dr. Reed Rolfman, showed great confidence in her abilities and hired the 22-year-old inexperienced teacher as an assistant professor to teach classes in health and physical education. In September of 1971, Vivian married William Stringer.

Cheyney State was a wonderful place to begin. The president had told her, "we want you to come here and take your wings." Vivian started with a powerful vision of what she wanted to accomplish. She knew she could do anything she set her mind to, so she immediately envisioned a team becoming good enough to compete in a national championship. She was hired as an assistant professor to teach classes in health and physical education. Coaching appointments were distributed through a volunteer system. A faculty meeting was held and first it was requested that someone volunteer to coach softball. She raised her hand. Next was volleyball. She raised her hand, thinking that everyone would want to coach the volleyball team. Finally they asked who would like to coach basketball. She looked around and nobody put up a hand, so her hand shot up. Vivian recalls that being selected to coach basketball "gave me one of the happiest feelings of my life."

## DECISION TO COACH

Volunteering to coach was Vivian's beginning to a distinguished coaching career. Essentially she took a recreational-type program and steered it into a competitive enterprise. From 1971 to 1983 her teams went 251–51 (.831), and they played in the final four the first year the NCAA sponsored the national tournament.

In 1983 Vivian had two children: David, who was two and Janine (Nina), who was 14 months. Vivian felt like the happiest person in the world. Two beautiful children, a wonderful husband, a house, and a job she loved. She was living the American dream. Then in November little Nina contracted meningitis. They fought for the child's life over a six-month period of time. From November until April, Vivian never left the hospital. It seemed the Stringer family's whole life had turned around. Meanwhile, several schools tried to recruit Vivian to coach, including big-name schools. The Stringers loved where they lived and didn't want to leave, but they felt like they needed a fresh start. They wanted to go where they had access to great medical facilities. The University of Iowa contacted Vivian; Iowa had a large teaching hospital right on campus. This was a place that could fill their need for a fresh start and provide much-needed medical facilities for Nina to recover.

Financial support at Cheyney made running a high caliber program without offering scholarships a difficult proposition when competing against scholarship schools. What a shift! At the time she left Cheyney, they had just been ranked number four and played in the final four. Iowa, on the other hand, was ranked 298 out of 301. In the year before she moved, Iowa had won only seven games, but the administration told Vivian, "You will not be limited on your schedule, the players you recruit, or anything else." In the first year (1983–1984), the team went 17–10. In the second year, 1984–1985, they went 20–8, and by the third year, 1985–1986, they went to the second round of the NCAA tournament. Vivian coached basketball at Iowa for twelve seasons and established a record of 269–84 (.76).

Towards the end of her sojourn in Iowa, tragedy struck again. William suffered a heart attack and died. Later, Vivian learned William had gone to the doctor 5 to 6 times in the six weeks prior to his death, and he had gone to the hospital, too. He had not felt well, but he didn't tell Vivian because he knew she would worry. Vivian was traveling a good deal during this time, and she knew he was taking medicine to lower his cholesterol, but she didn't realize the severity of his health problem. Even when he complained about heartburn or an upset stomach, he made it appear insignificant. His death was a shock.

After William's death, Vivian lost the desire to remain at Iowa. In the spring of 1995, **Theresa Grentz** vacated the head-coach position at Rutgers University. Later that spring, Rutgers contacted Vivian to see if she was interested in coaching there. No longer happy at Iowa, even though she had just recruited seven high school All Americans, she walked away from Iowa. She knew she had to move on and get a fresh start. Vivian was named head coach at Rutgers on July 14, 1995. At the time of this writing, Vivian was in her third season at Rutgers. Her record is 22–10, and she is taking her team to the "sweet sixteen." This accomplishment makes her the only woman to take three different teams to the NCAA Tournament plus two different teams to the final four. On at least five occasions she has coached national teams: 1979, 1981, 1985, 1989, and 1991. (See Recognitions and Achievements for further details.)

## MEMORABLE MOMENTS

Vivian describes her two most memorable moments as a "two-edged sword." She had grappled with personal lows and had achieved professional highs. Her daughter Nina was sick in the hospital when the Cheyney team made it to the final four, and her husband died when Iowa made it to the final four.

Another memorable moment came after Vivian staged a televised appeal to Iowa fans to break the basketball attendance records. The fans responded 22,157 strong. Aisles were obliterated by the massive crowd. This was a wonderful greeting for the teary-eyed coach. The game was with Ohio State. From fewer than 400 fans in 1982 to an amazing 22,157 fans in 1984 was the community's show of respect for an outstanding coach who had orchestrated an enviable program.

## CHANGES IN ATHLETES

Athletes in former days, according to Vivian, were from families where they learned the value of work and how to accept responsibility. Today's athletes are more focused on themselves. Too many come from divorced families where one parent cannot handle all the responsibilities of parenting.

In Vivian's opinion, today's athletes are better skilled and have a more thorough knowledge of the technical aspects of the game. These athletes bring overwhelming issues with them. They have many more pressures than earlier athletes, they are more likely to blame others, and they are more fearful of failure. Many are searching for happiness; they tend to run away from difficult situations rather than face and resolve their problems. Vivian often wonders if she gives team members counsel that will assist them to build a positive life. Many present day athletes have tender egos that are easily fractured. She feels it is rare to meet a young person who is confident enough to accept the fact that winning, losing, risking, and happiness are all vital parts of life.

There was a time when she would not have considered using a sports psychologist for athletes. That, too, has changed because time does not permit a head coach the essential hours to resolve problems and attend to the duties of a head coach.

## ROLE MODELS/MENTORS

*Mr. and Mrs. Stoner*—Vivian's parents Charles and Thelma Stoner instilled in Vivian the belief that she could accomplish anything—but the price was hard work. They fostered a desire in her to work hard for the family and to work equally hard in her studies. What she learned at home has been vital to her role as a leader, a coach, and a teacher. From these experiences she knew that she, too, must teach others to pay the price for success. Her father never missed a day at the coal mines even though he had suffered the loss of both legs by the age of 42. Watching her father continue to risk his life in the mine without the benefit of legs painted a permanent picture of dedication. She is forever grateful for her roots and what makes her who she is. She attributes who she is and what she has become to a wonderful family background and the opportunities provided her at Cheyney College.

*Coach John Chaney*—John, more than anyone else in the world, shaped Vivian's philosophy. He taught her how to approach people. She calls him the most consistent and honest person she knows. He is a man filled with anecdotes of wisdom. He never sacrifices his principles. He is "absolutely brilliant." Chaney and Vivian have spent hours talking about basketball and life. He is one of two people she tries to emulate.

*Dr. Anne Griffith*—Anne was Vivian's basketball coach at Slippery Rock College. Ann taught Vivian what respect was all about. She was a young, strict coach, but Vivian could always see the soft side of her too. The two made a special connection during those years. Anne attended Vivian's wedding and was there for her during the deaths in her family. Vivian considers Anne one of her best friends. It was she who influenced William and Vivian to go to Iowa.

## PHILOSOPHY OF COACHING

Vivian's philosophy is scattered throughout everything that has been written about her. For example, the *Rutgers Press Guide* provides four of Vivian's philosophical statements; one is entitled "Success" and the others are "Dreams," "Acadamic Success," and "Personal Development."

### Success

Success is measured not only in wins and losses, but also in knowing where you came from and what you have accomplished. We measure our program in a total sense. We are trying to translate the lessons learned on the basketball court to the lessons in life. We have grown in our competitive attitude. Now we are prepared to take that growth to the next level.

### Dreams

To dream is one thing. To believe is another. And to work very hard to make those dreams become a reality is altogether different. Few people know the price that must be paid, and even fewer are willing to pay the price. If you work hard each and every day, you can make those dreams come true!

**Academic Success**

There is no amount of money in scholarship or any other form that can begin to pay for the amount of time and commitment that an athlete gives to maintain the balance that is necessary to be successful in the classroom . . . but the degree that they receive from Rutgers can never be taken away, and with it they can open the doors to life and success. The athlete cheats herself if she does not get a degree. It is my responsibility to point in the right direction, to arrange every bit of assistance that is humanly possible, and continue to encourage my athletes to earn their degree so they have choices in life.

**Personal Development**

It is important that the athlete grow in several ways: emotionally, physically, academically, and spiritually. All of these elements affect her personal developments.

Vivian reports that there are times when she is upset, even with winning, because she disapproves of the way the game was played. She is really satisfied when she sees the game as a piece of art. "It's like beautiful music. It's orchestrated and I see art." After seeing the game as art, she goes to her office and closes the door, puts her feet up, and just smiles because she loved the way they played defense: the intensity they had, the smart choices they made; and then she knows that they're learning the game. The more they become students of the game, the more the game moves towards consistency. The athletes learn to break down the game tapes, and they can explain the whys and the wherefores. Vivian teaches each team member to diagnose her own personal game as well as the team's game and teaches them how to choose to make the corrections. She believes coaching is teaching in the finest sense, and at this she is par excellence.

## LIFE BEYOND ATHLETICS

It is Vivian's desire to write a basketball book and create some basketball films. She has an interest in establishing a coaching school. Vivian believes coaches really need to be educated so they will be constructive in dealing with the young people. In addition, she would like to get into game commentating.

This talented woman loves music. She plays the keyboard, and she loves to listen to music. Jazz and gospel music are two of her favorites. Both impact her moods. She likes politics, and she likes to read—especially motivational rags-to-riches stories where people beat the odds.

Family is extremely important to Vivian. David attends college at North Carolina State University where he plays football. Nina and Justin are both at home with Vivian. She dearly loves her children and spends quality time with them.

## RECOGNITIONS AND ACHIEVEMENTS

### Coaching Recognitions in Division I

- Big Ten Conference Coach of the Year, 1991, 1993

- Big East Coach of the Year, 1997
- Regional Coach of the Year, 1985, 1988, 1993, 1998
- National Coach of the Year, 1982, 1988, 1993
- Black Coaches Association Coach of the Year, 1997–1998

### National Coaching Assignments

- World Championships, 1989
- World University Games, 1985
- Pan Am Games, 1991 Bronze Medal
- National Team, 1979, 1981

### Other Accomplishments

- Carol Eckman Award, 1993
- *Sports Illustrated* Coach of the Year, 1993
- *USA Today* Coach of the Year, 1993
- Former Member of Kodak All American Selection Committee

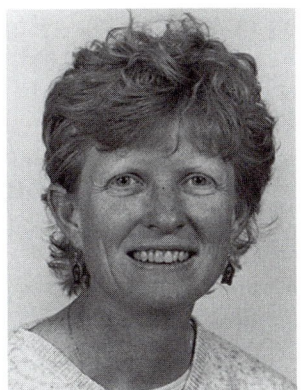

Photo courtesy of University
of Maryland

# CINDY TIMCHAL

*Lacrosse—University of Maryland*

## INTRODUCTION

After several rich competitive experiences as an elementary school youngster, Cindy Timchal put down her softball glove and hockey stick and stopped competing. The junior high cultural disease called "lack of confidence" took a bite. Once in high school she regained the confident part of herself, and sport regained its place as an integral branch of her life.

## PERSONAL DATA

*Born*: September 16, 1954, Upper Darby, Pennsylvania

*Father*: Daniel Timchal

*Father's Occupation*: Electrician for Gulf Oil

*Mother*: Anna Hamer

*Mother's Occupation*: Homemaker and government employee

*Sibling*: Mark

*Alma Mater*: West Chester State College—B.S., 1976

## FORMATIVE YEARS

Havertown, Pennsylvania, Cindy's hometown, was a new suburb where all the brick homes were built by the same contractor. The neighborhood was filled with games and fun. In elementary school, gym was Cindy's favorite class, and her first physical education teacher, Mr. Blessing, was a favorite. It was he who provided the encouragement for her competitive drive. Under his leadership she competed against other schools in field hockey and softball.

Family vacations were spent at Margate, New Jersey, playing on the beach and fishing in the ocean. Activity was important to the Timchal family, but Cindy waited until high school before again turning to athletics. She bypassed lacrosse and basketball for tennis.

Having lived just outside Philadelphia it was natural that she would attend the highly respected West Chester State College to seek a physical education degree. West Chester offered lacrosse teams and, because Cindy had never played lacrosse, she tried out for the lacrosse team and became one of three inexperienced freshmen to make a freshman team. She was good enough to play tennis but elected to do something different. There were four lacrosse teams, two freshman, a JV, and the varsity. The coach, Judy Wolstenholme, was an excellent role model, motivator, and teacher. Wolstenholme provided the environment where Cindy could continue to excel in the sport. Although not highly skilled, Cindy consistently improved through the challenging practices and competitions. She focused on doing the things she did well until she made the varsity team. Her next goal was to become a starter who could make an impact for the team. By graduation time Cindy had earned letters in lacrosse, tennis, and track and field.

Cindy did not plan to coach. Her focus was on becoming a physical education and health teacher. But the reality was that most physical education teachers also coached.

After graduation Timchal sought a full-time teaching position in physical education and health. She began as a substitute and then taught full-time at Unionville High School. The first year at Unionville High School she was assigned to coach three sports. After proving successful as a high school coach, Cindy was hired full time as the assistant lacrosse and soccer coach to Ann Sage at the University of Pennsylvania (1979).

Following a successful coaching stint at UPenn she stepped into a full-time coaching position at Northwestern University where she was hired to start a lacrosse program. She assisted Nancy Stevens in field hockey. During the years that followed, she compiled a 76–40 record with four finishes at number five in the nation. At Northwestern she had initiated a very successful program without the benefit of scholarship money—a great challenge as no other Division I program existed at the time in the midwest. Immersed in two programs, one season ended and the next began. The time passed quickly. Cindy remained nine years at Northwestern.

In 1991 Cindy learned that **Suzanne Tyler** at Maryland was giving up lacrosse to focus on field hockey and move into administration. Tyler had developed one of the top lacrosse programs in the country. Cindy learned about the upcoming changes and won the opportunity to become lacrosse coach. Cindy moved to the University of Maryland into a program that already had an established tradition. Since arriving she has set another standard of excellence for the sport. Athletes have been recruited from among the nation's finest lacrosse players, and she has hired an excellent coaching staff. The program has achieved extraordinary success. In eight years the school has won six national championships: 1992, 1995, 1996, 1997, 1998, and 1999. Her win–loss record at Maryland stands at a remarkable 148–11 (.930).

## MEMORABLE MOMENTS

The exciting 11–10 win against **Carole Kleinfelder**'s Harvard team in overtime stands as an exciting memory. Maryland was not favored to beat Harvard, and they had to come from behind. "It was pure drama, but it was interesting . . . when we were behind we were thinking we are going to get back in this game. Maryland had not won the national championship since 1986 so that was special. The team had picked up the nickname the "Silver Bells" because they had come in second in 1991. The win was exciting and rewarding."

There have been four more national championships for Maryland, back to back, from 1995 to 1998. Every championship was different. Cindy says some people may think it's overdone but it's not, as every one has been exciting. Every year her teams go out to play for the championship. In 1996 the challenge was especially formidable because no lacrosse team had ever won the championships back to back.

Certainly memorable was 1999. According to Maryland Sports Information, "Maryland established three National Collegiate championship game records in its 16–6 win against Virginia. The Terps scored the most goals in one-half (11), the most goals in one game (16), and established the largest margin of victory (10)."

## ROLE MODELS/MENTORS

*Judy Wolstenholme*—A fun, highly motivated teacher and coach, Judy taught game basics to freshmen. She worked with the players and helped them to develop into varsity athletes. This woman had a deep sense of commitment and obligation to making certain practice was based on hard work. Judy had the freshmen workout side by side with the varsity and better players—the better players became the mentors for the younger players. Judy facilitated an environment that produced athletic success.

*Vonnie Gros*—This Olympic field hockey coach coached Cindy's West Chester State field hockey team and is credited with providing Cindy with a solid field hockey background. Athletes performed well for Vonnie because they did not want to be a disappointment.

*Mr. Blessing*—Mr. Blessing was the elementary school teacher who got her started in competitive games.

Vonnie Gros and Judy Wohlstenholme put Cindy through "the best finishing school in the country." Cindy has admired other coaches from a distance, particularly Phil Jackson and Bill Walsh. Like watching the Tao of Sport Philosophy in action, she admires the ways they empower athletes to play to their talent. When their athletes step out on the court or field, their focus is to just go out and play their best. Cindy believes that as we need powerful male role models, we need to also see powerful female role models. Phil Jackson, former coach of the Chicago Bulls, has the attributes Cindy wants to emulate as a coach.


## PHILOSOPHY OF COACHING

These mentors laid a philosophical foundation for Cindy. Playing under the leadership of these important role models provided her with excellent preparation. Cindy believes only the misguided coach will feel she can control every outcome and that the greatest gift a coach can give to players is the confidence and freedom to make decisions on the playing field. These qualities are developed in practice, and the battle is within and not on the playing field. When this is done, the foundation for success has been laid.

Along with preparation, a major emphasis is placed on focusing on having fun. Believe it or not, "I think it's a misnomer that the National Champions must work so hard and be so rigid. The fun is in the execution, so you know you want to go out there and execute at the level they are capable of and kind of use that as a promise to themselves and to the team." Cindy focuses on affirmation. She says she can be very demanding, but she never yells at the kids. The aim is to affirm what athletes are capable of doing, and then allow them to actually do it. She emphasizes that every ground ball on every pass is important enough to make a difference in a game. A big emphasis is placed on the idea of "identifying the moments that really make the difference." Extra hustle and defense is also accented along with what most coaches never talk about—the possibility of losing. They also discuss the team's 50–game winning streak. Cindy told them, "Look, we might win, but we might lose; but we know that we can go out and play. We can't control the outcome, but we can control the way we play." Controlling their own play is the sturdiest foundation of Maryland's success. That loss finally came, but they had a rematch with the same team in the finals of the national championships and they won. Cindy's strategy is to do something different or do something no other team has done.

The big challenge in 1996 was to repeat their success. They try to keep players fresh and motivated. Cindy has learned that sometimes when you think you need to practice more or harder, it is actually better to do less. There's always that pressure to do more and sometimes you just need to take a step back and know that maybe rest is better than anything else you can do.

Cindy credits her assistant coach Gary Gait and their sports mentor Dr. Jerry Lynch with having the most influence on her coaching philosophy during the past five years. Gary "is able to communicate and demonstrate the simple execution and joy of the game of lacrosse, while Jerry has helped teach me and my team to NOT show up to win the game but to show up to *play as winners!*"

## CHALLENGES

Starting a program (at Northwestern) and scheduling competition with opponents hundreds of miles away was tough. The first few years were a struggle as the Midwest does not have the same appreciation for lacrosse as they do in the East.

Division I athletics has been predominately a male-dominated arena. It will take years to gain the same respect for women's programs that people have for men's programs. The women have come a long way, but there is still a lot more to do

Cindy feels the support of the university is critical to any athletic success. At Northwestern there was a time when the team was getting better and better—in fact totally exceeding expectations. Cindy knew it would flatten out because they didn't have scholarships to offer and the other programs brought in the money. It was discouraging for her to realize she had reached her peak. At that point Cindy wondered where she should go, and the University of Maryland opportunity arose; she competed at the top level while there.

Another bothersome problem was to find little connection between salary and success. Cindy found that many universities do not reward success; and success goes far beyond what is read on the scoreboard.

She has loved her years at the University of Maryland. Title IX has done a lot for women's programs and has been especially helpful for the lacrosse programs. She feels Maryland has been appreciative and respectful of her many accomplishments.

## CHANGES IN ATHLETES

Cindy does not notice a lot of change in athletes. In her opinion, the athletes who come to Maryland are hungry to compete, to win, and to get better. They are highly motivated. She knows many think the athletes have changed, but she claims one might just have to handle them in different ways. She feels mutual respect makes a very compatible working environment. She sees too much verbal abuse and lack of trust between athletes and coaches and believes that coaches need to provide a safe environment for athletes. She finds giving team members autonomy and decision-making responsibilities also provides confidence and assurance that the coach is counting on them.

## LIFE BEYOND ATHLETICS

Cindy likes to play golf. She enjoys working out and especially likes to run. Reading is another one of her favorite pastimes. Some of her favorite books are *Thinking Body and Dancing Mind*, *Soul Master*, and *Coming for the Soul*. A favorite movie was *Braveheart*.

Cindy has her sights on a long-time coaching career and is hopeful that professional or national coaching opportunities will arise for her.

## RECOGNITIONS AND ACHIEVEMENTS

### Accomplishments as a Player

- Member of the National Lacrosse Squad
- Philadelphia Colleges first team

### Coaching Recognitions in Division I

- ACC Conference Championships: 1997, 1999
- ACC Conference Coach of the Year, 1999
- Regional Coach of the Year, 1999
- Six National Championships, Five Consecutively: 1992, 1995, 1996, 1997, 1998, 1999
- Seven Players of the Year
- Thirty-One All Americans
- Twelve on the U.S. Developmental Team
- Eight National Team Players
- Only team to win 50 games consecutively, men or women, 1995–1997
- Third Winningest Career Coach in the U.S. Division I

### National Coaching Assignment

- U.S. Developmental Squad, 1999–2000

Photo courtesy of University of
California, Los Angeles

# JACKIE TOBIAN-STEINMANN

*Golf—University of California, Los Angeles*

## INTRODUCTION

One who begins coaching at 49, when some contemplate retirement, must have an invincible spirit. Invincible or indomitable, Jackie Steinmann is an "optimist." Now in her seventies, she was a latecomer to coaching but not to teaching. A twenty-five year veteran ski instructor, she started a golf coaching career as a UCLA volunteer. When she was hired, her salary was $2,000 per year.

Jackie was raised in Detroit in an affluent and athletic family. Her father was a professional baseball player, and her brother was a diver on the U.S. Olympic teams from 1956 to 1960. One of the pleasantries of her young life was walking in the woods and picking violets and other wild flowers.

## PERSONAL DATA

*Born*: April 3, 1927, Detroit, Michigan

*Father*: Marcus Tobian

*Father's Occupation*: Professional Baseball Player/General Contractor

*Mother*: Marion Melburne

*Mother's Occupation*: Nurse

*Siblings*: Bruce and Gary

*Children*: Heidi, Gregor, and Lance

*Alma Maters*: UCLA—A.B., Zoology, 1953; University of Toronto School of Medicine—DAAM (Degree of Art as Applied to Medicine), 1952

## FORMATIVE YEARS

Growing up in the Tobian home was fun and family focused. Until Jackie was ten years old, she spent summers on her grandfather's farm learning to milk cows, gather eggs, feed pigs, pitch hay, chase chickens, and ride horses. When farm work got tiring, her grandfather squirted warm milk, directly from the cow's udder, into the children's mouths, or they dashed across the field to their great grandmother's for cookies.

The Tobians owned a beautiful home in Huntington Woods where they spent hours walking dogs and picking wildflowers. Their other home was a lakeside cottage near Detroit. It was here they all learned to swim. When the depression reached their doorstep, it swept her father from wealth to near poverty. In the aftermath they moved to Sarasota, Florida, and then to Santa Monica, California. While her father searched for work, they resided in a small trailer on the beach. After working at several jobs, this determined man, who knew the value of hard work, started a contracting business. Her mother worked as a public health nurse for many years.

Jackie attended Bancroft Junior High and Hollywood High School where she excelled academically. Her brother, Gary, was an accomplished diver who was a silver medallist in 1956 and a gold and silver medallist in the 1960 Olympic Games. She took ballet and acrobatics lessons and studied piano for many years. A gifted person, Jackie is also a talented artist.

Jackie wanted to study medicine, so she began at UCLA, which was close to her Hollywood Hills home. She started with a major in pre-med. During that first year she was informed she would never make it through college. Her response was "I'll show you, just watch me." When she learned about the medical illustration profession, she changed majors so her medical interests could be combined with art. After three years at UCLA, she entered the graduate program in art as applied to medicine at the University of Toronto, Canada. For the first two years of this program, all the classes were taken with medical students. She took classes in pathology, embryology, histology, and dissected an entire human cadaver in anatomy. These classes were augmented with studies in medical drawing.

Throughout college Jackie participated in many aquatics activities both at UCLA and the University of Toronto. In Toronto she was on the synchronized swim team, and at UCLA she performed comedy diving and organized Esther Williams–type aquacades. Spare hours were spent lifeguarding at the local pool. Jackie graduated from the University of Toronto with a degree in medical illustration.

When Jackie wasn't teaching skiing, she worked as a medical illustrator at Children's Hospital in Los Angeles illustrating books on urology and pediatric anesthesiology and for the *Journal of Obstetrics and Gynecology*. She also worked as a medical illustrator for the U.S. Government at Tripler Hospital in Honolulu. Between 1955 and 1957 she did modeling and served as a modeling instructor for the Caroline Leonetti modeling agency. From 1957 to 1974 she taught biology, physiology, math, sewing, typing, and physical education in the Los Angeles City School District. From 1960 to 1963, she taught sewing in a private school. Next (1962 to 1969), she taught painting in an adult program. Then from 1963 to 1977 she was owner, operator, and co-director of Holiday Hill Ski School with her husband in Wrightwood, California.

## SPORTS HISTORY

Even though Jackie had been a varsity high school and college swimmer, her serious interests began when she met and married (1953) Hans Steinmann. Hans' parents owned the Holiday Hill Ski Resort in Wrightwood, California. She learned to ski and became a proficient skier. After Jackie and Hans were married, they owned and operated the ski school. She became a certified instructor and taught full and part time over a twenty-year period along with raising her children. After twenty-five years of marriage, Hans and Jackie were divorced (1976), an event that devastated Jackie. Needing something to occupy her time, she turned to the game she had "taken up with vengeance" nine years earlier at age forty—golf. By this time she had become quite proficient, learning from whomever she could, winning club tournaments and some local amateur events.

As the divorce neared the final stage, she met Genny Davis who also lived in Valencia, California, where Jackie and the children lived. Genny had earned a partial scholarship in golf for the UCLA women's golf team. The school was just starting a fully funded golf program.

## DECISION TO COACH

Through Genny, Jackie learned UCLA was in the market for a golf coach; Genny suggested she apply. Knowing she had nothing to lose, Jackie applied for the job. After interviewing, she was offered the job. She knew little about coaching and had no one to ask about exactly how to coach, so she learned by experience, "stumbling" at times. Soon she could see the fruits of her labors and by the end of her second year (1978–1979), UCLA was ranked number nine in the country. Sometime in these early coaching days she became involved in a program called "Lifespring." This program was a popular self-enhancement program sweeping the country. She became one of the teachers in the program. Always the teacher, Jackie attributes her success and longevity to the fact that, like her father, determination undergirds everything she does. She has employed a lifetime attitude that she will be very good at whatever she does. She also loves what she does, and this passion for doing and becoming is an invaluable asset. Finding fun in whatever she does makes greeting each day an adventure. Imagination and creativity have paved Jackie's success channel. As these qualities have been coupled with an insatiable desire to learn, and to learn from the best, it has produced longevity and success in all quadrants of her life. This is illustrated with Jackie entering her twenty-second year as UCLA's head golf coach (1998–1999). She has won six conference championships in the Pacific 10 and has been Pacific 10 Coach of the Year several times, as well as Regional Coach of the Year, National Coach of the Year, and Taylor-Made Coach of the Year. She was the driving force in organizing the Women's National Golf Coaches Association and served eight years on its board of directors.

## MEMORABLE MOMENTS

At a team meeting a few years ago, Jackie remembers stepping out of her coaching role and becoming an actress. Jackie has a vivid memory of her version of a "Win One for the Gipper" speech. It had to do with teaching the team the value of compassion, and how energy put into negative thinking takes away from the ability to focus on what is really important. Carefully plotting the night before in order to sound spontaneous, Jackie gave an Academy-Award winning performance as a hurt and disillusioned teacher who was disappointed with the behavior of her students. She knew that threatening to quit would give the team a wake up call. After closing the door and leaving them in the room to ponder their behavior, she walked down the hall saying, "Yes! Yes! Yes!" She had finally gotten through to a tough team. Not only did she teach her team something, but she, too, learned something. It was all a part of coaching.

It was that same tough team that produced another memory by winning the national championship. They struggled through the year, but when it came to the national championship, it was for Jackie "memorable and magical!"

Receiving awards have been special, but the friendships made over the years have been most rewarding to her. To Jackie, "Golf is a wonderful sport and it attracts gracious and loving people," and it has been wonderful for her to be associated with such people.

Another choice memory occurred when several coaches from across the country met at the University of Georgia, at the national championship in 1986, and wanted to organize a coaches association. Jackie took the lead and wrote the constitution and bylaws patterned after the ones she used as president of the Far West Ski Instructors Association. That was how the organization got started; and Jackie was elected and reelected president of the organization and served four more years as past-president. In 1987 and again in 1999 the association recognized her an unprecedented second time for her pioneering efforts and contributions to golf with the Rolex Gladys Palmer Meritorious Service Award (first awarded to her in 1986).

## ROLE MODELS/MENTORS

*Heidi, Gregor, and Lance*— Each of Jackie's three children has been a great support to her. Together they have shared many long talks about coaching, life, and the road to success.

*Chuck Hogan*—Jackie's role model and mentor, Chuck is a very wise and trusted advisor. She commends Chuck for his friendship, his support, and for teaching her a great deal through the years.

*Renee Baumgartner, Ph.D.*—Baumgartner is golf coach and senior women's administrator at the University of Oregon, and Jackie describes her as "a best friend." They support each other, and Jackie respects her wisdom. Renee is much younger and they are complete opposites, but Jackie values her friendship and often thinks of her as another daughter.

## PHILOSOPHY OF COACHING

On the inside cover of the *UCLA Golf Press Guide* can be found a well crafted statement of Jackie Steinmann's coaching philosophy. The statement is entitled "UCLA Women's Golf: Purpose and Philosophy." The first paragraph follows verbatim by permission of the UCLA Athletics Department.

The Goal of the UCLA Golf Program is to be a leader in Women's Golf. We have a vision to make the world a better place by just being in it, and being the best that we can be with dignity, charity, and respect.

This statement of purpose and philosophy is followed with a list of thirty-five different aspirations. At the bottom of this dynamic collection is the statement, "GOLF IS ONLY JUST A GAME!"

## CHALLENGES

Learning to coach by trial and error has been a challenge. Some obstructions have been beyond her control, but not worrying about them has been a conscious decision. Coaching hasn't always been easy. Jackie has become better with age and, now in her seventies, she fancies herself a pretty darn good coach: "At least I screw up people a lot less than I used to."

Jackie believes that by the time a quality player gets into a college program, she already has a solid golf swing and, when one has that foundation, it is time to transcend the level of mere mechanics and to start thinking, acting, walking, and talking like a winner. She believes that the "mental" aspects of golf have not usually been well taught, and teaching golfers how to be successful, after swing mechanics, takes priority and practice.

In earlier years when the team needed uniforms, Jackie persuaded manufacturers to supply them as a public service. Supplying uniforms and places to practice and play were necessary to compete against formidable opponents. Hours and hours were spent pleading for practice time and thanking the course managers for their cooperation. Because of the generosity of many local country clubs and their members, Jackie was able to find enough places to play on some of the best courses in the country. She also found corporate sponsorship for the golf program, which enabled her to host a very successful yearly collegiate tournament. In the early years show business celebrities and sports figures lent their prestige and names to help the team. All of the efforts paid dividends. The Golf Team contributed to helping UCLA being named the #1 Athletic Program in the country.

## CHANGES IN ATHLETES

Women's golf has undergone great changes over the last twenty-two years. The scores have come down dramatically. Equipment has improved and so has teaching and coaching. All of these items have contributed to better performances, advancement of players, and the popularity of the sport. On the other hand, Jackie does not like the way recruiting has changed. Athletes often go to programs because they get caught up in getting a full scholarship instead of making better educational choices or finding programs that may better suit other needs. She also believes athletes are much more demanding these days, and they probably get too much and expect even more. It is her opinion that it is the fault of times and athletics in general. Too often the pressures of winning affect both coaches and players in negative ways.

According to Jackie, coaches should be role models. This means a coach should assist the athletes with their lives and their preparation for the future and not dwell solely on sport. She feels strongly about this aspect of coaching and recognizes there are some coaches who miss the boat. Winning is not everything. What is learned in the process of getting there is of more value and importance.

## LIFE BEYOND ATHLETICS

Jackie retired on June 30, 1999. She wants to do many other things including writing a book on coaching. She would like to assist other college and high school coaches. In her more ambitious moments she thinks about learning to fly an airplane, going to culinary school, getting a Ph.D., and running a bed-and breakfast inn. She even claims, "When I am 90 I would like to start a new career."

A gourmet cook, Jackie loves to have company for dinner, brunch, or tea. She creates unique menus and tries new recipes on friends. Each meal is accompanied by a printed menu with an elaborately set table. Her home is on the top of a mountain in the Hollywood Hills with a spectacular view. The beautiful decor is traditional with French country flair and plenty of antiques.

Time permitting, she likes to read. She is a pushover for romantic novels. She loves movies such as *Forrest Gump*, *The Sound of Music*, *Gone with the Wind*, *Angels in the Outfield*, and *Fly Away Home*. Gardening is especially fun for Jackie. She grows her own herbs and vegetables.

Her son, Lance, a general contractor, lives close by. Another son, Gregor, also a builder, lives in Jackson Hole, Wyoming, and Heidi, her only daughter, is an intelligent, very talented person who works in the advertising business. She has four grandchildren: three boys and a girl.

It is obvious that this talented, creative, and fun-loving woman finds joy and contentment in life and in the challenge of a lively coaching career. Certainly she is a role model for excellence!

## RECOGNITIONS AND ACHIEVEMENTS

### Coaching Recognitions in Division I

- PAC 10 Conference Championships: 1979, 1982, 1983, 1990, 1991
- PAC 10 Conference Coach of the Year, 1990, 1991
- Regional Coach of the Year: 1983, 1984, 1985, 1991, 1996
- National Coach of the Year, LPGA, 1989
- National Coach of the Year, National Golf Coaches Association, 1990
- National Champions, 1991
- Four First-Team All Americans, 9 Second Team
- Thirty-one players playing professionally

### National Coaching Assignment

- Coach of U.S.A. vs. Japan, 1989, 1992

### Other Accomplishments

- Rolex's Gladys Palmer Award, 1986, 1999
- Collegiate Women's Golf Hall of Fame
- Member of Rolex Executive Committee for College of Golf Education
- Member of California State Amateur Committee
- National Golf Coaches Association established the Jackie Steinmann Scholarship 1999
- NCAA Presidential Award, 1999
- UCLA established the Jackie Steinmann Endowment Scholarship, 1999

Photo courtesy of University
of Maine

# SUZANNE TYLER

*Lacrosse/Field Hockey, Athletic Director—University
of Maine*

## INTRODUCTION

Suzanne Tyler has Olympic blood in her veins. Her Olympic ties reach back to
1896 when most of the U.S. Olympic team either came from Princeton University or the Boston Athletic Club. Tyler's grandfather, Albert C. Tyler II, was
a Princeton man and represented the United States in the most famous
reenactment of the ancient games in Athens, Greece, in 1896. Albert Tyler distinguished himself and his country by winning a silver medal in pole vaulting.
The medal is on display at Princeton University.

Although Albert Tyler passed on before Sue was born, she feels a deep connection with her grandfather. Sue's father often told her about grandfather Tyler and his athletic feats, causing her to feel a bond with the grandfather she
never knew.

## PERSONAL DATA

> *Born*: March 24, 1947, Philadelphia, Pennsylvania
>
> *Father*: Albert Clinton Tyler III
>
> *Father's Occupation*: Tool Room Mechanic, Philadelphia Navy
> Shipyard

*Mother*: Emma Groff

*Mother's Occupation*: Homemaker

*Sibling*: Albert Clinton Tyler IV

*Husband*: Dennis Casey

*Children*: Andrew and Alexis

*Alma Maters*: Northeastern University—B.S., Physical Education, 1969; Pennsylvania State University—M.S., Physical Education/Sport Psychology, 1972; University of Maryland—Ph.D., Physical Education and Sport Psychology, 1986

## FORMATIVE YEARS

The Tyler family remained in Philadelphia three years after Sue was born before moving to Chew's Landing in southern New Jersey. The neighborhood had enough interested children to keep Sue active in games and play.

Sue Tyler was a good student, achievement oriented, and attracted to the sciences even in elementary school. Being achievement oriented, she focused on getting straight As and maintained a perfect attendance record for five straight years. The serious nature of this youngster kept her busy and involved in school and in all the available extracurricular activities.

Many summers were spent at her grandparents' farm. Challenging surroundings stimulated her inquisitive nature, and she enthusiastically engaged in farm work. She drove the tractor, rode horses and cows, and fished in a nearby creek.

She played games with the neighborhood children and most often with the more skilled boys. When the boys were not available, she used rocks and sticks as play objects since they did not have any balls.

## SPORTS HISTORY

Tyler played on her first softball team at age ten. She was coached by a young high school girl named Monica. Eventually, Monica became Sue's idol. Monica had struggled with rheumatoid arthritis and could no longer play the game, but she maintained the will to compete and passed her same competitive will on to the youth she coached.

Play day activities, public fairs with running and wheelbarrow races, or any competitive, energetic activity attracted Sue. High school provided her first encounter with field hockey and when she saw the game, she fell in love with it and worked hard to make the team. Her first starting position was goal keeper, the only spot open on varsity, but she soon moved to "inner." Surprisingly, her parents offered little support other than providing transportation to games. They never stayed to watch her play. They were not against her playing; they just did not understand the attraction. Still she mustered the enthusiasm to continue playing.

Not only did she play field hockey, she competed in track and played JV basketball. The school offered five sports, and she competed in four. As a junior and senior in high school during the 1960s, Sue never realized that South Jersey and Philadelphia offered a good roster of activities for girls and women when compared to other areas of the country.

Playing field hockey was a major factor when choosing which college to attend. She wanted to play field hockey as a freshman, major in biology, and become a veterinarian. The school of choice was Upsala College in East Orange, New Jersey. She knew they had a great biology department and the school was relatively small in comparison to the big high school she had attended. Although it was not known as a field hockey school, it provided her the opportunity to compete. During her first year at Upsala, she was the best of the freshmen and really wanted the challenge of not being the best. She wanted to compete at a much higher level. She felt she might be a star if she transferred to another school program. Also during this year, she decided she wanted to teach physical education and coach so she could teach others how great it was to be an athlete. She wanted others to know being an athlete didn't make one less of a woman or a person. Athleticism was a positive human quality. At college she had her first experience of the stigma associated with being an athlete; she had not felt this in high school. She was disappointed because a negative association was attached to something she dearly loved. That realization changed her career goal and the path she next chose to follow.

Changing schools had athletic, academic, and economic implications. Family finances necessitated a scholarship and she had a scholarship at Upsala. So she searched for a school with a field hockey program which would offer an adequate scholarship. Rutgers, Ursinus, and Bouvé at Northeastern were all under consideration. Northeastern was rumored to have a great team, and team members played with a higher-skilled hockey club on the weekends. Bouvé awarded her a huge scholarship and set up a loan system for her so she could go to school almost free. There were no athletic scholarships at the time; her money was based on academics and need.

## DECISION TO COACH

She entered Bouvé still planning to teach but also intending to do research in exercise physiology. She planned to work after graduation as a researcher in an exercise physiology lab for one or two years and then to enter an exercise physiology graduate program. This plan did not last long as she was seized by a love for teaching and coaching. However, she wanted to teach where students were not required to take a physical education class. After applying at several different schools, she accepted an appointment at Cornell University in Ithaca, New York, where physical education was an elective not a requirement; now she could teach where students wanted to learn. She taught swimming, badminton, field hockey, volleyball, canoeing, and bowling. She assisted with the field hockey and lacrosse teams in her second year and both sports became coaching passions. Three years at Cornell gave Sue the motivation to go to Penn State and work on a master's degree.

At Penn State she learned that volumes of information were available on exercise and fitness, but the valuable information did not reach out and convince people of the need to exercise. This need was usually contained within each individual's psyche. Now a reason existed for her to turn to graduate work in sports psychology. Upon completing a degree in sports psychology, she accepted a year's appointment at the University of Maryland. She took Margarita Arrighi's position as head lacrosse coach and a full load of physical education classes. Margarita returned after a year and Sue remained to assist with the JV team and be head coach for field hockey. At the end of that year Margarita moved to the professorial track, opening the way for Sue to again take on the head coaching reigns for the 1976 season. In the next ten years, Sue took the team to the national finals eight times and won two national championships, first in 1981 and then in 1986—the same year she completed her Ph.D. program. Four of the coaches she lost to in the finals were **Pam Hixon** (1982), **Tina Sloan Green** (1984), **Marisa Didio** (1985), and **Carole Kleinfelder** (1990) (all women featured in this volume). For fourteen of the sixteen years she coached the lacrosse team, she also coached the field hockey team. The lacrosse team compiled a 141–60–4 record during those sixteen years. The next year after her 1987 lacrosse team won the national championship, the field hockey team also won a national championship. This team finished a fourteen-year record with a 147–86–26 ledger.

By 1989 Tyler had demonstrated the ability to be a two-sport coach and win national championships in both. She also displayed an aptitude to be a fine administrator. Acknowledging her coaching and managerial abilities, the administration appointed her associate athletic director in 1989, acting athletic director in 1990 (overseeing 23 sports), and, in 1995, she was named University of Maine's athletic director. This designation spotlighted her as one of the few women athletic directors overseeing both men's and women's sports in Division I schools from 1991 to 1995. The senior athletic director asked her to apply for the University of Maine position in 1991. When hired she took the reins of a troubled program. Since that time she has balanced the budget, built a new stadium and turf field, added two new women's sports (ice hockey and volleyball), and taken several teams to new heights: top 20 for field hockey, highest attendance for both men's and women's basketball, most number of wins for men's basketball and top 25 ranking for football. Women's basketball has received its first NCAA tournament win, and a national championship in 1999 for men's ice hockey. She now takes pride in coaching the coaches toward success!

## MEMORABLE MOMENTS

Winning three national championships were standout events for Sue—two in lacrosse and one in field hockey. Sue observes that "nothing is quite as much fun as such wins." Going to the finals a total of nine times in twelve years and taking second place six times in those years was exciting, and it was especially exhilarating when her team defeated Penn State 11–6. Another great experience was to be voted lacrosse coach of the year in 1984 and 1986. Coach of the year was a great honor and especially significant to Sue as her own peers cast the votes and recognized her abilities even though she did not win the championship either of those years.

Knowing that her grandfather had left her a great legacy, even though he died before she was born, has conferred on her a great deal of inspiration. Her father often expressed to her his wish that she could have known her grandfather because he had bypassed him and passed his athletic attributes to Sue. He said they were alike in their will and their determination to accept challenges that moved them to the next level.

## ROLE MODELS/MENTORS

*Emma Mutchler*—Emma was Sue's high school physical education teacher. Sue's family was not well-off financially, and few young people in her surroundings went to college. No one in Sue's family liked sports nor had they received a college education except, of course, her grandfather. Emma Mutchler inspired Sue to do her best and never say she couldn't do something unless she had tried. Such encouragement fostered within her a fearless resolve to always do her best.

*Vonnie Gros*—Of Vonnie Gros, Sue reports, "I first saw her play field hockey against Australia in the early 60s. Then I found out that she was also on the United States Lacrosse team. She was a great player and coach! She was a person who seemed not to be confined by societal restrictions. She was true to herself and followed her passion."

## PHILOSOPHY OF COACHING

Ms. Mutchler's teaching "to be the best you can be" forms the cornerstone of Sue Tyler's philosophy in the classroom and on the playing field. Tyler fervently believes that a team can always achieve more than anyone can on an individual basis. Understanding this idea simply means that the fully functioning whole is greater than the sum of its individual parts. If each individual performs an assigned role equal to her ability, then the team will be able to meet its goal. If Sue's goal is a game plan she has figured to beat the opposition, then it is extremely important that all athletes do their jobs. When athletes did not fulfill their assigned roles, they would have to figure out why. Side-line players were expected to be involved in analysis and suggest remedies and possibilities. The bottom line was "never say can't." If the plan does not work, try something else. If athletes apply all they know to winning and they lose, then they will have the satisfaction of knowing they have done their best. Sue has both a master's degree and a Ph.D. in sports psychology and her understanding the psychological dimensions of an athlete has contributed to her teams' successes.

## CHALLENGES

Reflecting back on the 1970s and the early 1980s, Sue said, "facilities were never really ours to use." Often her teams had to use a recreation field. Weight rooms and many facilities were simply off limits. One of the reasons Maryland teams were better to start off was because of the innovative things they did on the field. Sue realized men were successful because they were stronger. So the women tied ropes on to fences with pulleys and tried to do resistance training with the pulleys. Sue lobbied for access to the weight room and Maryland became one of the first women's lacrosse and field hockey programs to have women lift weights. However, the women were always seen as second-class citizens no matter how successful the teams were. They never got decent field space and the funding was much less than that given to their male counterparts. The other difficult aspect was knowing that "if you complained you were gone. The squeaky wheel did not get the oil, the wheel got taken off and a new wheel was put on." Coaches did the best they could and refrained from speaking out too much as that assured the team could keep on developing.

According to Sue, "There still is no equity as much as people say there is equity. Women still need equity, equity does not necessarily mean equal but fairness, true acceptance. There are people that accept us because we are here, but it is going to take time and generational changes to have true acceptance of women's involvement in sports both at the participation and the administrative levels."

## CHANGES IN ATHLETES

Tremendous changes have taken place in sport since Sue's entry. The skill levels of athletes are much higher because they have had opportunities to develop earlier. They are coached better, and they are usually taught proper techniques early on. Skill development and equipment in some sports has improved dramatically. Athletes are faster, stronger, and more skillful. Women do not hide the fact that they are athletes. In the 1970s most of the athletes pretended that they didn't care about being athletic. Now, women show they care, and they demonstrate their commitment enough to get dirty and sweat. They are willing to do what they have to do to get better. Psychologically they are tougher and stronger. Tyler believes being accepted as an athlete has helped in this area.

## LIFE BEYOND ATHLETICS

In 1987 Sue married Dennis Casey. She describes Dennis as a great guy. He is the burser at the University of Maine. In 1990 Sue and Dennis adopted a little six–week-old boy from Romania named Andrew. In 1992 Sue and Dennis added Alexis, a little Russian boy, to their family. The family lives on a scenic hill near a lake. Their home was built in 1820, so it is a natural for Sue to enjoy collecting antiques.

Reading is a favorite pastime, and she is especially drawn to authors like Dick Francis and John Grisham. Francis writes mysteries about horses and Grisham writes mysteries. Along with reading she enjoys fishing on the nearby lake and gardening.

When asked what advice she would give to the upcoming generation she says, "Follow your passion. Follow it, just do it, and it will work out. If you back away from your passion, then you are not true to yourself."

## RECOGNITIONS AND ACHIEVEMENTS

### Accomplishments as a Player

- All Region Lacrosse, 1968, 1969
- All Region Field Hockey, 1967–1968

### Coaching Recognitions

- National Championships in Lacrosse: 1981, 1986
- National Championship in Field Hockey: 1987
- National Lacrosse Coach of the Year: 1984, 1986
- One Olympian
- Two Field Hockey Players on National Teams
- Twelve Lacrosse Players on National Teams

### Other Accomplishments

- University of Maryland Athletic Hall of Fame, 1995
- One of three women who are Division I Athletic Directors for Men's Sports
- One of the few women ever to coach national championships in two sports

Photo courtesy of Brigham
Young University

# ANN VALENTINE

## *Tennis Coach/Associate Athletic Director—Brigham Young University*

## INTRODUCTION

Antoinette Marie Valentine, the ninth of ten children, was born to first-generation Italian parents in Sykesville, Pennsylvania, on New Year's Day, 1932. By the time she turned nine, both parents, Mary and Carmen Valentine, had succumbed to untimely deaths. Under these somber circumstances, and amidst offers from relatives to raise the young children, Fran, the eldest, said "No!" She was determined that the family would remain together; and they did.

Under Fran's leadership, the ten children organized a plan to bolster the financial and emotional needs critical to withstand their colossal misfortune. The plan required each person to become a contributing family member. Earnings from work at grocery stores, cleaning establishments, newspaper deliveries, house cleaning, and other menial jobs were contributed to the family coffers for food and clothing. Although they were short on money and material possessions, an abundance of love and kinship overrode their adversity and melded a solid family unit. Fran's parental instincts fused the large family with stability and direction.

## PERSONAL DATA

*Born*: January 1, 1932, Sykesville, Pennsylvania

*Father*:  Carmen Valentine

*Father's Occupation*:  Coal Miner

*Mother*:  Mary Fratto Valentine

*Mother's Occupation*:  Homemaker

*Siblings*:  Frances, Pat, Jenny, Sally, Gemma, Viola, Louie, Joe, and
Sam

*Alma Maters*:  Slippery Rock University—B.S., 1955; Pennsylvania State University—M.S., 1961

## FORMATIVE YEARS

Two older brothers and one younger brother provided the perfect cohort
for Ann's athletic inclinations. The foursome fashioned their own game ball
from a tin can and used the Catholic church's ample playground for a football
field. They even folded chairs for the school custodian in exchange for an
hour's playing time on the basketball court.

Ann's athletic interests were partly satisfied while playing on the high
school basketball team. The competitive schedule was limited, but it was the
only sport offered for girls. An older brother and sister introduced Ann to tennis. They played on a farm-side clay court with the local doctor. Ann often
tagged along to spectate and shag balls. Her efforts were rewarded with five
minutes playing time at the conclusion of each match. This began Ann's love
affair with tennis.

## SPORTS HISTORY

Two local men, Dr. Fugate and Russ Kramer, entered Ann Valentine's life
at the right moment. Fugate, also the family's physician, provided Ann a
square-headed wooden racket with a smooth grip. Later, Russ Kramer, an
employer noting her interest in tennis, encouraged her to hone solid skills.
These men took her to Pittsburgh to watch a pro tennis tournament. This
rousing experience opened a whole new world for the youngster from
Sykesville.

The goal to attend college and become the first member of her family to
earn a college degree was set in Ann's youth. To do so required dedication and
hard work. While she was a senior in high school, her commitment required
her to leave school at 4 P.M., catch a ride with the English teacher, and commute
seven miles to work in a grocery store. Work finished at midnight and after a
short walk to her brother and sister's restaurant she assisted there until 2 A.M.
before returning home. After high school, she worked to save for college.
While staying with a sister in New York, she availed herself of the ample opportunities to compete. She performed well in tournaments and lauded her
Sykesville teachers for enabling her to compete so skillfully.

## PLAYING CAREER

After saving money for two years, and with the financial support of her brothers and sisters who shared her same dream, she confidently entered Slippery Rock University in Pennsylvania. She intended to major in music. Upon discovering that a music major required $500 more than any other major, she chose a physical education major instead. Slippery Rock afforded many competitive opportunities that a small high school could not. While there, she competed for four years on the tennis team (only losing one match in her career) and at the same time competed on the field hockey, volleyball, and basketball teams. Her only male coach was the tennis coach who was also an English professor. Valentine credits him with teaching her the finer points of strategy. Summers in New York or in Pittsburgh provided work and opportunities to enter tennis tournaments where she became more competitive, vastly improving her sprouting tennis skills.

## DECISION TO COACH

Valentine's determination to coach was a natural outgrowth of teaching physical education and competing. Slippery Rock did not offer a coaching emphasis, but she was a rated official in a variety of sports and spent a good deal of time officiating high school sports as well as working twenty hours per week as a secretary, thus enabling her to help finance her education. This exposure to rules and coaches held her fascination. When she claimed her first teaching job, the contract package included coaching gymnastics and basketball. A successful first year of coaching attracted her to the prospect of coaching as a career. The next year Valentine changed schools to be closer to the young man she dated. This time coaching the men's and the women's tennis teams accompanied her teaching position. Her teams took the Pennsylvania state championship that was held at Penn State University. While at the tournament, the Penn State tennis coach, Sherm Fogg, watched the matches and wanted to recruit one of the young men. The latter was from a poor family and was unable to afford a college education. At the time Ann's brother Sam played football for Penn State. Due to Sam's familial relationship to Ann, Rip Engle, the football coach, gave up a scholarship to Fogg so he could use it to bring Ann's young tennis athlete to the university. This was a thrilling experience for Ann Valentine.

After a three-year stint of coaching and teaching in the public schools, Coach Valentine accepted an assistantship to Penn State with the prospect of coaching the women's tennis team. In this assignment she decided she loved the sport and enjoyed the rewards of working with young people. By semester's end she was invited to join the faculty and become the tennis coach. Ann and the Valentine clan were ecstatic, but the young man in her life was much less pleased, knowing the huge chunk of time this new assignment would demand.

Dr. John Lawther, an expert in sports psychology and dean of the College of Physical Education, became her faculty mentor. From him she learned valuable lessons about the psychology of teaching and about friendship and life. He took time to instruct in a way most professors would not. For example, he often drove by the tennis courts to observe Ann teaching. On one occasion he poked his head out the car window and stated, "Ann, remember, less talking and more doing provides greater skill." Lawther became a dear friend. Her favorite memories of him stem from the Penn State tennis courts where neither would call "quits" to a tennis match come rain or snow.

While at Penn State Ann suffered several severe bouts with asthma, forcing her to a climate where the asthma would subside enough to regain her health. Utah's climate offered that opportunity, and, to the fortune of Brigham Young University, she relocated to Provo, Utah. Subsequently she accepted a position at the church-owned university. Still weak from her bouts with asthma, Valentine slipped into the shoes of BYU women's tennis coach.

It was here, at Brigham Young University, that Ann created her lofty tennis tradition. Looking back to the early days, she notes tennis was a "glorified play-day." The team schedule involved a month of competition with little time for conditioning. Valentine claims that today intercollegiate tennis places an athlete in a sphere of strength and aerobic conditioning, mental preparation, video skill analysis, technique practice, and nutritional education. Now athletes are exposed to unlimited competitive opportunities and coaches who use motivational techniques unheard of in the 1960s. Today's coaches focus on the positive, and they teach athletes that they are each imbued with "the seed of greatness."

## CHANGES IN ATHLETICS

Competitors of the 1990s are surrounded with superb equipment and facilities. They are bedecked in attractive athletic attire. Sixteen-hour car journeys have been reduced to six-hour, cross-country airplane trips. Support systems like Brigham Young University's Cougar Club have arisen to provide recognitions like the Scholar-Athlete Program. This program illustrates to athletes and the public that the era of the dumb jock is past history. This is exemplified by the tennis team's 3.36 cumulative GPA. In addition to these enhancements, athletes have gone from no scholarships, to partial scholarships, to full scholarships. Athletes' performance has improved greatly. Valentine shares a view similar to other coaches—that women's athletic advances are charged with pros and cons. One thing she would like to change between the past and present athletes is their attitudes of appreciation. It appears to her that many full-scholarship athletes feel the university owes them everything; Valentine would like to correct this notion.

## MEMORABLE MOMENTS

Valentine's accomplishments as a tennis coach are multitudinous. In 23 years of coaching her teams have placed in the top 20 nineteen times and the top 10 ten times, and she coached 17 athletes to win 32 All-American awards. Flanking these achievements are a multitude of prestigious awards such as induction into the National Utah Summer Games Hall of Fame, the Wilson ITA Coach of the Year Award, and the ITA Rolex Meritorious Service Award. These accomplishments are especially impressive to sports writers, athletes, and administrators. Most striking has been her resolve to take unpopular ethical stances in behalf of right actions.

## COACHING PHILOSOPHY

As teacher and coach she has imprinted her special brand of integrity upon untold students. When newsprint and record books are brown and consumed with age, the premier record of her success will be etched in the oft-silent chamber of individual memory. These inscriptions will continue to guide and direct the once-indecisive and confused former athletes whom she would not allow to be less or do less than was appropriate and right. Their map of conflicting values needed Valentine's strong directive to right action and conduct. The oft-honored Coach Valentine is unpretentious and humble when her extensive accomplishments are recognized. Foremost, she is deeply appreciative to four brothers and five sisters whose unity, love, and financial support provided the anchor to escalate her to the top seed of her profession. She encourages her athletes to do likewise.

## RECOGNITIONS AND ACHIEVEMENTS

### Coaching Recognitions in Division I

- Fifteen Conference Championships:
  Intermountain Athletic Conference: 1977, 1979, 1980, 1981, 1982
  High County Athletic Conference: 1984, 1985, 1986, 1987, 1988, 1989, 1990
  Western Athletic Conference: 1993, 1994, 1995
- Eleven Regional Championships: 1977, 1979, 1980, 1981, 1987, 1988, 1990, 1991, 1993, 1995, 1996
- IAC Conference Coach of the Year, 1980, 1981, 1982
- HCAC Conference Coach of the Year, 1983, 1984, 1985, 1986, 1989, 1990
- WAC Conference Coach of the Year, 1993, 1994, 1995
- Regional Coach of the Year, 1988, 1990, 1994, 1995
- National Coach of the Year, 1995
- Seventeen All Americans, 23 awards
- Two players on National Teams
- Team of the Year, 1994

- Nine ITA Scholar-Athletes
- Second Winningest Coach

## National Coaching Assignments

- World Games Committee
- World University Games Committee

## Other Accomplishments

- Utah Network Girls' and Women's Sports Hall of Fame, 1993
- Board of Directors, ITA
- NCAA Tennis Committee
- Central Region and National Ranking Committee
- UAHPER Honor Award
- ITA Rolex Meritorious Service Award, 1996
- Thirty-one national, regional, and conference administrative assignments

Photo courtesy of Arizona
State University

# LINDA VOLLSTEDT

*Golf—Arizona State University*

## INTRODUCTION

After soaring near the top of the salary scale, Linda Vollstedt, a high school math teacher, resigned to become Women's Golf Coach at Arizona State University for one-third of her salary. The year was 1980. The extravagant move required selling stocks, retirement funds, insurance policies, and land to subsidize the salary loss. Friends and family shook their heads in disbelief, but Linda understood destiny's price.

## PERSONAL DATA

*Born*: November 2, 1946, Portland, Oregon

*Father*: Lyle Vollstedt

*Father's Occupation*: Meat business

*Mother*: Norma Vollstedt

*Mother's Occupation*: Homemaker

*Siblings*: Gary, Billy (deceased)

*Alma Mater*: Arizona State University—B.S., Math Education, 1969;—M.S., Math Education, 1971

## FORMATIVE YEARS

Linda attributes her competitiveness to the elder of her two brothers. He was smart and didn't apply himself, so Linda applied herself in an effort to out-do him. Her dogged attention to goals positioned her as number one in a high school graduating class of 550 students.

## SPORTS HISTORY

Linda's passion for golf began in high school. Her love for the game blossomed into a dream of coaching, even though she had never been mentored by a golf coach. In 1964 few colleges had women's golf teams. Arizona State University was one of a few schools with a women's golf team, so Linda procured an academic scholarship from ASU and played golf for the school.

## COACHING

A degree from ASU in math education qualified Linda to become a public school teacher. After twelve years as a public school teacher and golf coach, she took her successful coaching vita and applied to be golf coach at Arizona State University. The father of Lauri Merten, one of Linda's former high school golfers, encouraged her to seek the position. Linda did not receive the job that year, but the following year she was hired to replace the coach who had been an ex-tour player. This was the next step in pursuing a coaching dream and fulfilling what she believed was her destiny as a coach.

It took three years for the job to escalate to a full-time position, but the budget, the work load, and the salary lagged miserably below an acceptable standard. Finally, after suffering years of inequity—the money discrimination alone totaled about $100,000—Title IX and gender equity flexed its muscle in favor of women, and Vollstedt's salary was matched to that of her male counterparts. Vollstedt claims her greatest obstacles have been salary conflicts and the implicit and explicit discrimination foisted towards women.

Golf programs for women were either just emerging or unheard of on most college campuses when Linda took on college coaching. ASU wanted a top-ten program for women's golf. But with inadequate administrative support, Vollstedt's success was limited to good teams. In time she was able to convince the administration that building a great program necessitated their support. Once this task was accomplished, she was able to drive her program to the top.

## PHILOSOPHY OF COACHING

Like her own early golfing circumstances, she still finds today's recruits rarely come from a high school where they have had a golf coach. In most cases her golfers have been coached by either a good teacher or their own father. Vollstedt's coaching style is best exemplified in the way she views her role as a significant person in the lives of those she coaches. She is forging a new way of viewing the coach. Knowing a difference can be made in the lives of athletes, she teaches principles that can be used for a lifetime. She decries the "football mentality" that extols yelling and screaming and breaking a player's spirit through the use of negative expletives. She clearly does not identify with coaches that get upset with an athlete who misses a putt or makes a wrong choice in club selection. Her philosophical stance provides an encouraging structure where athletes can become better in weak areas. The core of Linda's coaching philosophy is to "teach them to be their own coach; to learn from their mistakes; to emphasize what they are doing right; to have positive thoughts at all times." Her greatest desire is to create an environment where athletes feel good about themselves. Thus, Vollstedt fashioned an environment that will make a difference in the lives of those she coaches.

Ultimately Linda's life is encircled in her work. The golf team has become her family, and they are carefully nurtured with love and kindness while being imbued with values planned to sustain them in golf and in life.

## MEMORABLE MOMENTS

Linda Vollstedt believes she was destined to be a coach and a teacher. Her record sparkles with the positive results of a destiny being fulfilled. Reflecting on the greatest or the most memorable of these experiences, she declares winning her first national championship to be the greatest coaching moment in her life. This event, at Hilton Head, South Carolina, in 1990, was the culmination of ten years of coaching. Although the first big win always seems best, Vollstedt maintains the most exciting coaching memory was to win the championship again in 1993. It had been a tough year, and ASU was not expected to win. Vollstedt was determined to have the team do things her way. Ultimately, the team recognized the coach was trying to cultivate better people and at the same time help them to achieve their personal goals. The win was especially thrilling because it had been a stormy year, but the components for success melded, the team peaked at the right time, and it captured the national title.

The 1994 conference championship was another come-from-behind victory. This accommodates sweet memories of a collage of miracles. Heather Farr, a former ASU player and LPGA team member, had lost a long battle with cancer, and a team member's sister had also succumbed to cancer. This was a sad period for the team. The year had been dedicated to Heather. When they approached the last 4 holes, team members claimed they could literally feel Heather's spirit enter their own bodies. The last three or four shots were miraculous. One athlete chipped in from behind a tree, a shot that would be impossible to duplicate. Another player chipped in on the eighteenth green. One had to hit a driver off the fairway just to get it to the green. She hit it a foot from the hole and made it for a birdie. Another team member hit into the green about two feet from the pin, and also made a birdie. The team began discussing this event and soon realized that each one had been part of a shared spiritual experience. Coach Vollstedt firmly believes there is a constant spiritual energy operating around all of us and it is available to everyone. She believes we must learn to tap into the energy and, if we do so, we would find greater meaning in life and lessen its stresses.

Winning three NCAA championships in a row—1993, 1994, 1995—and going undefeated in 1995 was a thrill for Vollstedt and a real feat. No other team had ever done either.

Another exciting year was 1997. The team consistently placed in the top three but was never expected to win the NCAA championship. They peaked at the right time and won regionals by only one shot. That win provided the confidence needed for a smooth transition going into nationals. Each player made a contribution, and each knew she had to perform her best. It was a team performance, one without a super star. Team members had complete confidence in each other. They all had faith channeled in the right direction and kept the energy flow positive throughout the competition. It became another mystical experience.

The 1998 NCAA championship was bittersweet for Vollstedt. At the site of the championship in the fall preview, Linda had a golf cart accident and severely injured her leg. She was out of coaching for four months, but was able to come back in two months before the final event. Her team went on to win by 18 strokes, setting a new collegiate golf scoring record.

## CHALLENGES

While coaching has eminent moments, it is rarely without challenges and obstacles. Vollstedt mediated the obstacles with wisdom and patience. Wisdom teaches her not to expend energy on unchangeable particulars, and patience reminds her that in time some things do change. These obstacles are an assortment of administrative traditions, women's rights, and the accompanying issues such as salary, newspaper and television exposure, and the NCAA's exhaustive array of rules. One of her strategies for success with administrators has been to ask them for suggestions; often one of their suggestions has been a solution to a problem. This approach has linked the golf team and the administration in a cooperative endeavor.

Women's golf at Arizona State University has become the premier athletic program. This acclaim is the result of the dedicated work of Coach Vollstedt and her progeny of dedicated athletes. Linda has made a concerted effort to teach players that successful people have recognizable characteristics. These characteristics are manifested in the way the players walk, talk, and dress. They are also displayed in hard work on the playing field and in the academic arena. In addition, Vollstedt emphasizes the need for social skills and encourages players that women have their own style of competing in sport. She feels that the female style could enhance and benefit the male competitor, too.

Coach Linda Vollstedt has never been mentored by a golf coach. However, she does credit Chuck Hogan for his part in making a big difference in her life.

He operates a company called Chuck Hogan's Learning and Performance Center. His efforts have helped advance her understanding of the mental side of golf and life. Although Linda has coached without the benefit of mentors or role models, she has taken some ideas and ideals from Hogan and has gleaned bits and pieces from others in order to strike her own method and style of coaching. Even so, Vollstedt has an extraordinary talent for coaching and a superb record affirming it. For example, in nineteen seasons her team has placed in the top five nine times, and they have won five national championships, six total, five in the past six years. This is an incredible record. However, Vollstedt knows the value of a personal mentor, and she intentionally teaches and mentors others to pass on what she has learned. Ultimately, to teach and mentor a generation of coaches and athletes will be her gift of sharing—Linda Vollstedt's destiny fulfilled, a teacher and a coach.

## RECOGNITIONS AND ACHIEVEMENTS

### Coaching Recognitions in Division I

- Nine PAC 10 Conference Championships: 1981, 1984, 1985, 1987, 1988, 1993, 1994, 1995, 1996
- PAC 10 Coach of the Year, 1989, 1993, 1994, 1995
- Regional Championship, 1993, 1997
- Western Regional Coach of the Year, *Golf Week*, 1989, 1993, 1994, 1995, 1997
- National Golf Coaches Association Coach of the Year, 1993, 1994, 1995
- NCAA National Coach of the Year, 1984, 1985, 1986, 1989, 1993, 1994, 1995, 1997
- National Championships: 1990, 1993, 1994, 1995, 1997, 1998
- Twenty All Americans, 37 Awards
- Fourteen Players Playing Professionally
- Three NCAA Individual Champions
- Ten U.S. Curtis Cup Players
- Ten USGA Amateur and Public Links Champions
- LPGA Teaching Division Coach of the Year, 1993, 1996

### Other Accomplishments

- Member of NCAA Golf Committee
- Golf Coaches Hall of Fame, 1994

Photo courtesy of University
of Kansas

# MARIAN WASHINGTON

*Basketball—University of Kansas*

## INTRODUCTION

It took an exceptional teacher to note the dimming light of boredom encasing one of her most capable young math students. The student was Marian Washington, and the teacher was Ruth Redding. Ruth ignited the light of a possibility into young Marian Washington.

## PERSONAL DATA

*Born*: August 16, 1946, West Chester, Pennsylvania

*Father*: Goldie Washington

*Father's Occupation*: Self-employed

*Mother*: Marian Jane Lomack

*Mother's Occupation*: Homemaker

*Siblings*: Four sisters and one brother

*Child*: Josie

*Alma Maters*: West Chester State College—B.S., Health and Physical Education, 1970; University of Kansas—M.S., Biodynamics and Administration, 1975

## FORMATIVE YEARS

Marian's parents not only taught the value of hard work; they also taught the importance of taking pride in work that represented quality rather than mere quantity. The entire family had to work to make ends meet.

Although the Washingtons did not have an abundance of money, they had a mother who balanced their lives with an abundance of love. She was a religious woman, and her father was a highly respected member of the community. He was respected because he had integrity and it showed, and the townspeople showed the entire family respect because of their father's admirable ways. All of the Washington children acquired their parents' enormous capacity to work hard and to love others.

## SPORTS HISTORY

Marian was raised on a farm just outside of West Chester. In junior high she discovered sport skills came easily, and through sports a sense of self-worth developed: "I thought it was the one avenue that if you were able to start at the same starting line as everybody else, it didn't matter what your color was, it didn't matter how much money you had or what clothes you had, it was what was inside you and what gifts you were blessed with that really mattered." Marian became an accomplished track and field athlete and aspired to become an Olympian.

Ruth Redding awakened Marian to the possibility of going to college. Ruth taught ninth grade math at Henderson High School. She was black and she helped Marian realize she was physically gifted, but she recognized that Marian was also intellectually gifted and capable of receiving a higher education. This was important because it gave Marian a same-race role model which was not very available in that period of time.

In the early sixties, black students were usually scheduled in manual-skills classes such as typing. Although Ruth taught some of these classes, she also taught upper-level classes. Upon Ruth's suggestion, Marian took more challenging math classes and did very well.

The following year Ruth had Marian sign up for the college prep courses. However, after signing up for the classes and going to school the first day, she had been put back with her friends in the pre-preparatory classes. Ruth called Marian that evening to ask her how the first day had gone, and Marian told her what had happened. Ruth sorted it out, and the next day Marian was back in the college prep courses.

As she approached high school graduation, she was looking for a scholarship opportunity because she didn't have any money. Marian wanted to attend Tennessee State where Wilma Rudolph had gone, but Tennessee was too far from home and she had too little money. After applying to several schools, only one replied offering a partial scholarship for track. The best solution was to remain at home and attend nearby West Chester State College. By this time she really wanted to play basketball, and West Chester State was the number-one school in the country for athletics. Marian attended Cheyney State College for a year and then transferred to West Chester State.

At West Chester Marian "auditioned" for the basketball staff. Her stellar performance left no question that they wanted her on the team. The coach was Carol Eckman, a stand-out performer, but her vision of West Chester was way ahead of the game.

Like most women athletes at the time, Marian majored in health and physical education. Without question, she wanted to be a teacher. Her basketball career at West Chester State was very successful and resulted in an invitation to try out for the U.S. national team. She became one of the first two black women ever to make the team. That same year, West Chester State won their first national invitational basketball championship.

Her continual success in basketball pushed her track and field career into the background. In 1970 Alberta Lee Cox talked to seven All Americans about moving to Kansas City to play on the same AAU team in order to get ready for the 1972 Olympics. Even though they prepared, the Olympic committee had too many events to add women's basketball to the schedule. The impact from that decision was traumatic. Marian was twice an Olympic trialist for throwing the discus and had once been the national indoor shot-put champion.

## DECISION TO COACH

While in Kansas City, Marian taught two years at Martin Luther King Junior High School. This assignment allowed her to teach and play for Bert's AAU team. She played basketball three additional seasons, then returned to throwing the discus. In 1972 she looked up the legendary throwing coach, Bill Easton, at the University of Kansas, and started throwing under his direction. Bill and another friend encouraged Marian to take a leave of absence and go back to college and complete a master's degree. That fall, 1972, she enrolled in the University of Kansas and combined studies with assisting the women's basketball team. At this same time, she was competing nationally with the basketball team and throwing the discus with the track and field team. The following year (1973), Marian was invited to take over the basketball program at the University of Kansas, and the next year (1974), she was appointed athletic director for women. It was an unbelievable task, but she felt it was her destiny. Marian was taught to deal with long work hours and a large volume of work.

In 1974 she started the University of Kansas track and field program for women. With the passage of Title IX, she was responsible for overseeing eight sports and was looking for qualified coaches. Then in 1975, Marian was able to get scholarships in place. Marian is now in her twenty-seventh year at the University of Kansas.

## MEMORABLE MOMENTS

Being part of the first women's national basketball championship team is an historical first. The second was to be one of the first two black women ever to be selected for the national team. The other black athlete was Colleen Bowser from Augusta, Kansas. Playing for the United States in the 1971 world championship in São Paulo, Brazil was really a highlight.

Marian was the first black woman to coach a United States team in international competition. In 1983 her U.S. Select Team compiled a 7–1 record in Taiwan, losing to Canada in the finals. Being the first black person on an Olympic coaching staff is certainly another highlight, as was being part of the gold medal experience in 1996 in Atlanta. Finally, being the first woman to be the president of the 3,000-strong, 99 percent male Black Coaches Association was a distinct honor; she served twice as president—1993 and 1994. Marian received her honorary doctorate degree from West Chester University in May of 1999.

## ROLE MODELS/MENTORS

*Parents*—Marian credits her parents as the first and foremost of her role models. From them she learned the value of hard work, integrity, and how to maintain a balanced life filled with love and God. All of these qualities have carried over into her life and her coaching career.

*Ruth Redding*—This woman was Marian's advocate. She got her into college prep classes, inspired her to think about college, and assisted her in applying for college. Ruth Redding saw that Marian was a bright, capable young woman, and she endowed Marian with a picture of herself that she had never before seen.

*Coach Fascioli*—Coach Fascioli started the track program at Henderson High School. Marian credits Fascioli with helping her to achieve in the track and field program. He drove athletes to the limits and more. He pushed her to do her best.

*Carol Eckman*—Carol, coach of the West Chester State basketball team, provided another driving force and a wonderful role model. Her vision of success was passed to her players as she foretold women's potentials and urged them to organize and work together for unified success. Carol organized the first invitational that produced a national championship.

*Alberta Lee Cox*—Cox was Marian's AAU coach, the one who would have been the first women's Olympic basketball coach in 1972 had there not have been a boycott. Through Cox's efforts, Marian was able to perform well enough to play for the national team. Marian felt Alberta Lee Cox probably did more than any other person in developing the foundation for the U.S. team. She coached and inspired them and had them ready for the 1972 Olympics, but, due to overscheduling, women's basketball was not included. According to Marian, Carol Eckman and Alberta Lee Cox did whatever was necessary to promote women's basketball. Their impact is still felt today.

## PHILOSOPHY OF COACHING

It is important for Marian to know and understand each athlete. She explains that finding the connection is critical. "It's like going in to a dark closet. You know there is a light switch, and my job as a coach is to find that switch so I can turn athletes on to their potential." It is her hope that athletes will come to trust her. She does not play games with athletes; she is truthful and direct. She never wants to hear athletes say, "Well, coach, if you had only told me."

Many of her athletes have had to battle all of their lives, mostly because of their backgrounds, and, as a result, they only know one way to fight for survival. To counter these difficulties, she teaches alternative ways to fight and skills for coping.

Diversity requires everyone to learn to work together. She finds it is a challenge to help young people learn how to live with each other and how to respect and appreciate differences. Society doesn't do that well, but Marian is determined to add her unique touch to creating a better world. The heart of her philosophy, while putting winning teams on the floor each year, is to take young people and teach them how to care for each other, to be positive with each other, and to live together and work to achieve common goals.

## CHALLENGES

Marian is a true pioneer. In the sixties she was part of an integrated high school when the civil rights movement was at its peak; she was one of the first blacks on a national team; she was an athletic director at the age of 28; she was the first black woman to coach a U.S. national basketball team; and she was the first woman president of a male-dominated Black Coaches Association. Marian has personified aspiration, discipline, and hard work. Marian is a Christian who believes enthusiastically in the Lord Jesus Christ for all things.

At times the challenges seemed unfair; in some cases, it was difficult to determine if they were challenges because she was a woman, or because she was a black woman, or both: "Every time there was something that was difficult, it seemed like the good Lord would find something very positive shortly after for me to experience to keep encouraging me. So as I look back over the years, truly He has graced me with some wonderful friends and loved ones to help me, but it was truly because of Him that I was able to survive."

Her biggest challenge for the first five years was merely trying to change attitudes towards women's athletics. Another challenge was to establish eight sports programs, and another was to go from zero scholarships to fully funded athletic scholarships.

## LIFE BEYOND ATHLETICS

Marian has dreams of what she would like to accomplish. She is business minded and would one day like to have a business in the sports industry. She has been offered professional coaching positions, but feels the time is not right for such a job. Artistically inclined, she would like to pursue some of these interests, like the martial arts, photography and, art. One of the next plans on her agenda is to start workshops for young women coaches—particularly black women—so they can better understand how to prepare themselves to break into the coaching ranks.

Marian's idea of an ideal vacation is going to the beach. Reading is a favorite pastime, especially inspirational books. She collects classic movies.

Marian has one daughter, Josie. Josie is a 1984 graduate of the University of Kansas. Josie and her husband, Rick McQuay, and their two children, Lauren Nicole and Ricardo, reside in Pennsylvania.

## RECOGNITIONS AND ACHIEVEMENTS

### Accomplishments as a Player

- Twice AAU All American
- National Team: 1969, 1970, 1971, 1972, 1973, 1975
- World Championship Team, 1991

### Coaching Recognitions in Division I

- Big Eight Tournament Titles: 1979, 1980, 1981, 1987, 1988, 1993
- Big Eight Conference Championships: 1979, 1980, 1981, 1987, 1992, 1996
- Big Twelve Conference Championship, 1997
- Big Eight Coach of the Year, 1992, 1996
- Big Twelve Coach of the Year, 1997
- Black Coaches Association Coach of the Year, 1992, 1996
- Three Kodak All Americans
- One Olympian

### National Coaching Assignments

- Olympic Festival, 1981
- Olympics Assistant Coach, 1996
- National Team Coach, 1983

### Other Accomplishments

- Olympic Selection Committee, 1984, 1988
- Carol Eckman Award, 1991
- Kansas Basketball Coaches Association Coach of the Year, 1992
- President of Black Coaches Association, 1993–1994
- Kansas Women's Athletic Director, 1974–1979
- Member of Kodak All American Selection Committee

Photo courtesy of University
of Florida

# MARY WISE

*Volleyball—University of Florida*

## INTRODUCTION

Mary Wise has taken her University of Florida Volleyball squad to the NCAA final four five times in the eight years she has been coach. This noteworthy accomplishment also distinguishes her as the first and only female volleyball coach to have achieved such a feat. In the 1990s, she won more games than any male or female coach of a female volleyball team.

## PERSONAL DATA

> *Born*:  August 8, 1959, Evanston, Illinois
>
> *Father*:  Richard Fischl
>
> *Father's Occupation*:  Dentist
>
> *Mother*:  Lila Freshour
>
> *Mother's Occupation*:  Homemaker and manager of Richard's dental office
>
> *Siblings*:  Michael, Paul, John, Cathy, and Tom
>
> *Husband*:  Mark Wise
>
> *Children*:  Matthew and Mitchell

*Alma Mater*: Purdue University—B.S., Physical Education, 1981

## FORMATIVE HISTORY

Mary, the fifth of six children, was raised in a neighborhood enriched by prolific Catholic families with 8 to 12 children per family. Hence, neighborhood play was a prime event with children who created year-round outdoor activities.

The Fischl family engaged in tent camping and a yearly week at the YMCA family camp in Fremont, Michigan. Although neither parent had a keen interest in sports, the neighborhood kids did. They always had a pick-up game in progress, and, of course, Mary and her close-in-age siblings were always participants. Their closeness in age encouraged them to play with each other, too.

## SPORTS ENTRY

Mary attended the same elementary school for eight years. In the seventh grade she attended Saint Athanasius. This school offered an advanced basketball program for girls. The seventh-grade team was permitted to travel and compete in the Chicago area. During this time a favorite teacher emerged— Tannie Braigel, a parent and an athlete, volunteered to coach the seventh- and eighth-grade teams. She devoted the time and effort to make it a successful experience for the young girls. The team was good enough to play in DePaul University's Alumni Hall for a city championship.

It was a drastic switch from the small elementary school to a 4,000–student public high school. At Evanston High School, Mary found a niche in the athletic program where she moved with the seasons from one sport to another. First to volleyball, then to basketball, and finally to softball. Playing on three teams for four years kept her absorbed in activities she loved.

Evanston High School also featured track and badminton, sports for which they were well known, having established a long tradition. On the other hand, traditions had not been established in volleyball, basketball, or softball.

Mary expected to follow the example of her parents and siblings who all attended college. The decision of where to attend a university was easy because Purdue University offered her a volleyball scholarship. Timing was good as it was the first year scholarships were offered to women (1977). Originally her plans were to attend where her brothers and sister were attending, because tuition and living expenses were less at an in-state school. But Purdue had lost a prime recruit to the University of Southern California giving Mary the volleyball scholarship.

Carol Dewey was Purdue's volleyball coach. At the time, Carol was the all-time winningest coach in the history of Purdue's sports programs. Purdue won the Big Ten Conference championship in both her junior and her senior years. Both years the team went to the national tournaments. The volleyball team's success motivated Purdue to increase volleyball scholarships, travel budgets, and support systems in order to elevate the sport to a true intercollegiate sport.

## DECISION TO COACH

Tannie Braigel, Mary's seventh-grade coach, aroused Mary's interest in physical education as a college major. Four years with high school coach Alice Simpson again ignited in her the spark to teach and coach, and shortly after meeting Purdue coach Carol Dewey, Mary knew for certain that she wanted to coach college students. This fine coach was a mentor and a guide to Mary. By the time Mary was a senior, she was teaching, and Carol Dewey was instructing her in the art of coaching.

Mary graduated from Purdue in May 1981 with a bachelor's degree in physical education. She was offered and accepted the head volleyball coaching position at Iowa State University. Mary was just 21 years old and an inexperienced coach. Associate Athletic Director Elaine Heber could have hired an experienced male coach, but she insisted on a female hire. She had strong feelings that women should coach women, so she risked hiring an inexperienced young woman. However, Elaine Heber knew that Mary had been carefully tutored by Carol Dewey for four years, and that permitted Elaine to feel comfortable with the decision to hire Mary. Looking back, Mary states, "At 21 I didn't know much. I just worked hard and tried not to hurt anybody."

The Iowa State years were productive for Mary as she dated and married Mark Wise whom she had met at Purdue. She also logged an 81–63 win—loss (.550) record, with a second-place finish in the Big Eight Conference. The last year (1984) was her best season; the team established a 21–9 (.700) record. The young couple planned to moved to Tampa, Florida, for Mary to work on a master's degree at the University of South Florida. Just prior to the move, Mark was hired as head basketball coach at Lindsey Wilson College in Columbia, Kentucky.

Wilson College did not have a volleyball program, nor did the nearby high schools. Mary decided to volunteer as an assistant for a couple of months at Western Kentucky Univeristy in Bowling Green. Afterwards she contacted Kathy DeBoer, head coach at the University of Kentucky. In 1986 Kathy was asked to take the dual role of assistant athletic director for women and head volleyball coach. She agreed to accept the assignment if she could hire a second assistant. The timing was perfect because Kathy DeBoer needed an assistant. For the next two years Mary and Mark had a hundred-mile commuter marriage so each could coach. When Mary became pregnant, Mark resigned his position and moved to Lexington. It was a financial challenge to live on $14,000 per year until Mark began teaching at a local high school and was hired as assistant coach at Transylvania University. With both employed and both coaching and both in the same town "it seemed like heaven." Neither were head coaches, but both were doing what they loved to do.

Mary remained as assistant at the University of Kentucky from 1986 to 1990. During the time she was at UK, the Wildcats won two Southeastern Conference titles and went to the NCAA tournament three times. She also advanced from graduate assistant to associate head coach.

In the spring of 1991, the University of Florida head volleyball coaching position became available. Mary interviewed and was offered the job in March; they immediately moved to Gainesville. Earlier she had competed with Florida and thought coaching at the University of Florida would be "a dream job." The job was especially attractive to her because she knew that the University of Florida offered great support to athletics, the quality of academic support was great, and the environment was very appealing to recruits. In short, Florida had all of the ingredients for a successful mix.

When Mary arrived, there were two highly skilled German players on the Florida team. These two talented players provided an outstanding base from which to build. One, Gudula Staub, was a two-time All American. Mary was successful in getting better recruits early in the season. Right away another two-time All American athlete from Turkey joined the team. Her name was Aycan Gokberk.

Since 1991, Mary's teams have made five final-four appearances and have won eight SEC Conference titles. In eight seasons at the University of Florida, Mary's record is 271–27 (.909). Overall, with the years at Iowa, her record as a head coach is 352–90 (.796). Currently she has the winningest volleyball program in the country, by total victories, since 1991. No woman volleyball coach has had so much success in that period of time.

## MEMORABLE MOMENTS

One of the greatest moments for Mary occurred when she was a senior setter at Purdue in 1980. Purdue was in the conference championship finals playing against Northwestern. It was "a five game screamer." The second major highlight occurred during Mary's first year at University of Florida (1991). They were matched against Louisiana State University. It was a home game, and LSU went on to the final four, but the Gators beat them. According to Mary, "The match went five games and that really put us on the map."

The third highlight happened in 1993. After losing some talented seniors to graduation, Florida went to the final four. The 1993 team was playing against number-one ranked University of Texas. Playing at Texas, the team lost Aycan Gokberk to a knee injury in the third game. In spite of losing Aycan, they beat Texas, and Florida made it to the final four for a back-to-back second year.

## ROLE MODELS/MENTORS

*Tannie Braigel*—Tannie Braigel was the volunteer seventh-grade coach. "She was devoted to kids, supportive, competitive, and she was a wonderful teacher who possessed great teaching skills."

*Alice Stimpson*—Alice coached Mary in three sports for four years at Evansville High School. "Her superior teaching skills qualified her to teach anything. She was a role model, and she took students to another competitive level."

*Carol Dewey*—Purdue's volleyball coach, Carol Dewey, became Mary's coaching mentor. "Without a doubt, Carol Dewey had the most significant impact on my coaching."

## PHILOSOPHY OF COACHING

Mary sums up her philosophy this way, "We think to be successful everyone must have a role, and we are really big on fulfilling goals. How will each player help us be successful from the leading kill-getter to the player coming off the bench. It's all about fulfilling roles, and that we learn how to compete, and we relish and we love competing. Competing is a good thing. Work hard and treat people well. Playing volleyball at college was such a good experience for me that I strongly feel I want to do everything I possibly can to make it a positive experience for the players. I want them to enjoy this time. And, when it is all over, I want them to miss it. I don't want them to count down the days until it's over. My hope would be that they really had enjoyed it."

Mary believes a coach must have a game plan and understand it. Different roles factor into her game plan: "When each of the team, including the coaches, contributes to the assigned role, success results. Athletes know the areas they must be good at to defeat any given team. When this approach is taken, then all they have to do is go out and play hard."

## CHALLENGES

Mary is appreciative of the fact that she has been blessed with good health and good support. During her senior year in high school, a new coach was assigned to volleyball—she had never coached a volleyball team. The experience was so unpleasant that six of the seniors quit, leaving Mary and one other as the only seniors on the team. Volleyball was the sport she wanted to play in college. Things went from very good to bad and worse.

Fortunately, in 1977, when the sports were under the AIAW, high school athletes tried out for scholarships, and coaches wrote letters of recommendation. This worked in Mary's favor. Other coaches knew of her playing ability and wrote recommendations for her to Purdue. Actually, Mary believes she was recruited to Purdue more on personality than on skill. However, Carol Dewey saw her potential and employed her know-how to develop her into a highly skilled competitor.

## CHANGES IN ATHLETES

Mary describes the change in athletes as a "lost innocence." Certainly the participation is based on intrinsic motivations; playing for the love of the game has seriously diminished. Players playing high school volleyball are playing to see if they can get a scholarship to compete in college. The accountable levels have increased. Coaches and players are held far more accountable now than in the past. One can verify this by looking at the rule book. Coaches are expected to win much more now than previously. One of the major consequences is that the game is now coached at a much higher level, and the women play at a much higher level.

## LIFE BEYOND ATHLETICS

Mary and Mark's second son, Mitchell, was born in 1993. When not involved with volleyball, Mary likes to spend time with her boys. Family activities include Little League Baseball, flag football, and University of Florida games. Mark is a television broadcaster for men's basketball and enjoys his profession. In his free time he takes the boys to the dentist and the pediatrician.

The family takes a yearly ski vacation. Mary also likes to read, but presently her reading is confined to reading while lying next to Mitchell. Matthew attends the games with Mary. The younger son, Mitchell, travels with the team in the University of Florida plane.

## RECOGNITIONS AND ACHIEVEMENTS

### Accomplishments as a Player

- All Conference Big Ten, 1979, 1980
- All Region, 1979, 1980

### Coaching Recognitions in Division I

- Eight SEC Conference Championships, 1991–1998
- Conference Coach of the Year: 1991, 1992, 1993, 1995, 1996
- Regional Championships: 1992, 1993, 1996, 1997, 1998
- Regional Coach of the Year: 1991, 1992, 1994, 1995, 1996
- AVCA Coach of the Year: 1992, 1996
- Ten All Americans, 11 awards
- Winningest Team in NCAA volleyball since 1991: 271 wins, 28 losses (.906)
- Only woman coach to take a team to five Final Four

### National Coaching Assignments

- Olympic Festivals, South Squad, Gold Medal, 1993
- World University Games, 1995

Photo courtesy of Fresno
State University

# MARGIE WRIGHT
## *Softball—Fresno State University*

### INTRODUCTION

Perhaps Margie Wright's disappointment as a youth at not being allowed to participate on a recreation league softball team girded her with the will and determination to cultivate an enviable softball program at Fresno State University. It all happened in Warrensburg, Illinois, and is now being realized in the Fresno Bulldog's $3.5 million stadium in Fresno, California.

### PERSONAL DATA

*Born*: December 28, 1952, Decatur, Illinois

*Father*: Kermit Wright

*Father's Occupation*: Truck driver for a corn processing plant

*Mother*: Eva Mears

*Mother's Occupation*: Homemaker and then school playground director

*Siblings*: Janet, Betty Jane, Betty Fern, Jeannie, and Paul

*Alma Mater*: Illinois State University—B.S., Physical Education, 1974

## FORMATIVE YEARS

Margie's hometown is Warrensburg, Illinois. This small farming community of about 700 people is located in downstate Illinois. Her parents not only raised their own children, but they raised 15 foster children, too. So plenty of children and lots of boys were around to interact with in games. Little money was available, so everyone took turns coming up with a dime. With the dime they purchased a rubber ball and played baseball all day long. By the end of the day, the ball would be worn-out and someone would find another dime for the next day. Margie's mother hit ground balls, her father played catch, and Margie and her sisters fielded the ground balls and pitched the ball. The family did little else for active recreation, but they played cards and board games. The community had one television station, and they listened to a lot of radio. They were active in their local Church of God congregation. They retired to bed early and arose early as Margie's father always left for work by 5 A.M.

Money and summer softball prevented extended vacations other than visits to an uncle and aunt who lived in Memphis, Tennessee. It was hard to go on extended vacations because the kids played softball and Margie's father coached a team.

The elementary school was two houses from the Wright's house. In the sixth grade the children were bused to another small town. Margie had a favorite science teacher, Mr. Garbs. She described him as "very hard, but he had a great sense of humor." A social science teacher impressed her, too; he was very strict, but had a great sense of humor. In the seventh and eighth grades the students went to a school in Warrensburg. Here, in junior high, she met Mrs. Southern, director of the National Honor Society. Mrs. Southern gave Margie a lot of direction and held students accountable, much like her own parents. During study hall hours, Margie worked for Mrs. Donna Baldwin, her physical education teacher who was strict but fun. The junior high and high school years in Warrensburg were very enjoyable to young Margie.

## SPORTS HISTORY

The family and the neighborhood kids played street ball and Indian ball. Margie also played softball in the summer and basketball in the winter. When Margie was ten years old, she made cuts on the little league baseball team. The very night she was going to start as the pitcher, while in the park ready to play, a member of the women's club came to the park to inform officials a meeting had been held and it had been decided that girls were not allowed to play on the team. The announcement was made 15 minutes before the game started. Upon hearing the news, Margie ran home and cried for the next two days. It was a devastating event for the youngster. Her father took things in hand and had her play on the city park team he coached, along with her two sisters. She was the youngest and the smallest on the team, as a result she got walked. Her growth didn't spurt until she was 12. One day an older sister, the pitcher, quit, and Margie became pitcher.

The decision to attend college came when she was a senior in high school. Knowing the financial conditions at home would not allow her to go, she never entertained the idea. None of her older sisters could go, and it was assumed she would marry soon after high school like most everyone else. A good friend, Cheryl Binklead, played on the same summer softball team. Cheryl was a year older than Margie, and her parents had sent her to Illinois State. Margie remembers thinking how "neat" it was for Cheryl to go to college and play college basketball. Margie was a high school cheerleader because they didn't have a girls' sports program. The more she thought about it the more she realized "that is what I want to do. I want to go to college." After talking to her parents, on several occasions for long periods, it was apparent they could not give her financial assistance. But with her father's help, she obtained a student loan enabling her enroll at Illinois State University in Normal, Illinois.

When Margie got to Illinois State, she played softball, basketball, and field hockey. Jill Hutchinson and Gooch Foster coached both sports together. These women became the first female role models she had known beyond her mother and sisters. In addition to softball and basketball, Margie played field hockey during the last three years of college and then played AAU field hockey for two years after graduating. At Illinois she earned four letters each for basketball and softball and three for field hockey. As a junior she led the ISU softball team to a second-place finish in the NCAA softball nationals.

## DECISION TO COACH

Jill Hutchinson and Gooch Foster affected Margie's pursuing a physical education major. She wanted to be a high school teacher and actually acquired a teaching position before graduating. She still lacked one summer term to graduate. The job was at Metamora High School, with a student body of just 800 students, in Metamora, Illinois. At the school she coached five sports: volleyball, basketball, softball, track, and bowling. She was the only coach at the school. In addition to coaching five sports, she oversaw the Girls' Athletic Association Intramural Program. She held this heavy load for three years before burning out; breaking up with the young man she planned to marry added fuel to the fire. She decided to move on to Eastern Illinois University where she took a pay cut, but she only had to coach volleyball and be assistant softball coach and teach some classes. Margie remained at Eastern two years. Gooch Foster called to say she was leaving ISU to go to UC Berkeley and Jill Hutchison was going to focus on basketball. ISU offered Margie the job, and she began coaching there in 1980. In six seasons at ISU she accumulated a 149–80–2 record.

In 1985, Gooch Foster, now coaching basketball at Berkeley, called to report that Fresno State College was looking for a softball coach. Gooch also called Fresno and told them about Margie. After a few conversations between

Gooch and Fresno, they called Margie to see if she was interested enough to apply.

When she started thinking about coaching softball on the West Coast in comparison to the Midwest, especially in terms of weather, the change became very appealing. This was her first experience being interviewed; other positions had been offered without an interview. After the interviewees were narrowed to four, she interviewed, and within two weeks Fresno offered her the job. The downside of the decision was that she would leaving her family and her alma mater. However, the opportunity would allow her to accomplish goals held since her freshman year of college.

In 1986 Margie became the softball coach at Fresno State. In addition to coaching, she stayed an active competitor until being selected as the assistant coach to the U.S. Olympic Softball Team in 1996. In the late seventies, 1977–1979, after graduation, she played in the Invitational Women's Professional League for three years for St. Louis. She also played for the Moline Red-Birds. After arriving in Fresno she organized a team of kids to play for her, and she was player and coach. The name of the team is the Fresno Force. Her amazingly competitive life came to a close at the age of 44.

## MEMORABLE MOMENTS

Winning the Olympic Gold Medal heads Margie's list of memories. Even today the thing that gives her goose bumps is listening to the national anthem and listening to the roar of the crowd as the game was finishing and then being awarded the gold medal. "It was such an unbelievable feeling, and the special part for me was I had five players that had played for me at Fresno State on the medal team. It was just a thrill that they could all be part of something so great." At that point Fresno State had not won a national championship. They had been in several world series but had never won.

The second stellar experience was winning the national championship in 1998. Margie explains, "Winning this national championship was, oh my gosh, the thrill of a life time. I'm around these kids everyday, and I know how hard they worked, and how much they wanted it. And I know how much pride they had in the program from past years. To beat the team that only had three losses all year and to know you had to be perfect was a thrill."

The third highlight was the 1998 tour of Japan for the world championships. Margie says, "Anytime I'm representing our country I am so proud to wear those three letters: USA. It is just a phenomenal feeling to walk out in front of other countries and be proud that you're wearing USA on your chest, it is just great." Again there were six Fresno State kids on the team: "It was so nice for them to be able to celebrate that, and to win, because it was a lot tougher this time than it was in the Olympics."

## ROLE MODELS/MENTORS

*Eva Mears Wright*—Margie holds her mother, Eva Wright, as the most impressive of all her role models.

*Mr. Gaabs and Mrs. Southern*—These two elementary school teachers combined strict expectations with good humor and left a lasting impression on young Margie.

*Jill Hutchinson*—College coach Hutchinson taught Margie a valuable lesson in temper control. Margie was blocking out to get rebounds during a basketball game, and the defense kept shoving her in the back, but the referees did not call it. Margie lost her "cool" in the process. Hutchinson sent her to the bench and then said, "If you ever act like that again, you will never play another basketball game for me." Margie remembers this like it happened yesterday. She also remembers "it straightened me out immediately."

*Gooch Foster*—Foster challenged Margie to stretch her capacity as a pitcher. About an hour before a game, Gooch came and asked Margie to do something she had never asked her to do before. She wanted her to throw at four or five different speeds. Margie went with the catcher beyond the outfield. Between them they came up with five new signals, and using the new strategy won the game. In the final they lost the game in 16 innings.

**Billie Moore**—After college Margie became a collegiate basketball referee. Many of the games she officiated were games involving UCLA and Billie Moore. Billie invited Margie to try out for the 1972 World Games team. Billie helped Margie improve her jump shot. "I always looked at her with a great deal of respect because she was very tough and her teams were always very good, and they left everything out on the court and that's what I always respected."

*Darlene May*—Darlene was coach at Cal-Poly, Pomona; she was not only a great basketball coach, she also earned Margie's respect as a great official.

## PHILOSOPHY OF COACHING

Margie's philosophy is based on winning but not in the usual sense. It's mostly the individual winning as a person. She says she will give any player that plays for her the tools and the opportunities to become the best they can become. She tries not to get wrapped up in mere wins and losses. From her perspective, the most rewarding thing from athletes she has coached has not been the trophies that they have won. The most rewarding part is knowing the kind of persons the athletes have become, such as what they have done in their own lives to be role models for others. The philosophy Margie uses has more to do with life in general than it does sport: "Because you can't play softball all of your life even though some would like to. But you can't. You have to work hard at anything good that you get." She believes these qualities show when she looks at all the Fresno State athletes who have made the Olympic team and World Championship teams. She sees young people who haven't given up. She sees young people who "have fought, and fought, and fought and have gone through a process in which they have done everything in their power to not give up and to set a goal and to work as hard as they can to make it."

## CHALLENGES

One of the biggest challenges has been being a female in a male-dominated profession. Going through all the Title IX battles has been difficult for Margie. Some difficult situations have occurred recently at Fresno State. Margie was brought up to do the right and the fair thing, but the coaching environment has not been totally fair to women and women coaches. She also believes it will probably remain this way for a long time. She also states, "You have to be better than everyone in order to get recognition. And that is the toughest thing." The battles have almost been enough to drive Margie out of coaching.

Recalling her high school teaching days, she claims it was especially bad. Coaching five teams for example, holding one practice at 6 A.M. and another at 8 P.M. Prime practice time was usually not available for most women coaches during those times.

At Illinois State there was only one indoor facility, and softball, her sport, was last on the scheduling list. At Fresno, the softball program has led the nation in attendance for many years. Here she feels she has sold her soul to get community support. In addition, they played on a field with bleachers, but without lights or a fenced outfield. Women could not practice at night like the men. Luckily for Margie, Fresno State was picked randomly for investigation of gender equity and inequity. The investigation by the Office of Civil Rights exposed the many inequities; in fact, Fresno State was out of compliance in 11 of 13 areas. With all of the inequities, Fresno State has come a long way, and now they have a $3.5 million Bulldog Stadium. Margie fought for and raised money to make the stadium a reality.

Another problem occurs when women try to promote women's sports. She claims they are told, "You don't get paid as much as the men's sports because you don't bring in revenue." Revenue does not automatically increase without a marketing and sports information support system to promote sports. Another problem happens when people are jealous of "your program because it is the most successful on campus. Slander does not help morale, especially when it drains one's energy and filters down to the athletes and you have to take supposed colleagues to court, it is not pretty."

Now Fresno has the best attendance in the country for softball. They draw as many as 6,000 for top games like UCLA and Arizona. So after three years she described as "hell," things are much better. The softball program brings in almost $200,000 a year. It brings a lot of recognition through the national championship and players on the national and Olympic teams. Recently she negotiated the best contract she has ever had.

Margie has a stubborn streak, and she is not a quitter. She has built an excellent softball program, fought a battle for a stadium, and received an out-of-court settlement from a law suit. She refuses to allow discouragement or jealous others to impede her progress. She stayed at Fresno and won the battles. It has been extremely difficult, but adds that she does not regret staying. Now she describes herself as very, very happy, but those three years were very difficult.

## CHANGES IN ATHLETES

The opportunities for athletic young women to compete, to be stronger and be better at softball, has made the sport better. She feels our society in general and the younger players have not been held to any level of accountability, which makes coaching more difficult. The lack of accountability can be seen, especially at Fresno State, where Title IX battles have been fought and female athletes expect to be treated like some of the male athletes; that is a very ugly change. When men athletes get things just because they ask for them, it causes problems. Margie's philosophy is, "You work for what you get here, if you want to have more than one uniform, then we need to show we deserve more than one uniform, and you need to respect the one you have." Leaving $100 bats around overnight on the field after they have been graciously donated by bat sponsors is simply one indicator of poor acceptance of responsibility and accountability. Many are not learning some of life's most important lessons in the earlier parts of their playing careers.

Finally, the kids that come to college today are more physically prepared: "Yet, sometimes that's a disadvantage because you may have to break bad habits." Athletes work out, use weights, and run to condition. They understand physical conditioning much better than earlier athletes.

The quality of competition continues to improve. Softball is becoming an Olympic sport and the World Championships and media coverage have made all Olympic sports more attractive to viewing audiences. Finally, athletes are learning the interview process, qualifying them to be great ambassadors for women's sports and the country.

## LIFE BEYOND ATHLETICS

Running and keeping in shape are important parts of Margie's life. She likes working in her garden; it's good therapy, and she takes pride in her 31 rose bushes. She loves Charlie Chan movies, *The Wizard of Oz*, and watching old movies like *Casablanca*.

Reading is another favorite pastime for Margie, and Patricia Cornwell's books are her favorites—she has read every one she has written. Cornwell writes about a female pressing forward while working in a male-dominated environment. Cornwell's books are detective stories; the main character is a coroner. She also reads John Grisham's books and enjoys books focused on law.

# RECOGNITIONS AND ACHIEVEMENTS

## Accomplishments as a Player

- International Pro Softball Association Rookie of the Year, 1977
- Played three years for the WPSC St. Louis Hummers, 1977–1979

## Coaching Recognitions in Division I

- Nine Conference Championships:
    NORCAI: 1978, 1982, 1983
    NORPAC: 1985, 1986
    PCAA: 1987, 1988
    Big West: 1989, 1990, 1991, 1992
    WAC: 1996, 1998, 1999
- Regional Championships: 1982, 1984, 1987, 1988, 1989, 1990, 1991, 1992, 1994, 1997, 1998, 1999
- Regional Coach of the Year, 1986, 1987, 1988, 1998
- National Championship, 1998
- National USOC Coach of the Year, 1986, 1987, 1988, 1998
- NCAA Coach of the Year, 1998
- NFCA Coach of the Year, 1998
- Forty-Four All Americans
- World Sonics appearances: 1987, 1988, 1989, 1990, 1991, 1992, 1994, 1997, 1998, 1999
- Second Current Career Winningest Coach in Division I
- Six Olympians, 1996 team

## National Team Assignments

- Olympic Festivals, 1993, 1994, 1995
- World Games assistant coach, 1996
- Junior World Games, 1995
- World Games, 1998
- World Games assistant, 1993
- Pan Am Games assistant, 1991 gold medal
- U.S. Junior National Team, 1995
- ISF World Champions, 1998

## Other Accomplishments

- Illinois State Hall of Fame, 1998
- All American Selection Committee, 1987–1999
- Decatur Athletic Hall of Fame, 1997

Photo courtesy of University
of Georgia

# SUZANNE YOCULAN

*Gymnastics—University of Georgia*

## INTRODUCTION

Bill Allen's daughter Suzanne was the son he never had. She was the one who played baseball with him in the backyard and at the same time learned the meaning of discipline and hard work. She recalls, "My dad was a disciplinarian. He worked nearly all the time. He definitely instilled a strong work ethic in all of us. He used to tell me there were two things he couldn't tolerate—disrespect and laziness. I've used those words a million times because I feel the same way he does."

## PERSONAL DATA

*Birth*: June 16, 1953, Fort Worth, Texas

*Father*: Bill Allen

*Father's Occupation*: Buyer for Montgomery Ward

*Mother*: Doris Allen

*Mother's Occupation*: Homemaker

*Siblings*: Denise, Gretchen, and Becky

*Husband*: Sam Yoculan

*Children*: Adam and Alexis

*Alma Mater*: Pennsylvania State University—B.S., Therapeutic Recreation, Dance emphasis, 1975

## FORMATIVE YEARS

Growing to adulthood in a family of girls, Suzanne spent a good deal of time with her father as she was the type of child that was in continuous motion and was not satisfied to just "sit around." She began gymnastics at age thirteen.

## SPORTS HISTORY

East Brunswick High School's gymnastics team was the state AAU champion. Suzanne was on the team from 1967 to 1971. The team was coached by Ann Burmeister, a former Olympian, and Don Weider, a talented coach and a strict disciplinarian. Ann's daughter, also named Ann, was an outstanding gymnast for East Brunswick, and her daughter, Talya Vexler, is a freshman gymnast for the University of Georgia. This makes her a third-generation gymnast.

East Brunswick's gymnastics program was so good that it attracted as many as 3,000 spectators to a match. After Ann Burmeister graduated, Suzanne won her first all-around competition; previously, she had always taken second place to Ann Burmeister. Suzanne learned to survive without a lot of attention and became a team player, because Ann was the star. Finally in her senior year she won the AAU all-around title.

Recruited to Pennsylvania State University for gymnastics, Suzanne quickly learned the program was more like an intramural enterprise: a cadre of about 40 girls and a situation where anyone could just walk in and join the team. Not being the kind to stand in line even at a grocery store, Suzanne soon found waiting in line to perform a cartwheel or any other gymnastics skill consumed too much practice time. Standing and waiting did not set well with one so energetic. Gymnastics should not have been her sport. She lacked the necessary flexibility and she did not have a low center of gravity. The practice floor was not padded nor were the beams, producing a continuous round of shin splints. Finally, her goal-oriented personality would not allow her to play for mere fun; she loved to compete and she competed to win. Consequently, she only remained on the team for a few months.

Her next venture was coaching part time for the Nittany Gymnastics Club. She also worked in a parks and recreation program in Altoona, Pennsylvania, while attending college.

## DECISION TO COACH

While replacing performance with coaching, she discovered she would be much better as a coach than a college gymnast. It was satisfying to know she could enjoy the sport and develop talented youngsters to become better gymnasts than she could have become.

No actual decision was made to coach; the process was very gradual. The more she coached, the more certain she was she could coach. First she coached 20 hours per week, then 30, and then 40. The change from performer to coach was so subtle, no one in her family reacted. Hence, becoming a coach was a process rather than a conscious decision. Over time she realized she had a talent, and she continued to coach.

One career decision she did make was settled while student teaching special needs children in New York. After a month, she determined she did not have the temperament to work with emotionally disabled and autistic children with whom she could not communicate. She left the program.

After marrying Sam Yoculan, the two purchased the parks and recreation program where she had been working part time. They incorporated it as Gemini Gymnastics. Sam kept the books, handled the payroll, and mopped the floors on Sunday afternoons. Buying the gym was not a deliberate decision; it just fell into their laps. Right after Suzanne graduated, the people who managed the gymnastics club offered, "You have been working here, we want you to run this thing." The parents and the city of Altoona wanted to get out of the business, so they offered it to her.

This was a good opportunity for a couple without other plans, and there was no need to invest any money. The real decision came when they sold the gym. They made a decision based on the fact that it didn't make sense for Suzanne to spend all of her time with other people's children instead of their own. Club coaching was strenuous and involved the coach from 3 in the afternoon until 10 at night. When their son, Adam, was young, Suzanne cared for him in the morning, and Sam took over in the evening. When Adam started kindergarten, Suzanne had little time with him, and she did not want to raise Adam in the gym where he would not get her undivided attention. Suzanne and Sam preferred not to put themselves or Adam in such a position, so they sold the gym.

Suzanne still continued to coach eight national-level gymnasts at Nittany Gymnastics in State College. They were the only kids she coached—it just involved some weekends, and it was not a year around job. Ed Isabelle of Nittany Gymnastics asked her to run the summer camp at his Woodward Gymnastics. Suzanne agreed to be the director at Woodward.

After two years at Woodward, in 1983, the University of Nebraska men's team came to the camp where Suzanne was teaching other coaches how to spot; she was one of a few females who could spot. They were the powerhouse in men's collegiate gymnastics, and several members of their team were going to be on the 1984 Olympic team.

The Nebraska guys told Suzanne Nebraska was looking for a women's coach, and she would be "a great college coach." Ed Isabelle also promoted the idea, and between Isabelle and the Nebraska team, Suzanne got excited about the possibility. Sam thought it would be fine—especially since she was back working evening hours in club coaching.

Suzanne applied for the job, was told she was one of two finalists, and was promised an interview. They never afforded her an interview, and they hired Rick Walton, from Georgia. This first experience with college athletics was also her first realization women didn't have the same opportunity as men. She reasoned Rick was hired because he had coached college gymnastics, but she was disappointed being denied the promised interview.

Ed Isabelle suggested she apply at Georgia, but Suzanne refused his suggestion based on her disappointing Nebraska experience. Ed just went ahead and signed her name on a Georgia job application and also sent a recommendation with his signature. Shortly thereafter she received a call from Liz Murphy, Director of Women's Athletics at Georgia. Suzanne explained she had not applied, but she went for an interview and was offered the job. The idea of going to Georgia never appealed to Suzanne until she was offered the job, and then she wanted to go. This happened at a time when she desperately wanted to coach a college team at a big institution. She was aware, too, that Georgia was coming to grips with Title IX and that there were problems with keeping the gymnastics program at the school, but she wanted the job and she took it.

## CHALLENGES

Athletics, according to Suzanne, "is the most sexually discriminatory profession in existence." This belief is not just directed to Georgia Athletics. It applies to anything involved in supporting and promoting athletics. It is her contention, and rightly so, that columnists write about familiar areas, and they are not familiar with gymnastics. "They don't care about gymnastics because they don't know about gymnastics."

It is also Suzanne's deep-seated belief that because gymnastics is not a backyard sport or a school sport, children are not exposed to it, and therefore the public's unfamiliarity with gymnastics tends to hurt the sport. She further explains that kids can grab a ball and throw or kick it around, but very few kids have the convenience or skills to easily engage in gymnastics, so they are not attracted to the sport. Obviously this leaves few gymnastics-knowledgeable people to become the sports writers to promote gymnastics. Many knowledgeable writers think the only people interested in gymnastics are women, and others believe those interested in gymnastics are interested because they have a child in gymnastics. This narrow vision does little to develop the sport. So the biggest obstacle to Suzanne is not just the attitude toward women but the attitude toward gymnastics in general. Suzanne calls this a "double whammy negative attitude." In her mind, this translates into, "Women should not be coaches, this is a man's occupation. Women can't be hard, women are supposed to be soft. They're supposed to be sentimental. They're supposed to be sensitive. They think you can coach if you're like that. All of those old stigmas and stereotypes are still in existence."

Basically the most discouraging moments to Suzanne are related to the media's and the athletic administrators' unfamiliarity with the sport. She claims, "People aren't receptive, in general, to other people's decisions. People are receptive to things they're familiar with and the things they understand. Football's already a success. It's already popular. Football already had 80,000 people at games, so everybody's behind it. People aren't interested in jumping in and being a part of a cause or a mission."

Suzanne felt, "It was hard to get people to have the same passion toward the sport that I had." Finding people who were passionate about the fact that college gymnastics could be a huge spectator sport in a community like Athens has been a key to her success. It was not easy, she found. "Ten were turned off before one could be found that could be turned on to the sport."

Suzanne prepares for every meeting she attends. Beforehand she tries to find out what will be discussed. When she gives a talk she wants to know about her audience in order to develop a rapport with them.

She wants people to identify with her not just as a gymnastics coach, but as a person with a wide range of knowledge beyond gymnastics. To do this she familiarizes herself with sports in which others have an interest. "I definitely don't try to get them to think of me as a Woman Coach. I'm not on a mission—'poor me, I've got to take care of a house and kids.' I'm no different from anyone else. My job is my choice. I don't want to be a 'Joan of Arc' kind of coach. I don't have any big issue that I'm championing. I just love what I do. When people around know you love what you do, they can't help but accept you. I don't think I come across as somebody who has all the answers. I'm a good listener. I'm sensitive to other people. How do I get along in a man's world?—I laugh at their jokes. I don't cop an attitude about sexist jokes. My husband's Italian. If they make an Italian joke, I laugh at it. I'm not sensitive about any of that stuff—gender, ethnicity. If you want to be around a group of people, you have to roll with the punches. You can't personalize everything that comes across your desk."

## ROLE MODELS/MENTORS

*Ed Isabelle*—When Suzanne was a freshman in college, Ed Isabelle started her out in coaching. Ed taught her to be a gymnastics instructor and a coach. He taught her the foundation for what she knows about gymnastics. He encouraged her to go to clinics, to acquire the technical aspects of the program, and to take advantage of every possible learning experience as he felt she had "natural instincts" to be a good coach.

According to Suzanne, Isabelle sees things in a very simple way; to him, "Nothing is complicated. He sees everything as an opportunity, and he turns problems into opportunities. He is optimistic and positive. If I ever tend to get a little negative or discouraged, he's definitely the one who turns it around for me." Suzanne maintains telephone contact with Ed at least once every month.

## MEMORABLE MOMENTS

As with most coaches, winning the national championship is memorable and exciting. Suzanne recalls the 1989 championship as more memorable than the 1987 championship. Winning at home by 0.05 points, with the air of excitement and the support of fans was a wonderful moment for Suzanne.

The second most memorable moment was when the University of Georgia Gymnastics Arena was filled for the first time, drawing the state of Georgia's highest-ever attendance for women's athletics. This was a beginning goal realized. When she first started coaching, she had pictured what it might look like with the arena full of fans, and it happened.

The third moment happened with Lori Strong (a gymnast between 1993 and 1995), in the locker room, after a big win over Alabama on ESPN. It happened as Suzanne was correcting the team on some of the things they did wrong and reprimanding them on some of their behavior even though they had just won. Lori looked up at her and exclaimed, "You are never satisfied. You are never happy, and you are never satisfied." That was a memorable moment for Suzanne because she learned from the comment. She learned that Lori was exactly right. "*I am* never satisfied, and *I do* have high expectations. It was a memorable moment to me that an athlete could recognize that and make that comment."

## PHILOSOPHY OF COACHING

Professional challenges and working with athletes are rewarding and a source of Suzanne's happiness. Watching young women reach potentials they never thought within their reach is a significant dimension of her coaching.

Suzanne feels the only way to be successful is not to be afraid of failure and to fight adversity, and she feels these are some of life's lessons one can learn in sport. She teaches it is very motivating to watch athletes figure out that the more they have to overcome adversity, the more successful they become.

In terms of job satisfaction, Suzanne rates herself as 9 out of 10. Just after another successful season, the rewards and the satisfaction are a lot greater than the disappointments. Ten years ago she had many days when she wanted to leave and never return. "Success helps. Respect helps. And respect comes from success. Basically, everything comes from success. There's no question about it."

Having claimed everything comes from success, she claims she feels no more stress to win today than she did during her first year coaching. Her first year attitude was, "We're going to the national championships—we're going to be a national championship team. I feel the same way today as I felt ten years ago. I don't feel any more pressure today because we won last year. It's exactly the same. We want to defend what is ours, the national championship. Before we had it, we wanted to go out and get one. It's not pressure—it's life. It's wanting to be a climber—not a camper."

Expounding further she states, "I feel like the competition is won or lost in the practice gym. I try to approach the competition day as much as possible like I approach the practice day. When we get up on the balance beam and have to do a routine, it's the same routine we do in the practice gym—it's not having an opponent who's going to physically influence what you do. If we make a big deal out of the competition, that just adds unnecessary pressure. The gymnasts prepare before practice with treatments in the training room with their metric strengths, and they eat a certain way. Most of the girls don't eat a lot before practice—they do the same thing before competition. We don't have a big meal before competition, because we don't do that on a regular basis. We have a big team meal after we win."

Many of the Georgia team is made of elite athletes: "These athletes have been preparing for competitions for ten years before they get to Georgia. They prepare themselves in different ways. They know what works and doesn't work for them. If something doesn't work at Georgia, it is changed, but it is not changed on the day of competition. Change is more of an on-going process."

The gymnasts all do different things to prepare themselves mentally: "We have girls who listen to motivational tapes, girls who listen to soft music, girls who take a nap—and we have some who want to get up early and go exercise. We don't say 'no exercise'; and we don't say, 'you have to take a nap.' Lucy Wener used to nap before competition—she also napped before practice everyday."

If they want a massage, the massage therapist is there for them. We make sure that we stay at a hotel where there are exercise bikes, because many of the girls like to exercise before competition. We make whatever they need available, and then it's up to them to decide what they need to be successful in competition. The mental and physical preparation are blended together, because a lot of the gymnasts prepare mentally by doing physical activity. We don't require team activity before competition—other than a short meeting, 15 minutes before competition. But that's not mental preparation. It's a team unity meeting."

Team members are well aware that the two things Suzanne cannot tolerate are laziness and disrespect. This has been an undergirding detail of her philosophy. For example, she considers an athlete who is always late is showing disrespect for team members.

Suzanne wants athletes to have no fear of failure. When failure is associated with fear, it precludes athletes from taking risks. To Suzanne there is no such thing as failure. Failure, to her, is not trying new things, not pushing oneself, and not having high expectations. Pushing oneself and having high expectations may cause one to readjust or transfer into something else. If transfer does occur, it merely suggests one should not be disappointed because the person did not fail to try. Hence failure to try is the failure component.

Losing a competition should cause a transfer in energy. It is expected that Georgia athletes do the highest level of difficulty in gymnastics. Coaches who espouse the idea that they lose a competition based on level of difficulty irritate Suzanne. She claims, "We have not *lost* anything. If we didn't try difficult skills, *that* would be a loss. We don't want to win by doing mediocre gymnastics—doing the easiest and safest skill at each level of difficulty. And we don't want to win because everybody else falls. I wouldn't feel any glory in winning if we hit 22 (of 24) routines and everybody else hit 17 and that is why we won."

Winning is what they did in 1993 and in 1998; they hit all of their routines and were far superior to other competitors. Although other teams had outstanding performances, Georgia was better.

Returning to the effects of the fear of failure, she claims it hurts children's development. For example when the teacher tells a child he needs to read five books this month, and the parent phones the teacher to say, "That is ridiculous, my child can't even read one. The expectations are too high. He can't do that. He'll fail." Suzanne believes the child should try to read five books and determine if it is possible. If the child reads three it is not a failure in Suzanne's book; it is three more than if the teacher had not given the assignment. It's partial success. It's not failure. To her, complete success may mean expectations are not high enough.

## CHANGES IN ATHLETES

According to Suzanne, the changes for women are almost endless: budgets have increased and support staff and benefits provided to women have undergone enormous changes.

There are now awards, such as the Sears Cup, recognizing the number-one athletic program in the nation; the Honda Awards, for the top athlete in each woman's sport; and the Broderick Award, for the overall woman athlete.

## LIFE CHOICES

Life choices are some of the hardest things for Suzanne. She still deals with the tug between work and family: "Mainly because I love my work so much. I get jazzed about my work. I don't like cleaning house. I like going to my daughter's soccer games. I like the family activities. I am not good with monotony. That's why I do well in my coaching job, it is always changing. It's going at a different pace. But at home, it's the same job every day. Dealing with family activities is routine. For a lot of people, their job is routine. So going home is refreshing." The mundane tasks of caring for a home make it difficult to balance her activities and not work too much.

For the present, Suzanne wants to continue the thing she loves—coaching. She wants to get all 12 scholarships endowed. She also wants to win more back-to-back championships, as she did in 1998 and 1999, and have 4,000 permanent season-ticket holders. If this can be done, the gymnastics team will be able to provide two endowed scholarships a year.

## LIFE BEYOND ATHLETICS

A variety of non-thinking, easy-reading books appeals to Suzanne. She likes to read at bedtime. Other times, she likes biography, self-help books, motivational books, books about speaking, and business books. Pat Riley's *The Winner Within: A Life Plan for Team Players* is a favorite because he puts a premium on cooperation, diligence, positive thinking, preparation, teamwork, respect for authority, and resilience. These characteristics are consistent with her own experiences and reinforce many of her own ideas. She enjoys the beach and likes to kayak, snow ski, hike, and play tennis.

In addition to these interests, Suzanne has been inspired by Mel Gibson's portrayal of the thirteenth-century Scottish warrior William Wallace in *Braveheart*. She especially likes the line pointed out by a William Wallace follower, "If they know you, they will respect you. And if they respect you, you can lead them." Suzanne has "found the need for people to know you indispensable in both leadership and promotion."

## RECOGNITIONS AND ACHIEVEMENTS

### Coaching Recognitions in Division I

- Ten SEC Conference Championships: 1986, 1987, 1991, 1992, 1993, 1994, 1996, 1997, 1998, 1999
- Twelve regional championships
- SEC Coach of the Year: 1986, 1987, 1998
- Five National Championships: 1987, 1989, 1993, 1998, 1999
- NCAA Coach of the Year: 1987, 1993, 1998
- Thirty Athletes, 137 All American awards
- Top-Ten ranking all 16 years, 14 of which were Top Five
- Six Olympians
- Twenty-four individual NCAA champions
- Five Honda Award winners

Photo courtesy of North Carolina
State University

# KAY YOW
## *Basketball—North Carolina State University*

## INTRODUCTION

The sporting world has long recognized that the will to win transmits tenacious tentacles into many dimensions of a competitor's life. Kay Yow explains the phenomenon: "I've faced a lot of tough opponents on the court, but the toughest foe that I've ever faced is cancer. I am grateful for the experiences I've had in sports which required a fighting spirit, determination, perseverence, etc. These same qualities, to a large extent, were what I needed for my fight against cancer! My sports background helped prepare me to battle this disease as well as often tough situations in life. I thank the Lord for blessing me with competitive sport opportunities and for inner qualities such as determination, perseverance, fighting spirit, etc. I am grateful for my battles in sport which have helped prepare me to battle in life. I think the Lord blessed me with a fighting spirit, a perseverance, and determination to compete with this foe. It was those same qualities, to a large extent, that I needed for my battle against cancer."

## PERSONAL DATA

*Born*: March 14, 1942, Greensboro, North Carolina

*Father:* Hilton Lee

*Father's Occupation:* P. Lorrilland Company, machine operator

*Mother:* Cora Elizabeth Yow

*Mother's Occupation:* Hairdresser

*Siblings:* Ronnie, Debbie, and Susan

*Alma Maters:* East Carolina University—B.S., English, 1964; University of North Carolina, Greensboro—M.S., Physical Education, 1970

## FORMATIVE YEARS

Yow's youthful sporting experiences began in backyards and on side roads. Her organized basketball debut started in high school where her skilled performances won her all-state honors and a berth to play in the East-West games. Although thoroughly absorbed in basketball, precious time was also dispensed to compete in track and softball.

## SPORTS HISTORY

Endowed with ample energy and myriad leadership abilities, Kay wove herself into the sustaining fabric of school life. In high school she was voted president of her junior and senior classes. She was editor of the school's annual and held offices in the Monogram (athletic club) and in virtually every other club offered.

Kay's motivation to become a teacher originated with three high school teachers: Mr. Ted Bowne, Mrs. Vivian Davis, and Mrs. J. A. Hunt. They taught her favorite subjects, math and English. Ted Bowne's excellence inspired her to register for each math class he taught. The total impact of this high-power teaching team forced Kay to choose between becoming an English teacher and a math teacher. English finally topped the fray.

After earning a B.S. degree in English from East Carolina University, Yow applied for an English teacher opening at her old rival high school, Allen Jay. The post included coaching the girls' basketball team, too. She was shocked when offered the job as she felt ill-prepared to coach, but Doyle Early, the principal, had observed her play high school basketball and felt the former All Stater had the basic qualities necessary to coach. Early's confidence, coupled with former coach Earl Swigget's promise to assist until she felt comfortable, nudged her to accept the offer.

A good school support system and outstanding athletes spurred Yow's team to a first-year double—the conference championship and the tournament championship. Following a four-year stint of success, Yow felt the need to pursue a graduate degree in physical education. This time she selected the University of North Carolina, Greensboro. At UNC-Greensboro, the once high school salutatorian discovered coaching to be the best educational mechanism to help youngsters develop life skills. She felt the classroom did not provide the same promise of profound occasions to touch students as did the basketball court. The hardwoods afforded physical, mental, emotional, social, and spiritual growth in a host of spontaneous situations. Thus, Yow re-entered the coaching arena fortified with a new vision for sculpting young lives.

As she finished graduate school, Yow supported herself with a part-time job at Elon College. When the Elon job mushroomed to full-time status, Yow applied and was selected for the position. Leaving the high school students was painful as she loved that age group. The new assignment required teaching, coordinating the women's athletic program, and coaching basketball, volleyball, and tennis. After five years at Elon, Smith Barrier, executive sports editor for the *Greensboro Daily News*, encouraged Yow to apply for the head women's basketball coach position at North Carolina State University. Barrier had tracked Yow's career and felt she was perfect for the position. Although reluctant to break new ground, Kay took his advice. Shortly thereafter, the job was hers. In July of 1975 Kay Yow became the first full-time women's basketball coach at North Carolina State University and also in the state of North Carolina—a transforming move for Yow and women's basketball at the school.

At NCSU she was recast. With ready access to weight rooms, sports information services, and a free hand to order team attire, she hardly knew where to begin. Prior coaching jobs did not have elaborate facilities nor did they provide a sufficient budget for team uniforms or travel. From self-made uniforms to home and away uniforms with warm-ups, from no athletic meal tickets to an athlete's cafeteria, and from no weight lifting facilities to a fully rigged weight room, this was a quantum leap. It signaled a new beginning for Yow, and the start of a women's basketball tradition at North Carolina State University.

## MEMORABLE MOMENTS

Retracing thirty years of coaching summons fond memories for a coach. Yow's first-ever win against arch rival North Carolina in 1976 was especially sweet because they not only won, but the game was the first televised across North Carolina. Within that same memory bank is a stat of the team that posted a 13–14 losing record one year and the next year vaulted to the Sweet 16. This was a peak experience because, according to Yow, a turnaround of such magnitude took "people with tremendous outlooks and positive attitudes, not just talent."

Yow's coaching expertise has placed her in the international spotlight. Memories abide in stunning victories such as the teams that brought home the gold in the 1986 Goodwill Games and the World Championships later that summer. Her team defeated the Soviet Union twice on their own home court. Guiding the U.S. team to an Olympic gold medal in the 1988 Seoul games after a personal clash with cancer was a monumental accomplishment. As if these accomplishments were not enough, like the hot-handed shooter, her national teams have accumulated a 21–1 win–loss record as garnish to her other victories. These events are extremely satisfying to Coach Yow, but mere winning is not enough for a coach deeply imbued with Christian values and ethical purpose. The opportunity to see athletes become the first in their families to receive college diplomas is probably most memorable on her long list of accomplishments.

## PHILOSOPHY OF COACHING

The soul of Yow's coaching philosophy is to develop a genuine person with the characteristics to be successful no matter what the future brings. To augment this philosophy, Kay holds individual player goal-setting conferences, which include academic goals, basketball goals, and personal goals. She has involved players in a variety of community outreach programs, and she has had a professional enrichment program that brings professional people in at various times to meet, have dinner with the team, and offer timely advice about career opportunities. Player meetings are held frequently by her and her staff to reinforce the importance of every person on the team, thus bolstering the many roles that must be played on a team for the team to be a successful unit. When her players know how much the coaching staff cares about them, they become more eager to learn what the coaches know about basketball. Finally, athletes are helped to find summer jobs and internships while those who have finished eligibility are assisted in finding agents when they are interested in playing professionally.

## CHANGES IN ATHLETES

Noting how athletes have changed during the past thirty years, Yow is especially concerned about the "you owe me" attitude promoted by athletes who take rather than give: "The positive part of how athletes have changed is that they are more athletic, better trained, and have, I believe, a better grasp of fundamental skills."

## ROLE MODELS/MENTORS

Watching her athletes experience moments of joy is the essence of Kay Yow's allegiance to coaching. Yow does not coach for mere "W's and L's; it would be superficial to spend a lifetime career just for winning games. I am in this business to hopefully have a positive influence on young people and anyone else with whom I come in contact!" Surely this is to be expected of one who declares John Wooden as role model and mentor. The highlight of her career came when she flew to California and spent the entire day learning from John Wooden. He had already captured the respect and admiration of Yow by the way he went about winning. Kay had no female role model as she was the first full-time woman coach hired in the state of North Carolina.

Coach Kay Yow is world class. Her vision and reach extend beyond basketball boundaries; neither are routine or ordinary. Like others of her special kind, she is not aware of the magnitude of her influence on the courts or in the grandstands. She is an ambassador of humankind at church, community, and at North Carolina State where she models "in loco parentis." Her style is singular and radiant.

## RECOGNITIONS AND ACHIEVEMENTS

### Coaching Recognitions in Division I

- ACC Conference Championships: 1978, 1980, 1983, 1985, 1989, 1991
- Regional Championships, 1997, 1998
- National Basketball Coach of the Year, *College Sports News*
- Nine Kodak All Americans
- ACC Tournament Champions: 1980, 1985, 1987, 1991
- Coach of the Year, United States Sports Academy, 1988
- Six Players in the WNBA

### National Coaching Assignments

- World Championships, 1986, 7–0 Gold Medal
- World University Games, 1981, 4–1 Silver Medal
- Goodwill Games, 1986, 5–0 Gold Medal
- Olympic Games, 1988, 5–0 Gold Medal
- Win–Loss as U.S. Coach 21–1

### Other Accomplishments

- Carol Eckman Award, 1988
- Women's Sports Hall of Fame, 1988
- Women of the Year in Sport, National Organization of Women
- North Carolina Sports Hall of Fame, 1989
- Converse and WBCA Coach of the Year, 1990
- Fellowship of Christian Hall of Champions, 1991
- Girl Scouts of America Women of Today Award

# SUGGESTED READINGS AND RESOURCES

Anders, Elizabeth, and Myers, S. *Field Hockey : Steps to Success*. Champaign, IL: Human Kinetics, 1998.

Asher, Kinda S., ed. *The Best of Coaching Volleyball. Book I: The Basic Elements of the Game*. American Volleyball Coaches Association. Indianapolis, IN: Masters Press, 1995.

Bennett, John P. *Gymnastics for Everyone!* Boston, MA: American Press, 1995.

Burbank, A. *Beyond X's and O's: A Woman's Lacrosse Playbook*. Northampton, MA: Smith College, 1994.

Carr, Gerry A. *Fundamentals of Track and Field*. Champaign, IL: Leisure Press, 1991.

Cooper, P., and Trnka, M. *Teaching Basic Gymnastics: A Coeducational Approach*. Needham Heights, MA: Allyn & Bacon, 1994.

Cornelius, W. L. *Gymnastics*. Englewood, CO: Morton Publishing, 1983.

Craig, S., and Johnson, K. *Softball*. Dubuque, IA: WCB/McGraw-Hill, 1997.

Dorrance, Anson. *Training Soccer Champions*. Burlington, NC: JTC Sports, 1996.

Elliott, J. *Youth Softball: A Complete Handbook*. Carmel, IN: Benchmark Press, 1990.

Gould, Dick. *Tennis, Anyone?* Mountain View, CA: Mayfield Publishing Co., 2000.

Gregg, Lauren. *The Champion Within: Training for Excellence*. Burlington, NC: JTC Sports, 1999.

Herbert, Mike. *Insights and Strategies for Winning Volleyball*. Champaign, IL: Leisure Press, 1991.

Kahn, Liz. *THE LPGA: The Unauthorized Version*. Menlo Park, CA: Group Fore Productions, 1996.

Krull, Kathleen. *Wilma Unlimited: How Wilma Rudolph Became the World's Fastest Woman*. Troy, MO: Harcourt Brace & Co., 1966.

Nance, Virginia, and Davis, E. *Golf*. Dubuque, IA: Wm. C. Brown, 1990.

Neville, William. *Serve It Up: Volleyball for Life*. Mountain View, CA: Mayfield Publishing Co., 1994.

Potter, D., and Brockkmeyer, G. *Softball: Steps to Success*. Champaign, IL: Human Kinetics, 1989.

Sabin, Francene. *Women Who Win*. New York: Dell Publishing Co., 1975.

Scott, Bob. *Lacrosse Technique and Tradition*. Baltimore, MD: Johns Hopkins University Press, 1985.

Scott, John W. *Basketball Fundamentals for Players and Coach*. Englewood Cliffs, NJ: Prentice-Hall, 1989.

Sterling, Robert M., and Looy, M. *Athletes Tell Their Unforgettable Moments in Sport*. Champaign, IL: Leisure Press, 1986.

Stewart, Mark. *Florence Griffith-Joyner*. Danbury, CT: Children's Press, 1996.

Stolle, Fred, and Knight, B. *Tennis: Let's Analyze Your Game*. Englewood, CO: Morton Publishing Co., 1992.

Summitt, Pat (with Sally Jenkins). *Reach for the Summit*. Broadway, NY: Broadway Books, 1998.

Urick, David, and Woodward, B. *Lacrosse: Fundamentals for Winning*. (Sports Illustrated Winner's Circle Books), 1988.

Walter, Cyril. *Hockey the Gold Medal Way*. Auckland, New Zealand: TurBorren, Demi Holdings Ltd., 1989.

Walton, Gary M. *Beyond Winning: The Timeless Wisdom of Great Philosopher Coaches*. Champaign, IL: Leisure Press, 1992.

Amazon.com provides another good source for finding books related to a variety of sports.

We have used various web pages on the Internet as a major source of obtaining information for this project. Accessing web pages on the Internet provides current information posted by the Sports Information Offices of colleges and universities around the country. This can be done not only for the coaches in this volume, but for almost every college coach (at least those in NCAA Division I schools). The following example employs Yahoo! to access information on the University of Georgia's athletic program.

*Step One*: Get onto the Internet. In the search box, type "University of Georgia"; click on the first entry.

*Step Two*: A menu will appear that includes Athletics. Click on Athletics.

*Step Three*: A list of sports will appear. Click on either the Athletics official site or the specific sport.

*Step Four*: The Athletics official site will show a box listing sports (with a down arrow) in the upper left corner of your screen. Click the arrow, and it will give a list of all the sports at the University of Georgia which have web pages.

*Step Five*: Click on gymnastics. The menu includes coaches. Click on coaches.

*Step Six:* A list of the coaches for that sport will appear. Click on the name of the coach you want to know about. You may also check several other menu options, such as team roster, schedules, results, press releases, and history.

Each search engine will be slightly different, and each school will have information in varying locations. Search the different college and university sites and the different options using various search engines, and soon you will be able to quickly find all the information you might be interested in. Play with this example and then try some others. Happy surfing.

# INDEX

## About the Authors

NENA REY HAWKES is Professor Emeritus of Physical Education at Brigham Young University.

JOHN F. SEGGAR is Professor Emeritus of Sociology at Brigham Young University. He has published numerous articles on sociology and sports.